Sue
All The Best
Dave Eagleston

A Private Heaven
Two Brothers on
Separate Paths to Redemption

by
Dave Eagleston

Based on a true story

ALL RIGHTS RESERVED

Note:

As stated in the Author's notes, the events, names, and portions of the book, which took place in Canada, are true. The portions of this book that pertain to Marvin Eagleston are based on fact, but the dialog, names, and certain events were created from research. Any resemblance to real persons, places, or events is coincidental.

Copyright 2020 – Dave Eagleston Sr.

ISBN 978-0-578-91369-8

Eagleston Books

www.eagleston.com

For my wife Janie and children, Leslie, David, and Kevin

Chapter One

The stars faded as I stood on the breezy deck of the small oceangoing ship that ferried passengers, cars, and freight between Nova Scotia and the island of Newfoundland. The frigid air that morning, left me trembling even though I stood there with more layers of clothes on than you can even imagine. The boat boldly cut through the ocean water and layers of sea ice on that April day in 1970. We were sailing through the Cabot Strait, a few hundred miles west of the *Titanic's* watery grave, and during the night, the constant motion of this small ship made sleep an impossible luxury. Groggy but exhilarated, standing alone on the deck that morning, I took my first breathtaking look at a new, captivating sight. Across the water, in the gentle light of morning, stood a rugged rock of an island, and I could make out a small village tucked neatly into a narrow bay. The ocean's giant gray waves pounded relentlessly against the rocky shore as my heart pounded eagerly against my chest. I knew nothing about Newfoundland, but as I looked out across the cold, lashing waves of the Atlantic and laid eyes on Newfoundland's snow-covered hills, I stood in fearless anticipation.

A few days earlier, the US Army had given me an honorable discharge after a tour of duty in Vietnam as a combat helicopter pilot. Now, this beautiful island would be home for my family and me as well as the unique backdrop for my first assignment as a commercial helicopter pilot.

The sun rose slowly behind us, as the stars faded in the morning light, and my heart pounded with excitement, thinking of what great discoveries lay right before me. The winter wind against my face felt refreshing and mixed with the salty smell of seaweed and kelp. All my senses were alive and on full alert as the icebreaker pushed its way past the last traces of sea ice into smoother water, passing a towering blue-and-white lighthouse with a bright red roof. Strategically located, the lighthouse towered above a small, four- or five-acre rock island about a half mile from the main landmass. Across from the lighthouse, a base of snow coated the harsh cliffs surrounding Cape Ray. In a short time, our ferry would complete its intense pounding and chopping as we put into the dock, but I didn't want the excitement on the deck to end.

The powerful ferry continued through the icy water, and a few minutes later, I could see the docks at Port aux Basques, the closest point of land between Canada's mainland and her tenth province, Newfoundland.

My beautiful wife, Barbara, and our little energetic two-year-old daughter, Leslie accompanied me on this trip. Barbara didn't share my eagerness to migrate to this mysterious island, but I begged and pleaded with her to go. Of course, it would have been easier to convince her if she wasn't eight months pregnant with our second child. Traveling to a cold, isolated country, pregnant and chasing after a busy two-year-old, wasn't going to be easy. To make matters worse, we had no idea what town or village we would be living in. But after a night out, complete with a lovely dinner and a glass of wine, she relaxed, and I promised that if she agreed to go with me, she would never regret it. Perhaps she consented because of the wine or the promise of adventure, or perhaps she only wanted to believe in me. She finally consented, and now we were almost there.

The constant movement of the ship paused, and the large vessel slowly eased to a stop as we docked in Port aux Basques. Knowing we would have to drive our car off the ferry soon, I hurried back to our cabin to get Barbara and Leslie. In the tiny, cramped cabin, Barbara sat on the bed, brushing her hair. She turned toward me and looked spectacular. Still the shy, quiet woman that I had fallen in love with back in high school. Her eyes were a lovely sky blue, and her short blond hair gave her more the look of a college girl than a twenty-three-year-old mother expecting her second child.

We had met at Will Rogers High School during my senior year. With an attractive figure and eyes a cover-girl model would be jealous of, Barbara had been a gentle, kindhearted teenager. On the other hand, more of total cutup, I sang and acted in school plays and musical programs. Studying fell to the bottom of my list of things to do. A fact well documented by my infamous grade cards. The complete opposite, Barbara could easily be described as diligent, intelligent, disciplined, preferring to remain on the sidelines of society while shunning any form of attention.

Even after we were married, when I worked at a television station in Tulsa as a cameraman and sang on local TV programs, Barbara shyly avoided all invitations to visit the studio, preferring to watch me on our little black-and-white TV at home. To her, beauty wasn't a power to be used in subtle, self-serving ways, nor a person's most important quality. But her stunning picture gave me hope during my time in Vietnam. Pinned to an ammo box, her photo greeted me each night when I returned from flying a combat helicopter in and out of the Vietnam jungle.

At that moment, on the ice-breaking ship, with the morning light streaming in through our tiny cabin window and an uncertain future pushing against her like an iceberg, my wife looked even more beautiful than usual.

Beside her stood Leslie, our little pumpkin of a daughter, clutching Barbara's leg and chewing on her favorite pink blankie. A typical two-year-old, full of energy, enjoying games, and asking a hundred and one questions. She had always been such a good baby, so naturally her mother and I expected all our children would be easy to parent.

"Daddy!" Leslie yelled, looking up at me with a grin on her little face. I picked her up and held her to the cabin's only window to let her look outside. She grabbed hold of my face with both hands. "Cold," she said, squeezing my cheek.

"Are you ready, you little pumpkin?" I asked. "Wait till you see this place; you won't believe how pretty it is with all the snow on the mountains." I glanced at Barbara, and I could see the doubt in her eyes. But she smiled and put on her best happy face, hiding her thoughts and fears from Leslie. I could sense her fear, but Leslie didn't notice. I sat our little one on the floor, and she ran to her mother.

"Mommy, snow?" she yelled. "Mountain." Barbara gave her an enthusiastic smile, and Leslie kept up her excited chatter. "Play, snow," Leslie said.

"Not right now, but soon," Barbara answered as she stood.

I hugged Barbara and felt the familiar tension stirring within her. Barely over the night crossing, she now faced a daylong drive. I picked up Leslie, grabbed our bags, and went down to the lower deck, where twenty or thirty cars and a few trucks were jammed together like sardines in a can. The vehicles, packed with what appeared to be returning Newfoundland travelers, had their engines running, and the drivers seemed eager to drive off the ferry.

We found our little green Pontiac with our small wooden trailer safely hitched behind it. I fumbled my keys, then dropped them on the floorboard just as the car in front of us drove away. Our turn. Someone behind us tapped their horn as I located my keys, started the car, and glanced at Barbara.

"Are you ready?" I asked. She looked deep into my eyes but said nothing.

"Ready or not," I announced, "We're on our way."

I eased our car down the massive steel ramp toward the docks. On one side of the drive, three Newfoundland stevedores, dressed in black down-filled coats and sou'western caps, waved at us as we drove past them slowly. One of them leaned against a snow shovel and pointed at our license plate, sharing a good laugh.

"I guess they don't see many Texas plates up this way," I said jokingly, trying desperately to lighten the mood. Barbara kept silent. We followed the small caravan of cars leaving the ferry. Drivers eager to hurry past the edge of the little town and onto the open highway. Port aux Basques resembled some of the old fishing villages I'd seen on TV, but it looked nothing like the other parts of Canada we had driven through. Nothing like the lovely farms and beautiful cities of Ontario, or the straight rows of crops and perfectly manicured fields along the highway in New Brunswick. And not at all like the tree-lined hills of Nova Scotia with its little Scottish towns and villages. It seemed as if we had driven off that boat and into another world.

With the solid blue background of a winter sky above us and the dark gray carpet of sea beside us, we had our first good look at a Newfoundland village. The colorful houses sprinkled along the side of the hill were surprising. An astonishing mixture of small white homes and a multicolored collection of old weathered structures—well preserved but entirely out of touch with modern-day designs. Most of the cottages appeared to be somewhat cramped, with doors and windows covered by sturdy shutters to keep out the harsh maritime weather. Then we passed one colorful home, light green with black window frames and a brilliant red front door. Several houses were a fainter robin's-egg blue, and a few were bolder in vibrant canary yellow.

Several cottages had small boats in the yard, and almost every home had some visible connection with the ocean. Near the water's edge, a few houses were built on stilts, keeping them safely out of the water, and strangely enough, a few houses, without stilts, stood only a short distance from the sea.

I noticed one house with ten or twenty empty lobster traps stacked in the yard, and past it sat a small tugboat entirely out of the water atop a makeshift drydock. A quaint little boat with a dark green hull, black deck, and a tiny white cabin.

"Boat, Daddy!" Leslie said. "Go boat?" she asked, wanting badly to go and see it.

"No, Pumpkin," I said, glancing back at her. "We have a long trip ahead."

"Boat, Daddy!" Leslie repeated, now moaning with her eagerness to see the boat and escape the confines of the car. Barbara reached across and touched my hand, and I looked at the line of cars in front of us. We weren't moving fast, anyway. I checked the rearview mirror and could see several more cars tightly packed behind us.

"We might as well let all the cars from the ferry get past us," I said. Then a bit louder, in a kind of announcement, I said, "OK, let's go see the boat."

Barbara and Leslie started to clap their hands and cheer me on as I turned off the main road into the drive. When we got out of the car, a salty sea breeze and the hint of fish being cleaned filled the morning air. The wind brought with it both the scent and sounds of the Atlantic coast, and it provided a clean, fresh feeling. We weren't far from the water's edge, where the majestic, grayish-blue ocean blended beautifully with the colorful village. In the distance, toward the hills, stood a small, picturesque cemetery with rows of light-colored gravestones and a few white crosses.

With Leslie in my arms and Barbara at my side, I walked toward the little tugboat, held above the ground in a wooden, V-shaped platform. Suddenly sounds of shouting came from inside the boat's tiny cabin and what sounded like a hammer striking solid wood. We stood there, a bit shocked, as an older man emerged from the cabin, cursing and waving his arms.

A crusty old fisherman, dressed in shabby black slacks, a thick gray turtleneck sweater, and a black wool cap stopped shouting in midsentence, then stared down at us as if we were invaders. His gray-and-white nicotine-stained beard covered most of the wrinkles on his weathered face, but his dark brown eyes were sharp and crystal clear. He reached up with his right hand and wiped wood chips off his sweater, then removed his pipe and blew thick smoke toward us. He said nothing.

"Good morning," I offered, smiling, hoping he wasn't as grumpy as he looked. He said nothing, then took another puff from his pipe. I tried it again.

"We just got off the ferry from Sydney and thought we would show our daughter your tugboat," I explained. "It's a fine ship, sir," I added, trying to prod him along.

The old skipper frowned again and pointed at the tug. "Lord Jesus," he said. "She ain't no ship, b'y. She's only a little ting. Now I've pulled some ships," he continued, sticking his chin out proudly. "And I've worked about on some ships. Even did some swillin'. But this, this be a tiny bit of nothing, and today I might just make a good fire of it."

I wasn't sure what he meant, or what I should say. "Ah, yes, sir. But tell me, what's swillin'?" I asked.

"What?" he blurted, "You never heard of swillin'? Seals, b'y, hunting seals. You got a lot to learn," he informed me, pronouncing the word "boy" as "buy."

"Pretty," Leslie said, pointing to the tug and smiling up at the ole skipper. His face abruptly transformed from that of a hard, crusty old sea dog to a lovable elderly man who couldn't resist the appealing innocence of a child. At that moment, he seemed to forget the problems inside the cabin that had him all worked up. "This ole ting," he repeated. "You think this ole ting is pretty? Why it's as old as Buckley's goat." As he spoke, he smiled at Leslie and motioned for her to come up. "Hop your carcass up here, girl!" he ordered.

Barbara glanced at me, and I smiled to reassure her. I lifted Leslie up to the deck, and the old skipper took her aboard. Leslie giggled as he placed her softly onto the deck. She looked back at us for reassurance. "Look, Mommy!" she said. "Fun!"

Under the skipper's watchful eye, she walked around the cluttered deck and stumbled on something we couldn't see. The old skipper picked her up, and she tried another step or two, down she went again. As he pulled her up, Leslie giggled, but her mother wasn't amused.

"OK," I said. "This nice man let you have a look, Pumpkin, and he needs to get back to work." He handed her down to me, and I could see the relief on Barbara's face. The skipper took a puff at his pipe.

"So where ya from, b'y, and where ya to?" His accent sounded foreign to us, our first taste of a real Newfie brogue. Hard for us to understand him, but I suspect he may have felt the same about us.

"We drove up here from Texas, and we're on the way to Gander." You could see in his eyes that the Texas part took him by surprise. "Texas!" he shouted. "Lord jumping Jesus. I met nary a man from Texas." He glanced at Barbara. "Nor woman neither," he added. "But it's a fine day for driving, seems to me."

The old skipper looked into the sky, then added, "And you're lucky; it's not too windy. The place you're driving through this morning can be some dangerous when she's blowing a gale." I glanced at Barbara, who listened carefully. The old skipper pointed toward the highway and continued.

"When the wind blows from the west and it's storming, we seen nights when it blew the train right off the tracks, right up there in the Anguille Mountains, up along Coal Brook."

I looked at Barbara and couldn't resist a slight smile. He noticed.

"Nary a joke, b'y," he said, returning to his grumpy self. "That wind can blow through a little ravine in those mountains like a hurricane. By the time it whips across the valley, it blows cars off the road and trains off the track. Believe what you want, but you better believe that. Better not be out there when it happens."

"Thank you for your advice, sir," I said respectfully. This time keeping my doubts to myself. "And thanks for showing Leslie the tug. We better get moving, and I'll remember what you said about the wind."

We got back into the car and backed out of the dirt drive and onto the main road. We could still see the little green-and-white tugboat and the skipper, standing on deck watching us. He wasn't the most gregarious person I had ever met, but he had made a good impression on our family, and Leslie seemed to have brought out his soft, friendly side. I drove past the last cottages of Port aux Basques, and ahead of us, a large sign proclaimed the "Trans-Canada Highway." With a full tank of gas, a beautiful highway ahead of us, and a warm feeling for Newfoundland after our encounter with the old skipper, we turned onto the highway. I looked at my wife. "Gander, Newfoundland, here we come."

Chapter Two

We approached the town of Corner Brook around noon, and I could see that the trip wore on Barbara. Located midway between the island's northern and southern tip, on Newfoundland's west coast, Corner Brook loomed large in the distance.

Barbara looked in the back seat to check on Leslie, then whispered the good news that she continued to sleep. Leslie had not slept well on the ferry the night before, but now the little traveler seemed comfortable in her makeshift bed, complete with her pink blanket and a few stuffed animals. I glanced at her in the rearview mirror and it brought to mind something that had happened in my early childhood.

***

One horribly cold winter night, I stood at the back door of our neighbor's house looking out through a frosted window. Bright orange, sky-high flames rose from the house next door—our house. Firemen gathered in the yard, powerless to contain the burning structure. My brother and sister stood beside me crying, unable to understand the devastating situation. Our mother and father were somewhere nearby, but I could not see them. We had come home on a Saturday night to find our house ablaze and our neighbors waiting with my brother, Marve.

Standing with tears running down my cheeks, I tried to understand the chaos going on in the yard. Outside, a tall man stood on the porch. He wore a black leather jacket and seemed unusually calm while he watched our home being destroyed by the fire.

The man put out his cigarette, turned toward us, and came into our neighbor's kitchen. As he stepped inside, the shiny barrel of a pistol could be seen, holstered on his belt. A silver badge flickered on his shirt as he quietly and carefully scanned the kitchen, taking in everyone and everything. When he spoke, his voice did not quiver or threaten, but his simple words and his deep, direct voice emitted authority.

"I need to talk with these children," he said. "Alone."

***

I drove along the main streets of Corner Brook while glancing down the hill toward a large river running parallel to the street we were on. Near the river, white smoke rose into the blue sky from large, belching smokestacks near a paper mill. One of the travelers on the ferry, on his way back to Newfoundland, had told us about the famous Bowater Paper Plant. And his description was accurate about the plant being the largest structure around Corner Brook.

The smoke poured into the sky and drifted east over solid forest toward Central Newfoundland. Near the factory were several heaps of sawdust three or four stories high, and a pile or two near the river. Along the highway, a few miles past Stephenville, we had seen log-cutting operations, and now we could see the ultimate destination for those fresh-cut logs. Soon, they would become newspapers, stationery, and other products.

After finding a small restaurant, I parked the Pontiac and left Barbara to relax and look after Leslie. When I returned to the car, I sat behind the steering wheel and handed Barbara the paper bag stuffed full of sandwiches. A powerful, unfamiliar smell permeated our warm, overcrowded car.

"Good grief!" Barbara said, her face suddenly flushed, "What kind of sandwich is this?"

"It's something new," I said confidently. "They call it seal flipper pie, and we were lucky, too. That restaurant is the only place in Western Newfoundland that makes seal meat into sandwiches."

"You mean this sandwich is made with seal meat?" she asked, incredulous. "How do you expect us to eat this?"

Barbara rolled the window down and stuck her head out for fresh air. By that time the foul, powerful odor filled the car causing me to lose my appetite. I felt like a complete idiot and should have apologized. But as usual, when Barbara questioned my decision-making, I became defensive.

"Shit," I grumbled. "Don't you even want to try it?"

She looked back at me and didn't say a word. The stench from the sandwiches hung in the air and mixed with the tension in the front seat.

At that moment my temper flashed, and I snapped at Barbara, like the hundreds of times my father had snapped at my mother. Normally he did this at the supper table over something trivial right before he exploded. And too often, my older brother, Marve, got the worst of our father's rage. Often Dad would slap Marve hard enough to knock him out of his chair and onto the kitchen floor. Then my father, getting more worked up, would yell at Marve and call him a damn sissy while the ten-year-old, freckle-faced boy lay on the floor crying. Those family scenes haunted me all the way to Vietnam and were always close to the surface. For an instant, the thought of slapping Barbara or slamming my fist into the dashboard flashed across my mind, then faded.

As I sat in the car smelling the thick, pungent aroma of seal meat, I looked at my wife's disappointed face and tried to simmer down and think things out for once. Anyone could make a mistake and buy the wrong kind of food. But only a cruel person like my father would hurt his wife. I cooled off a bit, but still felt terribly embarrassed.

"Fine," I blurted out, trying to end the argument. "I'll take the damn sandwiches back." I jerked the paper bag out of her hand, got out and slammed the car door, causing Leslie to roll over in the back seat.

I walked back to the restaurant, bought some ham sandwiches, and by the time I got back in the car, I had cooled off. Tears showed on Barbara's ashen cheeks. I reached for her, but she turned the other way.

"I'm sorry," I said. "I didn't think about you having a funny stomach when I bought the seal. I'm sorry, really. I realize this isn't easy for you."

She sat quietly sobbing, gazing into the sky. Once again, I had let myself get worked up over nothing and wanted desperately to become a better man than my father. But deep down, I had my doubts.

"Let's just go," Barbara said, her blue eyes red-rimmed from crying. As I started the car, she turned back toward her window. Leslie moved in the backseat, making sweet coos as she slept. Perhaps dancing with a teddy bear in her dreams. Her little sleepy moans were the only sounds as we left the downtown area of Corner Brook.

Driving along the highway toward Gander, the Trans-Canada Highway climbs into the surrounding hills and straightens out as it passes a few small villages. At this point we were close to a large, beautiful lake that continued in the same general direction as the highway. Nearby were a few campgrounds and parks tucked into the forest and overlooking the lake.

In the backseat Leslie awakened, moved around, and broke the silence. Our little one, sleepy-eyed and unsteady, climbed up and slid between us. She noticed the bag her mother held.

"Sand-itch?" she asked. "Candy?"

"Hi, sleepyhead," Barbara answered. "No candy, but we do have lunch, and guess what? It's too cold for a picnic, so we're going to eat in the car. Fun?"

"Fun!" Leslie replied, and watched her mom prepare our little lunch.

We passed a small but well-maintained airport at a little town called Deer Lake. As usual, I searched in vain for helicopters as we drove by. Barbara took the ham sandwiches out of the paper bag and handed half of one to Leslie. She handed the other half to me. I smiled at her, trying to ease myself out of the doghouse. Barbara gave me a slight grin, then screamed, "Watch out!" She pointed toward the front window.

As I looked back toward the road, I saw an enormous bull moose right in front of us, almost filling our lane of the highway. The dripping wet moose stood twice the size of a large cow, and seemed to be in no hurry. We were headed right at him—about to run smack-dab into an animal large enough to destroy an automobile and everyone inside it.

I swerved to the right to miss the monstrous creature, and in doing so ran my tires off the edge of the highway into the loose gravel. I strained to keep control of the car and to avoid losing our trailer completely, then felt the trailer's pressure against the edge of the highway as we drove past the moose. The nonchalant beast, with its giant face dripping wet, stared into the car window as we passed.

Quickly, I looked back to the road, fighting to maintain control as the front right tire pulled toward the gravel and the trailer barely managed to stay out of a deep culvert a few feet away. Finally, I maneuvered the tires, one at a time, back onto the highway, and as the trailer bounced onto the smooth surface, I took a deep breath.

Leslie and Barbara were still looking out the back window at the moose as I glanced into the rearview mirror. The gigantic animal, seemingly ignorant of the danger seconds before, continued his sleepy saunter across the Trans-Canada Highway.

"Are you okay, Leslie?" Barbara asked.

"Cow, Mommy," Leslie said, pointing her little finger. In front of us on the right side of the highway stood a large sign with a picture of a moose and the warning: Moose Crossing.

"Gee, thanks for the warning," I said.

We laughed together at the irony of the sign's location and at the relief of being in one piece after the near miss.

I slowed down and put my arm around Barbara. We ate our crumpled sandwiches and took turns telling children's stories to Leslie. As we drove east toward Gander, Barbara and I shared a vague sense of euphoria. I know for sure I felt it, and I think she did too—that joyous moment immediately after escaping what could have been a tragedy. Perhaps that's the reason Barbara seemed so sweet the rest of the day and never mentioned the seal sandwiches. I wanted that pleasant feeling to last, and somehow it did.

***

A few hours later, Barbara yawned and looked up from her pillow. "Looks as though you had a pretty good nap," I said. "Welcome to Gander. Let's find the airport and have a peek at the helicopters."

"Don't you want to find a hotel?" Barbara asked, sounding worn out. "We're getting pretty tired." I glanced at her and knew I had better put the airport visit on hold and try to find a hotel. "Hey, back there!" I said, trying to change the mood. "Is anyone ready to get out of the car?"

"Me!" Leslie yelled. "Ready!" She jumped in the seat a couple of times, and Barbara looked back at her.

"Settle down now," Barbara said. "We'll be there soon."

"Boy," I said, in my best effort to sound like a two-year-old. "I'm ready to find a hotel room and do something fun and get out of this car. Mommy wanted to go and see the dirty old helicopters, but I talked her out of it. We're going to the 'o-tell.' Sometimes Mommy's a bad girl, right, Pumpkin?"

"Bad girl," Leslie repeated. "Mommy—bad girl."

"Daddy's a good boy. Right, Leslie?" I asked.

"Right," she said, playing along. "Daddy—good boy."

Barbara couldn't keep a straight face when Leslie chattered away. I glanced at her, and could see her relief, realizing we had completed our journey.

It was the end of a long, difficult trip from Mineral Wells, Texas, to Gander, Newfoundland. We had said goodbye to our Army friends in Fort Wolters and our family in Oklahoma, including my older brother, Marve, who seemed more worried than anyone that we were moving far away. Looking back, I thought it a bit strange it affected him that way. I wouldn't find out why for a long time.

Our little family of three and a half had driven well over 3,000 miles. We had crossed eight states, five provinces of Canada, one international border, and an ice-packed section of the Atlantic Ocean. We had passed a few hundred hitchhikers and had almost run over a slow-moving moose. Now, at the end of our long trip, our remaining assets were easy to calculate; thirty dollars in cash, a quarter tank of gas, and a small wooden trailer packed with all our belongings.

That night, as Barbara and Leslie slept, I thought about our quarrel over the smelly seal sandwiches. In the dark little hotel room, I lay quietly beside Barbara, thinking about the past and the future. The kind of father I had as a boy, and the type of father I wanted to become as a man. It wouldn't be easy. So much to learn, but even more to unlearn. In the dark, cozy room, a small glimmer of light glinted off the tiny kitchen table, reminding me of mealtime as a kid. Some of my best and worst memories as a child had some connection to the kitchen table.

***

One night, a night like many others, we sat around the kitchen table, the same way as a normal family would. Dad said a short prayer, then Mom passed food around to the five of us. My sister, Sue, always had a funny story to tell, but that night Mom, after a drink or two, interrupted Suzie with one of her telephone operator stories.

Mom giggled and said, "I told this guy, 'Deposit fifty cents for another three minutes, please.' And he says, 'I only have forty-five cents, lady. Will that be OK?' I told him, 'Sir, this isn't a garage sale. Fifty cents or I'll cut you off.'"

We chuckled at Mom's story, and for a few moments we were almost a normal family. The children in our family fell into three distinct categories: first, my sister Suzie, the oldest and smartest. Me, the youngest and silliest. And smack-dab between my sister and I, my brother Marve, the weakest and most sensitive child. In some families, being the middle child wasn't a huge issue, but in ours, it seemed to be an insurmountable problem.

My mother, a tall, dark haired beauty, had caught my father's eye back in eastern Oklahoma. A Golden Glove boxer-turned-soldier, Dad was a stocky, somewhat handsome man, with a charming personality and a lightning-quick temper that could flare up as fast as a rattlesnake. Even in his late thirties, he resembled a prizefighter with his jet-black hair, huge cauliflower ears, and large block-shaped fists. A mixture of booze, Irish temper, sudden mood swings, and a deadly left hook, he put an ungodly fear into all three of his children. But more than any of us, his ferocious temper terrified my brother, Marve.

By the time he turned twelve, my brother spent many a night trying his best to stay out of our father's way, fearing Dad's wrath should he drop his fork on the floor, or, God forbid, spill a glass of water. Those were the days when I developed a talent for staying out of Dad's way. Sure, I got my share of slaps and sometimes a fist, but I figured out how to keep my father happy and let him feel like the king of the house. But Marve—he wasn't that lucky, eventually becoming Dad's whipping boy. Dad always needed someone to pick on when the booze reached a certain point and his inner demons took over.

At the table that night, Mom chuckled and continued her story as Dad left the table to fix another drink. We knew that after a couple of drinks Dad's mood would change. Marve glanced at his father, then back to his food. A scrawny, sensitive kid with a freckled face and thick glasses, Marve often felt like an outsider.

"Pass the potatoes," Suzie asked, reaching toward Marve. My brother took hold of the green dish and handed it to Suzie. As he did, his right arm grazed his water glass. Marve froze in place as the glass wobbled slightly, then crashed to the floor. Broken glass scattered across Formica in every direction. Mom stopped talking in midsentence, and Marve jumped out of his chair, hurriedly picking up the mess on the floor. The kitchen grew silent for a moment, then Dad turned toward the table, holding a drink in his hand. He slammed the glass on the counter, took one step toward the table, then grabbed Marve by the neck with his left hand. He jerked Marve off the floor and the frightened boy tried to pull away, but couldn't. Dad made a fist with his right hand, paused for a second, then slapped Marve hard three or four times across the face, only stopping when blood gushed from Marv's nose and Suzie and I begged Dad to quit.

"You're nothing but a four-eyed little loser!" Dad shouted, slapping Marve across the face again. Trying to stop crying, Marve picked up his glasses and looked down, avoiding eye contact with his father.

"That's right, pick up your glasses, you weak little punk," Dad said. "By God, at your age, I worked hard for my family. I shined shoes. Damn right, and I sold newspapers on the street corners. Always brought money home to my mother." Dad looked at the rest of the family to make sure we listened, even though he'd spouted that a hundred times.

"All you need to do is go to school and stop pissing in the bed, but you can't even do that, can you?" Dad looked at Marve with disgust. "You'll never make anything of yourself."

"Sit down, honey," Mom said, in a weak attempt to cool Dad off. Sometimes Mom could calm our father down, but mostly she retreated into her scotch and 7-Up shell, numbing herself to it all.

Marve, demoralized and hurt beyond anything a child should ever endure, sobbed and wiped his face on his shirtsleeve.

"That's right," Dad said. "Go ahead. Cry like a damn baby."

Marve limped away from the table, then hurried into the bedroom we shared. He fell across his bed and cried into his pillow. I followed him into our room and stood at the door, watching. I wanted to help him but had no idea what to do. Even though I had seen this scene many times before, it still hurt to see my brother treated this way. Marve hid his face in the pillow, not wanting me to see him cry, but I could hear it. Pitiful, muffled sounds. Sounds of his heart breaking and his fragile character slowly eroding, one cruel beating at a time.

Chapter Three

The next morning as the sun peeked through the curtains of our crowded little room at the Gander Inn, I slid out from under the sheets of our warm, comfortable bed. Excited to see the helicopters I would be flying, I stood and stepped carefully across Leslie, who slept peacefully on her pallet on the floor. Hopefully Leslie would sleep in, and her mom would get some much-needed rest after such a hard trip. After leaving a note telling Barbara of my plan, I dressed quickly, closed the door to the room, and went outside. In my excitement, I almost drove away without unhitching the old wooden trailer.

As I approached the Gander International Airport, its impressive size and extensive service facilities surprised me. It seemed massive and almost out of place for a city of only 12,000 people. Most cities the size of Gander didn't have an airport at all, and this one was more suited for a city the size of Atlanta or Chicago. But I knew the rich history behind the Gander Airport. One of my friends back in Fort Wolters had loaned me a copy of Ernest K. Gann's classic aviation novel, *Fate Is the Hunter*. One section of his novel described the important role the Gander Airport played during World War II. I had discussed this with Barbara on our drive from Texas.

"What happened is this," I explained. "The United States and Canada sent hundreds of military airplanes over to England to fight in the war. They flew from various locations in the United States and Canada, and Gander became one of their last stops for fuel before crossing the Atlantic. Gander's location proved to be perfect for those warbirds, and the most direct route to cross the Atlantic. Of course, with that many aircraft trying to stretch fuel during bad weather and tough conditions, some of them crashed before they arrived in Gander, and some crashed in the Atlantic Ocean after refueling in Gander. But most of them made it, and Gander played an important part of that success story. And now it's a major airport catering to domestic and international flights."

At that moment I saw firsthand an updated, impressive version of the airport Gann had described. Now with a large, modern passenger terminal and a main runway two miles long. There were a variety of aircraft on the apron, such as the Twin Otter, McDonnell Douglas DC-6, a Boeing 727, and a Super Constellation, nicknamed the Super-Connie. Overall, everything at the airport appeared to be in excellent condition.

Impressed with the airport, I turned my thoughts toward my new employer, Universal Helicopters. Now feeling anxious about getting my first look at some of the modern helicopters I had driven so far to fly.

Off to one side of the airport, a small gravel road led to some hangars, buildings, and a sign which listed the two companies in that direction: Eastern Provincial Airways and Universal Helicopters, Ltd. A few minutes later I came to a small green hangar with a handful of parked cars, a pile of junked-out aircraft parts, and a large collection of dirty 45-gallon drums stacked haphazardly. The hangar wasn't like the pristine well-stocked facilities back in the military. And then I saw them, a strange, unfamiliar collection of helicopters.

The choppers were parked in no particular order and resembled some type of helicopter swap meet. One antique Hiller 12E, three or four obsolete Bell 47s, and a single, more modern but rough-looking Bell Jet Ranger fitted with large rubber flotation gear instead of skids. The Jet Ranger appeared to be the only turbine-powered helicopter in the flimsy collection. Rugged, with a well-worn green and white paint job and a "Universal EPA" sign on the fuselage. The Jet Ranger was a much smaller helicopter than the turbine-powered Bell Huey that I had flown in Vietnam. But I knew I could get used to it if that's the best they had to offer.

Feeling worried and disappointed, I parked my car, walked past the dusty collection of helicopters and into the hangar, where I noticed two mechanics working on a couple of torn-down Bell 47s. The older, cage-framed 47 was a Korean War helicopter recently adapted to civilian use. It had bubble-shaped Plexiglas cabin barely large enough for a pilot and a couple of small passengers to fit into its long, side-by-side bench seat. I had seen a few of them in Vietnam but had tried to avoid flying one at all costs. With almost 1,000 hours of helicopter time under my belt, I didn't need to worry about that old bird.

Inside the hangar, two mechanics worked on another Bell 47 and seemed upset about something. One of the mechanics, the oldest of the two, cursed and threw a large wrench across the hangar floor. As it banged against the concrete, he shouted at the younger man.

"Lord Jesus, Larry. I'm tired of hearing you complain about flying in a helicopter. Better get used to it and stop griping. How are you going into the bush without flying? You planning to drive up to Labrador? Or, maybe you're going to swim across the strait?"

The skinny younger man didn't answer right away but stood for a moment pushing his long, straight hair out of his eyes. He glanced over at me and frowned.

"What do you need, b'y?" he asked in his thick Newfie accent. He fumbled in his toolbox for something, then handed a replacement wrench to the older mechanic.

"Are ye looking for someone?" he asked.

"I'm looking for Gary Fields," I said, unimpressed with the maintenance team thus far.

They looked at each other and grinned. "You missed him by about two years and a thousand miles," he said. "B'y, are you thinking of working here?"

"That's right," I said. "Where is Mr. Fields?"

Grinning like the quick cat that ate the slow mouse, the young mechanic walked toward the offices and motioned for me to follow him. He led me around the two helicopters, past a couple of ladders, and into a small but neat office. The room had a wooden desk, a couple of chairs for visitors, and a large map of Newfoundland and Labrador on the wall. I noticed a few model helicopters perched on a waist-high bookshelf.

A man who appeared to be in his thirties stood looking out the window. He seemed to be in deep concentration and didn't notice us walking in. Larry, the young mechanic, stood by as the man I guessed to be the chief pilot turned in our direction. Larry pointed his thumb toward me.

"Jack, this Yank is looking for Gary Fields," he said, half grinning.

"Okay, Larry, thanks," Jack said as he walked over and put his hand out to me. "I'm Jack Murphy, the chief pilot," he said. "I'm guessing you're Eagleston."

"Yes, sir," I said, relieved to think someone expected me.

"What happened to Gary Fields?" I asked, as Jack Murphy sat down and motioned for me to do the same.

Jack certainly looked like a chief pilot. His gentle, expressive blue eyes, and his lean, intelligent face gave him the look of a man with experience. As he took a close look at me, he smiled, and I thought how different this seemed compared with a military interview. Well dressed in dark brown winter slacks, a white shirt, and a handsome brown leather jacket, Jack Murphy gave the impression of a humble, confident man. I notice the gold wedding band on his left hand.

"Gary lives in Carp, Ontario," he explained. "He isn't really involved in the operational side of the company." He opened a drawer in his desk and said, "So, where you from, eh?"

"I'm from Tulsa, Oklahoma," I replied as Jack pulled a folder out of the drawer.

"I just left the Army at Fort Wolters, Texas, and we got here last night."

His face quickly changed. His eyes narrowed slightly.

"We! What do you mean, we? Is your wife with you?"

"Yes, sir," I replied. "Is there something wrong?"

He pushed the file to one side and took a deep breath before answering.

"Well, I don't know." he said. "This job isn't easy, eh. And you're going to be gone a long time when things get started, which can be tough on a wife without her family around." He glanced out the window, then back to me. "Newfoundland isn't the easiest place for anybody's wife to live, much less someone from the States."

He took a few papers out of the file, which I assumed were my flight records. From the look on his face, he seemed worried about something.

"Well, Mr. Murphy, my wife does have a bit of family around."

"Good," he said, now smiling again.

"We have a two-year-old daughter, and in less than a month my wife will be having our second child."

"What?" he said, now looking more stunned than concerned. "You mean your wife is about to have a baby, and you want to fly in the bush? Do you understand you're liable to be on a project anywhere on this map?" He pointed to the large map of Newfoundland behind him.

"First," he continued, "I have to unteach you all the military crap. Next, I have to teach you something about commercial aviation. I'll tell you right now our luck hasn't been too good at keeping Vietnam vets around. Sure, some of them come up and make it through the summer. But come snowfall, when they're on their own and have to dig a forty-five-gallon fuel drum out of three feet of snow, they scoot back to the mainland faster than crap goin' through a goose."

"Sir," I said, trying to get a word in.

"And stop calling me 'sir,'" he interrupted. "Call me Jack."

"Yes, sir," I replied. "I mean, Jack. I know you're worried about my wife. And I can see you're worried about me, but I want this job. I mean I *need* this job, and I won't be scooting back to the United States. I had the chance to fly in Los Angeles for the sheriff's department when I left the Army, and I turned it down. I *wanted* to come to Canada, and I *wanted* to become a bush pilot. Call it adventure, or crazy, or whatever you want. But I want to do this, and I convinced my wife to come up here with me. If you give me a chance, I'll do my best to learn everything you throw at me."

At that point I didn't know what else to say. The hair on the back of my neck seemed to tingle as a chill of desperation caught me by surprise. I couldn't stand the thought of going back to the hotel and telling Barbara I didn't get the job.

Jack Murphy got up and walked to the window. He stared at something in the distance, then looked back at me.

"You seem determined, and that's good. But what about your wife, eh? Do you think she'll get on OK up here?"

"Jack, when I went off to Vietnam, I left my wife six months pregnant with our first child. She did OK through all that. After I got shot, I came back to the States on a stretcher and she didn't fall apart. She's little, but she's tough and she can handle this."

He walked back to his desk, and when he turned toward me, his face showed his concern.

"Okay," he said, with a slight trace of a smile showing again. "Find yourself a house or an apartment or a basement and get settled in. Things are slow right now. We're waiting for the snow to melt in the woods before most of the helicopter contracts can start. Let's get some company paperwork completed on you this morning. Later this afternoon and tomorrow you work on getting a place to stay. Come back in on Friday."

"Great!" I said, as I felt relief flow through my body. Then I remembered one more problem. As much as I wanted to leave things right where they were, I had no choice. I had to lay it all on the line.

"Mr. Murphy," I said hesitantly. "There's something else."

The chief pilot shook his head and squinted. "What now?" he asked, the remnants of a smile replaced by a stern look.

"Mr. Murphy, you already know I'm an American, my wife and daughter are here with me, and my wife will have our second child in less than a month."

"Yes, yes, I think we covered all that."

"Well, sir, what you don't know is—I'm broke. I spent everything I had to get us up here. The 3,000-mile trip from Mineral Wells, Texas, took all my money. I couldn't bring my rented trailer across the border, so I had to buy a small used trailer. Now I need help from the company just to pay my hotel bill."

His face changed back to the overly concerned chief pilot.

Tension rose in the pit of my stomach as sweat formed on my forehead. "Mr. Murphy, sir. You may have had problems with other American pilots, but I promise you I'll work hard, and I'll stay through the winter if you'll give me a chance."

He scratched his head, and his face appeared more compassionate and less concerned. Maybe he believed me, and maybe he didn't have a choice. But whatever went on in his mind he kept to himself. A soft, gentle expression crossed his face as he spoke.

"Yes, boy, we can get you enough to get by on, and the company might be able to reimburse you for your travel costs to get up here. Not all of them, mind you, but at least the expenses from the Canadian border to Gander. That might help, eh?"

I smiled and nodded, but didn't say a word. At that moment, I felt like a rescued man. A warm, glorious feeling of relief washed over me. Afraid to speak, fearing that I might cry, I remained silent, knowing full well that if I allowed even one tear to fall, it would put Jack Murphy right over the edge.

Chapter Four

Later that morning, Jack Murphy introduced me to some of the people working for Universal, and they were an interesting assortment. The managers and employees of the remote helicopter company were either from Newfoundland or one of the other Canadian provinces. The non-Newfoundlanders, or "mainlanders," were easy to identify. They were reserved, intellectual, and somewhat polished compared to Newfoundlanders, who are more outspoken and seem a bit backward at first. But this little group of pilots and mechanics had a lot in common. They seemed to love their work and enjoyed trading good-natured wisecracks about their cultural differences.

After the tour, Jack and I went back into his office, where the accounting manager, Bill Turner, had left an envelope on Jack's desk. Jack handed the letter-sized envelope to me, and inside I found my first check. I felt a mixture of guilt and relief holding it. Jack never mentioned a word about the advance; he simply turned toward a large Newfoundland map with several pins stuck in various locations.

"Dave, let's look at some of the places where we work," he said, pointing to several pins stuck on the map in the northern part of Newfoundland.

"This is St. Anthony," he said, pointing to a pin at the northern tip of the island. "There's a hospital there run by a British organization called the Grenfell Mission. They service several small outposts and nursing stations along the coast of Northern Newfoundland and across the water along the south coast of Labrador. Our helicopters go there in the summer and in the fall on temporary assignments. Next, we have several helicopters in Goose Bay, Labrador, and in the summer, we have a few jobs along the coast of

Labrador." He pointed at two or three other pins on the map.

"How do you get the helicopters across the open water?" I asked, pointing to the large area of open sea between Newfoundland and Labrador.

"You fly them across," he said. "All our aircraft have floats in the summer and special skis on the skids in the winter to make it easier to land in the snow. I'll go over all that with you later, but for now, here are some of the other locations," he said, resuming his map tour. When he finished, he asked me if I had any questions.

"How many Jet Rangers do you have, and what contracts are they on?" I asked, worried about which helicopter I would be assigned to fly.

Jack smiled and let the question pass. "Let's take that up on Friday, eh. You get back to your family and come in on Friday morning."

"Yes, sir," I said, quickly realizing my mistake. "Okay, Jack. See you on Friday morning. And . . . Jack, thanks for the help, sir."

***

When I arrived at the hotel, I found Barbara and Leslie in the lobby. Barbara stood at the front desk, talking to the man behind the counter. Leslie sat on the counter, held in place by her mother. Barbara had a worried look on her face. As I approached them, Barbara's expression changed from concern to relief.

"Here he is now," Barbara said. "This is my husband."

The man at the front desk, a stern, crusty-looking fellow in his fifties, snatched the key out of Barbara's hand and cast a look in my direction with an air of superiority.

"We need to talk about your bill," he announced in an irritable tone. "Last night you paid for one night, and your wife tells me you're planning to stay. You need to pay for your room, sir."

"I understand," I replied, smiling, hiding my anger. "I'm starting a new job here in Gander and spent a bit too much cash getting here. You know how that goes?"

"Well, yes," he said. "But we have rules, and I need a deposit for tonight."

I removed the check Jack Murphy had given me and said, "Of course you do, sir. I only need to cash this company check; then I'll settle with you. Will that be all right?"

"Well, I guess it will," he said reluctantly.

"Great," I replied, quickly grabbing the key back from him with one hand and swooping Leslie up with the other. "Oh. And thank you *so* much for being so kind and friendly to my family. We were worried about moving here, but now we feel we've made the right decision."

The desk manager wasn't sure how to take that comment and stood behind his desk as we walked toward the elevator.

When we were back in our room, I explained to Barbara what had taken place at the hangar and shared the wonderful news about the company advancing us enough to rent an apartment. However, I purposely avoided mentioning Jack's concerns about her living in Gander and her having a baby soon. And since seemed pleased and relieved with the good news, I didn't say a word about how long I might have to be away from home when the contracts started. I stuck to the good news.

"I don't have to be at work until Friday morning," I said. "Why don't we all go get some lunch and start looking for our new home?"

Barbara smiled and turned to Leslie. "Did you hear that? Let's go find a new home."

There weren't a lot of choices as far as finding a place to live in Gander. There were no houses to rent within our budget and only a few apartment complexes. As with most homes in the north, freestanding houses in Gander had basements, and these were often rented out. It didn't take long to look at everything available, and we finally settled on a furnished basement apartment.

The next day, after we moved everything in and put Leslie to bed, I put on a Carole King album and listened to our favorite music. Before going to bed, I took one more look at the photos, decorations, and personal things Barbara had placed around the living room. It wasn't much, and it certainly wasn't fancy, but in one evening, she had transformed our little basement apartment into a home. Our home.

***

During the next few days, Jack Murphy gave me a full orientation and overview of Newfoundland and an introduction to bush flying in Eastern Canada. I absorbed a lot information due to Jack's no-nonsense approach. You either took notes or committed everything to memory. I took notes.

To prepare me for almost anything, Jack gave me a list of bases, phone numbers, frequencies, and several maps. Also, he introduced me to some of the other pilots and mechanics based in Gander. The mechanics, I learned, preferred to be called engineers. They weren't shy about correcting anyone who referred to them as mechanics.

Jack would often speak about Newfoundland in general sweeping terms, like the extreme weather conditions, limited aviation infrastructure, and unforgiving north winds. Though a mainlander, Jack loved the island and its rugged, unrestricted outdoors. In some ways it seemed good for me to hear it from a mainlander, since he appreciated everything about the province including its wholesome, spacious atmosphere. But along with the positive aspects, he also cautioned me on its unique hazards: dense fog along the south coast, limited supplies of aviation fuel, unlimited supplies of wild animals such as bears, moose, caribou, and other animals capable of damaging a helicopter. *Several* times he warned about getting stuck overnight in a helicopter in some remote section of the bush, and how easily it could happen. And he cautioned me on the dangers of flying across the open waters between the northern peninsula of Newfoundland to Labrador, which meant flying across twenty to sixty miles of frigid water.

"The Strait of Belle Isle," he said, "often has hundreds of icebergs floating down from the Labrador coast. Floats on the helicopter or no floats, the Strait of Belle Isle is nothing to take for granted."

But with all his briefings, he never mentioned the strange social customs in Newfoundland. Those things I had to find out from other employees. And one of the men always eager to dispense free advice was a helicopter pilot known as Big Jim. Six feet tall, with a solid, muscular frame, Big Jim had a reputation as a scrapper and a pilot who took "no crap from man nor beast." He looked the part, with broad shoulders, thick nose, and scraggly blond hair peeking out from his baseball cap. And, of course, an ever-present cigarette dangling from his mouth.

"Look, Dave," Jim said, as he leaned against the hangar wall. "If you get stuck out somewhere and have to spend the night, land at any fishing village. The fishermen are the best people in the world. They will put you up for the night and give you a proper feed. Even the poorest man in the village will borrow food from his neighbor to make sure you get fed. It has happened to me more than once. Let me tell you about that time in the spring."

Jim's big brown eyes squinted in a kind of John Wayne, long-distance stare.

"I was flying from St. Anthony to Labrador, across the ice-covered Strait of Belle Isle," he said, "when the damn engine started sputtering and thumping, then she just quit. Complete silence. Flying right over a bit of pack ice floating along the edge of the Atlantic Ocean. Lucky for me, you could land two or three helicopters on that long piece of ice. And even better, it happened mighty close to Mary's Harbour."

Watching Jim, it became clear that he enjoyed telling his stories, and they ranged from crash-and-burn helicopter whoppers, amazing animal encounters, to bawdy, unbelievable accounts of the girls he knew. He loved his stories, his helicopters, and his cigarettes. Lectures were given with intensity of expression, attention to detail, and a tremendous consumption of tobacco. Jim's smoking was legendary, too. Before each cigarette went out, he lit his next one, and with it, started a fresh, new narrative.

As Jim lit his next smoke, across the hangar, someone worked on the HF radio receiver, and I heard a familiar crackle and static. The radio sounded like an old portable radio I had as a kid.

***

Around the mid-fifties, when the Space Race was in full swing, I received a four-inch-long, red AM radio in the shape of a rocket for my tenth birthday. A terrific gift, but I'd asked for a new baseball glove. My brother Marve and I loved baseball, and sometimes Dad would take us to an empty ball field where he hit lightning-fast line drives to us. Those were the glory days of Oklahoma's own Mickey Mantle, and deep down, I think Dad wanted one of his sons to become a Major League baseball player so he could be a proud, famous father. We tried, but we were average, at best. After missing several of his hard-hit balls, the sessions usually ended up the same miserable way.

"Get this one," Dad yelled, standing near the backstop. He swung the bat, striking the ball hard, sending a line drive into center field. The ball sailed through the air with enough speed that most high school players would have had a tough time catching it, let alone a couple of kids. The two of us pretended to field the ball, but knew we never had a chance. The ball fell to the ground and rolled past us like many other hard-hit balls that afternoon.

"What's wrong with you two," Dad yelled. "Are you afraid of the ball?" Then, he would rant and rave about us missing most of them—humiliating both of us, and eventually focusing his rage on Marve.

"Come on, you little four-eyed sissy," he said. "Hell, you get over there and sit by the car. Get off the damn field." Marve walked to the car, shoulders slumped and crying. He sat as Dad hit a few more balls to me.

Dad could have taught us how to catch the ball, but somehow that wasn't part of his program. He thought we should be able to catch anything he hit. A short time later, when Dad drove back home with Marve and me in the back seat, he turned around and faced us. He gave Marve a menacing look.

"Why in the hell can't you learn to catch a baseball, son? I barely hit those balls today, and you ran away from every damn one of them just like a baby." Then raising his voice, he repeated, "Like a baby."

Marve looked out the window at the houses we passed and didn't answer. He stopped crying before we pulled into the driveway, then sat in the car while Dad and I walked up to the house. On the front porch, I turned to check on Marve, when a brown two-door Ford pulled up to our curb. A man got out of the car and walked directly toward me. A tough-looking, unfriendly face that would normally fill a boy with fear. But I wasn't afraid because I had seen this man, or others like him, bring booze to our house. Just another bootlegger.

During the '50s, when it was illegal to buy liquor in Oklahoma, it wasn't unusual to have a tough, grizzled bootlegger come to our house and leave a few bottles of scotch or vodka. After Dad paid him, the man would walk into the living room, use our telephone to call his boss, and get the address for his next drop-off.

Tulsa bootleggers were colorful, formidable characters, and their visits to our house were as regular as clockwork. Rude, abrasive men who paid off the cops, knew their way around Tulsa, and, regardless of the weather, wore long coats with special pockets to carry liquor and hide a pistol. No one messed with a bootlegger, not even our dad. They drove fast, souped-up cars with trunks so overloaded with liquor, the rear bumpers sat only a few inches above the ground. Fascinated with these cocky, lawless men, my brother watched their every move. I guess, in a way, they became his role models.

***

"Hey, Dave, did you hear what I said?" Big Jim asked, frowning at me.

"Yes," I said, "but you never told me what happened when you landed on the ice."

Big Jim grinned, exposing his tobacco-stained teeth, but before he could answer, Jack Murphy walked up with a strange look on his face. I suspect he may have overheard the last part of the conversation.

"Excuse me," Jack said. "If you lads aren't too busy in here, I need Dave in my office." The group went silent as I followed Jack toward his office.

I sat down in Jack's office, expecting him to resume our earlier discussion about working in the bush and how to deal with customers. He had given me several tips on providing the customers with only enough information about the helicopter to make them feel informed, but not enough for them become experts. But this chat wasn't about customers.

"Is your wife settled in, son?" he asked, his blue eyes watching me closely. "Do you think she's all right so far?"

"Barbara is doing fine," I said, trying to guess where he might be going. "She has a doctor now, and we've already visited the hospital to have a good look around. My daughter has found some friends to play with around the apartments. I think we're fine, Jack."

"Good," he said, walking to the map behind his desk. "Be sure and tell Barbara to call my wife if she needs anything," he said, turning toward the map. "Got something for you to do, so I want to make sure she's comfortable. I want you to fly up to Labrador. It will only be two or three days at the most."

"Great," I said, sounding a bit overeager. "Which helicopter do you want me to fly?"

"Well, hold on," he said. "Jim's going to fly the Jet Ranger, and you're going along with him. You won't get to fly, but you'll get to see the country and visit a few of our bases. You'll cross the straits over to Labrador and see some pretty tough country. Jim's going to stay on there, and you'll hop on a commercial EPA fight from Goose Bay back to Gander."

"Jack," I said. "I can fly a Jet Ranger if you give me a quick checkout."

Jack gave me that look again. "I'm sure you can fly a Jet Ranger," he said. "But for now, let's go with this plan. It will give you a chance to see a lot more than you can see in this hangar."

Disappointed I wouldn't be able to fly, but excited because this trip offered than another day sitting in the hangar drinking coffee.

"Go home and pack a bag for a couple of days," Jack said. "This is where you're going and the route you'll be taking if the weather is flyable. One more thing. Jim's a good pilot, but don't put much stock in some of his stories."

He traced our route on the map, and I tried to remember all the names and locations but wasn't able to due to my high level excitement. My first trip for Universal Helicopters! It would be an easy ride up to Goose Bay and then an airline flight back. Piece of cake.

***

The weather the next morning was cold and a bit rainy. At the heliport near the hangar, Big Jim and one of the engineers were busy pre-flighting a green-and-white Jet Ranger. I grabbed my bag out of the car and hurriedly ran toward the aircraft. An engineer named Paul worked nearby, helping Jim. Tall and stocky with long busy hair and a scraggly beard, Paul looked more like a hippie than an aircraft specialist. He closed the passenger door and slowly strolled around the aircraft checking doors, panel fasteners, and anything that might appear out of place.

"There you are, Yank," Big Jim snapped, looking up at me. "We were wondering if you were on mainland time, Newfie time, or on your own good time," he quipped. He grinned at Paul, but the hippie-like engineer kept a solemn look his bearded face. Paul seemed to be trying to make up his mind about me.

Jim, sitting in the pilot's seat, turned to me and said, "Put your bag in the rear compartment and watch out for the fuel pump and safety gear. The aircraft's ready, the flight plan is filed, and we're losing daylight."

I had hoped to go through the proper starting sequence with Jim, but as I got into the front left seat, he engaged the starter. The main rotor blades moved in a slow circle above our heads and increased their speed as the Allison turbines spun and whined to a start. I closed my door and hurriedly fastened my seatbelt. As my belt latched into place, Jim pulled on the collective control, nudged the cyclic forward, and the helicopter hovered three feet off the ground for a few seconds. He nosed the cyclic forward while simultaneously pulling on the collective to add more power. I watched his takeoff and felt an adrenaline rush. On the ground, Big Jim came off as loud and boisterous, and he certainly wasn't handsome. But strapped into a helicopter, comfortable in his own element, what he lacked in charm, he more than made up for in raw talent.

Flying north, we crossed mile after mile of thick forest. Jim seemed lost in concentration, so I relaxed and enjoyed the scenery and the impressive pilot next to me. Jim seemed to know the direction of the wind at all times and embraced it, using it to his advantage. He executed gentle control inputs with the least amount of pressure. After a quiet thirty minutes in the air, having flown over a couple of thousand trees and at least ten moose, Jim finally broke the silence.

"From Texas, eh?" he asked. "It gets hot down there, don't it?"

"Oklahoma," I corrected. "I'm really from Oklahoma, and yes, it does get hot down that way."

"Family in Oklahoma?" he asked. "You have brothers and sisters?"

"Yep," I replied. "One of each. How about you?"

A call on the HF radio interrupted our discussion, and when Jim finished talking on the radio, he drifted away in concentration. Now, getting closer to the western edge of Newfoundland, I thought of Jim's question about my brother and sister. It reminded me of the many horrible weekends as we were growing up.

Chapter Five

One Friday evening after Dad had run out of scotch, he called the local liquor dealer for an urgent delivery. Bootleggers were regular visitors at our house on a Friday evening, yet this time things were different. For some reason, Dad was in a foul mood when the bootlegger arrived at our front door, and his attitude worsened when the man handed him a bottle of rum instead of scotch.

"What the hell is this," Dad asked.

The bootlegger frowned, shrugged his shoulders, and said, "Keep your shirt on. I got a bottle of scotch in the car."

"Don't stand around talking then," Dad said. "Go get the damn bottle." The bootlegger got caught off guard by my father's arrogance and sharp retort. The two men stared at each other for a few seconds. Marve stood near the front door watching closely. As my brother moved a few steps forward, the bootlegger looked down at him. The man's frown turned to a pleasant grin. The tall man sat the bottle of rum on an end table, then, with a calm, controlled manner, looked Dad in the eye and touched the right pocket of his overcoat, where I suspect he kept his revolver.

With a half smile, he replied, "As I said, buddy, I have Cutty Sark in the car, and if you're not satisfied," he patted his pocket, "maybe you'd like to talk with my boss."

At that point, I expected Dad's lightning-fast left jab to bring this stranger down, but Dad's hand never moved.

"Cutty Sark will be fine," Dad said, his face a bit flushed and his posture less threatening.

The bootlegger returned to his car and brought the bottle back to the house. Now Dad seemed friendly, kind to the point of being charming while he paid the man. Marve watched the whole thing, and for the first time in his life, witnessed our father capitulating. The bootlegger took Dad's money and looked down at my brother. A freckle-faced, twelve-year-old boy stared up at him in admiration.

"See you, kid," he said, then turned and walked slowly back into the darkness.

Marve ran to the window and watched as the bootlegger took off in his souped-up car. The little quarrel over Dad's favorite scotch may have seemed like nothing, but for the first time, Marve witnessed someone forcing our father to back down. My brother and I knew we had better steer clear of Dad the rest of the night. But Marve wasn't worried about our father—his thoughts were on the brave bootlegger. Years later, when he looked back on his early life, Marve would talk about the heroic man who had stood toe-to-toe with his father. Something Marve had only dreamed of doing. And he would say that it had changed his life.

***

In the helicopter, Jim made another radio call, this time on the High Frequency (HF) radio to the helicopter base back in Gander. Jack had explained that the HF was capable of a longer transmission distance than the VHF radio. It made strange, crackling sounds sometimes, but unlike the VHF, the HF was not limited to line of sight. In other words, unlike the VHF, you could be on the ground or in the air and still use the HF effectively.

Jim finished his radio call by giving his call sign: "X-ray Sierra Kilo, over and out." On my headset, Jim's voice sounded as if he were a thousand miles away instead of three feet. Then, without warning, he broke into an old Irish song I had heard on the radio recently:

> *Her eyes, they sparkled like diamonds,*
> *I thought her the queen of the land.*

And her hair, it hung over her shoulder,
Tied up with a black velvet band.

"You know that one, my son?" he asked. "I love it."

Looking at him at that moment, anyone could see that he loved the song and loved flying. Jim wasn't much of a singer, but he was quite a pilot, a pilot in his own north country element.

"Dave," he said, pointing to the map in my lap. "Keep up with our route with your map there. Now is a good time for you to get up to speed with the Northern Peninsula. Look up ahead; we're going to land at that village at our 10 o'clock position. Do you see it?"

"Sure," I said, finding the village on the map.

"What's the name of it?" he asked.

"Flower's Cove," I replied, holding my finger on the map.

"Right," he said. "This place, Flower's Cove, is one of the Forestry and Wildlife bases we service. I'll give them a call and let them know we need fuel."

Jim called the forestry office and said, "Did they call you from Gander and tell you were taking on some fuel? We're headed to Goose Bay, and if the weather holds, we're going to make it to Battle Harbour tonight."

"No," came the reply. "You're not going to Battle Harbour."

"Why not," Jim asked, surprised.

"Cause this morning an airplane crashed near Red Bay. An EPA mail plane. An Otter loaded down with mail bags, and looks like the pilot's alone, laid up there hurt. Need you to get there and pull him out."

"No shit," Jim said. "You got his location?"

"Sure," came the reply

From that point on, Big Jim remained all business. We landed and quickly refueled the helicopter, then took off for Red Bay. Thus far during the trip, we enjoyed good weather. A slight tailwind, and a high, overcast cloud formation. We were flying above the northwest edge of the Northern Peninsula of Newfoundland and would be crossing over to Labrador.

In front of us the spectacular, treacherous waters of the Gulf of St. Lawrence stretched from north to south as far as you could see, separating Newfoundland and Labrador. Now in the distance I began to make out a long, remote, section of land, my first glimpse of Labrador.

Leaving the rocky shores of Newfoundland behind us, we slowly started across the enormous stretch of frigid, open water, and a familiar fear grew in the pit of my stomach. Not far from the Atlantic Ocean, the crossing loomed longer and far more dangerous than any lake or waterway I had ever flown over. Our aircraft had fixed floats, designed for water landing, but I had my doubts as to how long we would last in the rough water below. Jim climbed to two thousand feet, leveling off below a thick layer of dark clouds. I had written down our takeoff and landing times, each leg of the trip, but this time Jim made sure.

"You always want to make sure of your takeoff time," he said. "Then, you have two ways of knowing your fuel situation: the fuel gauge, which has been known to break, and actual flight time. We don't know what we're goin' to run into trying to find this airplane or what weather system might creep up on us in Labrador. Fuel is damn scarce where we're headed."

"Okay," I answered, now more interested in something up ahead of us in the water.

"Another thing," he continued. "You noticed I climbed as high as possible? Always gain altitude before crossing the straits. Flying over the water, even with floats, shouldn't be taken lightly," he said. "If this baby pukes an engine, you need to make as many Mayday calls as possible and stretch your glide as far as you can. The only way to do that is what?"

"Altitude," I said, looking down at the gray mass of cold, windswept water with large car-size chunks of ice floating everywhere. The sight of all the water and ice made me feel frozen.

"Jim, how 'bout a bit more cabin heat?"

Jim changed the setting on the heater and grunted something I couldn't understand. I looked toward the northwest again and could make out the shape of a strange white object floating in the water. At first, it looked like a large boat, but now I could see it was one of several spectacular icebergs.

As we got closer to the one directly in front of us, I got my first look. Jim nosed the helicopter forward, losing altitude, and, like me, seemed interested in the enormous mass. He put the aircraft into a dive, flying directly toward the stunning, frightening shape.

A powerful, pure-white island made of ice and snow, and its center formed the shape of an arch. On the bottom surface turquoise water illuminated a small pond created by rain and melted ice. Near its brilliant, snow-white edges, several harp seals rode as tiny gray stowaways, their childlike, oversized black eyes peering up at us.

"First time to see an iceberg?" Jim asked. We flew low-level across it, nearly touching its edge, and sending several of the seals scattering over its side and into the water.

"It sure is," I answered. "But I always thought icebergs would be bigger."

"Are you kidding me?" Jim snapped. "How big do think that one is, right there? And how many tons do you think it weighs?"

"Maybe ten or fifteen yards long and 200 tons?"

Jim snickered and said, "That one might be twenty-five to fifty yards long, and weigh as much as 100,000 tons." He pulled back on the cyclic and climbed back into the air.

"It's hard to tell when they're out in the open water like this," he said, "but a bit easier when they run aground and you have something as a reference. Remember, about ninety percent of an iceberg is underwater—makes it that much harder to estimate size. Believe me, that one right there is a giant. Thousands come down from Greenland, and the ones that don't melt float into the Gulf Stream. That takes them along the east coast of Newfoundland, where some wind up in the bays along the coast or even in St. John's harbor."

"How big do they get?" I asked.

"Well, I don't know for sure," he answered. "Hell, they can be massive, fifty or sixty feet high, I guess. Now I haven't seen one of the largest ones, but they say there are bergs a mile long and that weigh a few million tons."

"Wow," I said. "How long does it take for them to float this far down the straits?" I asked.

"Maybe four or five days, I guess."

Ahead of us, toward land, a string of puffy white clouds dotted the horizon below our flight level. The tiny clouds seemed to float effortlessly while obscuring part of the rocky shoreline. We were flying right into a frontal system, and most likely more rain or even a snowstorm.

"Son of a bitch," Jim said. "Looks like a damn cold front. Just what we need."

"Do we try to go under it?" I asked, wishing I to be at the controls instead of sitting on my butt like a passenger.

"No, not yet," he grunted. "When we reach Forteau," he continued, pointing ahead and slightly to the right. "That's it, right there at our two o'clock. When we cross it, we can lose our altitude."

He reached across with his left hand and pointed at my map. "Now, look," he said. "As we cross into Labrador, keep your finger on the map and follow every pond we pass. There will be very few landmarks other than ponds. We've got no other navigation aid than dead reckoning."

He glanced at the fuel gauge and tapped it, then he looked at his watch.

We had flown about forty-five minutes since we took off from Flower's Cove, and I made a note when we passed Forteau at 3:30 p.m. If Jim's extra fuel calculations were correct, we would have another hour and fifteen minutes remaining.

"How are we on fuel?" I asked. Jim scratched the stubble on his unshaven chin and thought for a moment before he spoke. "Here's how I make sure we get home," he said. "We've got about an hour twenty. If we leave ten minutes reserve fuel for my wife, ten for my son, and ten for my girlfriend, that means thirty minutes reserve. That gives us fifty minutes flight time before I put his baby down and we start chopping firewood and plan to stay the night."

"Right," I said, grinning as I wrote down and circled 4:20. We passed the village of Forteau and Jim descended, trying to stay beneath a thick layer of cumulus clouds. Below us were several brightly colored homes along the coast and a muddy road leading west away from the village. To the west, I could see a soggy dirt airstrip, very short, rough, and soaked from rain and melted snow. Jim must have noticed my curiosity.

"That little runway's not much good in the spring or summer, as you can see. But in the winter with a layer of snow, it's not bad for a Turbo Beaver or any single-engine fixed-wing on skis."

He continued to guide the helicopter lower and lower through the additional layers of cloud until we were past the village and into the hills. As we crossed the first lake, I could tell by the shiny end of the water that the wind came directly at us. The best wind sock in the world is a pond or lake. If there is no wind, the water has a smooth, icelike surface when viewed from the air. When the wind blows, it causes the lake's surface to be rough except for the edge of the lake where the wind is coming from. That smooth edge of the water identifies the wind direction and is one of the most basic, critical things to look for when flying a helicopter or light airplane. From the direction of the wind, I could tell it would take us longer to get to the crash site than we had expected.

We were now skirting low-level under a more solid layer of clouds with about 300 feet between the ground and the cumulus clouds above us. As I kept my right index finger on the map, Jim continued inland and a light coating of rain and ice slowly formed on our windows. This could lead to blade icing, worse than running out of fuel, according to Jack Murphy. Suddenly we felt a blast of rain and the slush on the windshield disappeared.

"See that?" Jim asked.

"Oh, yeah." I answered. "How long can we fly with blade ice?"

"'Bout two minutes." Jim snapped. "Watch out for an ice buildup on the outside temperature gauge; it will build there and on the blades. You can't see it on the blades, but you can see this." He pointed to the engine gauges. "And don't forget, we can always have a flameout if the engine gets the right amount of ice or snow."

We continued inland and came across several lakes or "ponds," as Jim called them. In the United States, we would call a body of water 10 miles long a lake—not here. Jim switched the frequencies on the VHF radio, and I looked at my notes. I drew a circle around 4:20 p.m., our fuel cutoff time. The clock on the aircraft confirmed my fear; five minutes after the hour. We should be close to the crash site.

"Delta Foxtrot Charlie," Jim called on our VHF radio, using the call sign of the downed aircraft in his calmest voice. "This is helicopter X-ray Sierra Mike. Come in, Delta Foxtrot Charlie." After a short delay and no reply, he repeated, "Delta Foxtrot Charlie, this is X-ray Sierra Mike."

"Dave," he said, "You do the radio calls, and I'll circle around this area."

I did as Jim suggested and continued to call out to the crashed airplane. We heard nothing for what seemed like ages. I finally heard that wonderful sound—not a voice but the sound of a radio being switched on and off.

"Foxtrot Charlie," I said, shortening the name. "If you read me, key your mike twice." The distinctive sound of a microphone being keyed twice. "Roger, we read you, Foxtrot Charlie. If you can see us, click once for yes and twice for no." One click. More music to our ears. He could see us, even though we couldn't see him.

"Now, help us turn," I asked. "If we're headed toward you, one click, or away from you, two clicks." Two clicks. Jim started a slow turn to the right and quickly had us headed back in the direction we had come.

"Help us again," I asked. "For us to turn to *our* right, click one time; to our left, click twice." Two clicks, and this time a bit more clearly. Jim turned to the left, and we headed toward a large wooded area with a small creek on the opposite side.

Before I asked my next question, Jim spotted the wreckage.

"We have you in sight," Jim transmitted. He pointed to our left and turned slowly in that direction. There it was, a red-and-white wing and part of an aircraft, hidden in the snow like a secret treasure.

Jim landed as close as possible to the crash site at the end of a small clearing in the trees. We were near a creek, the only open area, and it appeared the pilot had attempted to land his airplane beside the creek but ran out of room, crashing into the trees.

Out of the helicopter now, walking toward the crash site, and it took all-out effort for me to keep up with Big Jim as we trudged through knee-deep snow. The single-engine Otter was mostly intact, with a severely damaged left wing and crumpled undercarriage. It appeared the aircraft landed hard, then skidded across the tiny open space near the woods, the pilot lucky to have lived through it.

Within the first few steps, my feet were freezing, my jeans soaking wet, and my laced street shoes were ruined. At that very moment I realized why people were looking at my shoes as if I were barefoot. How Jack had told me that I had a lot to learn. But we had no time for self-sympathy; we had to get the pilot out and somehow make it out of the bush before dark.

The injured pilot lay in the front of aircraft, his right leg twisted grotesquely. Blood oozed from a long gash across his forehead and streamed down his badly bruised face. At that moment we knew he suffered from pain but we were unable to tell what other injuries beneath his heavy coat and winter clothing.

"Lord Jesus," Jim said jokingly. "Did you think this was an airport?"

The pilot snorted, and a look of relief crossed his bloody face.

"And you, me son," the pilot said to Jim, "You think you could fly any slower to get here?"

"How's your leg?" Jim asked, pulling the man's wool slacks and long underwear up to inspect the injuries on his right leg. About halfway between his ankle and knee, a small bone protruded from the bloody skin, which meant the pilot had an open fracture.

"Looks like you won't be playing hockey with Phil Esposito any time soon," Jim said.

"And I been looking forward to the *Russian Championship* next winter," the pilot quipped.

"What happened?" I asked, speaking to the pilot for the first time.

"Don't know for sure, just lost an engine," he said. "Full load of mail bags on my way to Blanc-Sablon, and this is the best place I could find to put her down."

"You hurt anywhere other than the leg?" Jim asked.

"No, I'm fine," he replied.

Jim reached into his jacket and pulled out a couple of candy bars.

"How much fuel you have left in this starched-wing monster?" Jim asked.

"'Bout eighty gallons, I think," he replied. "If it hasn't leaked out. I didn't smell any after the crash. You guys running low?"

"Always running low," Jim said. "Dave, get that 10-gallon can out of the back and that red hose curled up back there. Bring it here, and we'll pump fuel out of this aircraft and put it into ours. Bring our first aid and survival kit, too."

I walked through the thick snow to the helicopter and noticed for the first time how quickly the sun was disappearing. If we didn't leave soon, we would all be spending the night. It took me three round trips between the crashed airplane and the helicopter before I had the thirty gallons for our flight out of there. Together, Jim and I carried the injured pilot through the snow and got him situated in the back of the helicopter.

As the sun's last remaining light went down near the crash site, I marked the location of the downed aircraft on my map and made a note of our takeoff time. Looking into the back of the aircraft, I checked on the pilot. He had that same dazed, indebted look, and peaceful expression that I'd seen in Vietnam after pulling wounded soldiers out of the jungle. I glanced over at Jim as he carefully gained altitude and headed toward Blanc-Sablon. The heater finally produced much-needed warm air, and the aircraft's instrument lights twinkled. We broke a few Canadian Air regulations by flying at night, but knew we had done the right thing flying at night in an emergency.

With the extra fuel we had stolen from the airplane, a nice stretch of clear visibility, and a brisk 15-knot tailwind, we would be in Blanc-Sablon in thirty minutes. The pilot rested quietly in the back seat, and Jim hummed another rendering of "Black Velvet Band." We cruised across the total blackness of Southern Labrador, and after a while, began to see tiny lights in the distance. Lights from the small village of Blanc-Sablon.

Now I knew why Jack wanted me to tag along on this trip. Of course, the most obvious part of his reasoning had to do with training. Every minute I experienced the rugged reality of aviation in Newfoundland and Labrador, while watching and listening to a seasoned bush pilot.

But the other, more subtle reason had to do with him trying to determine if I could handle the work in this tough, unforgiving country.

My first day in the bush hadn't been easy, and I felt hungry enough to eat anything that didn't move. I felt exhausted from running back and forth in the waist-high snow, wearing street clothes and dress shoes. But in spite of all that, I knew something that Jack didn't; I knew at that moment that flying a helicopter in Newfoundland would prove much more difficult and dangerous than I had ever imagined. And I would love every minute of it.

Chapter Six

The next morning, Jim looked completely worn out as we sat in the Jet Ranger flying low-level all the way to Goose Bay. After spending the night with one of the local girls, Jim sat in the copilot's seat trying to stay awake while I piloted the helicopter. Easy to handle, the Jet Ranger flew with little effort. We enjoyed clear weather all the way across the rugged interior of Labrador.

When we arrived in Goose Bay, Jim took me to an outfitter, where I purchased some much-needed outdoor gear. Since I didn't have much cash with me, I wasn't able to buy a parka, but I purchased good winter boots, wool slacks, and some proper long johns. Best of all, I found a little souvenir black bear for someone special back home.

The commercial flight from Goose Bay to Gander only took a few hours and gave me a chance to unwind. When I arrived at the airport, Barbara and Leslie were waiting in the terminal. Leslie, excited to see her dad, ran to me and jumped into my arms. Barbara joined in the hug, and I sensed her relief.

"Daddy's home!" Leslie said.

"I brought you something, Pumpkin," I said.

"What? Let's see!!" Leslie shrieked.

"I'm afraid I don't have anything for you," I said to Barbara. She smiled and gave me another hug and gentle kiss.

"You're home," she said. "That's my present."

The three of us went home to our little apartment and enjoyed the evening with a small homecoming dinner. Though I had only been away a few days, Barbara's face showed me the extent of the undeniable relief she felt. It seemed clear that she felt lonely and isolated in

Newfoundland, and concerned about being so close to having our second child.

After supper I tucked Leslie into her bed, read her a Dr. Seuss story, and once more told her about the animals, icebergs, and the baby seals I had seen from the helicopter. She lay in her little bed surrounded by a treasure trove of stuffed animals. She clutched her new black bear and stared at the ceiling. She listened carefully, taking in everything and trying to imagine it all.

Soon, nature overcame her valiant efforts to stay awake. Her weary little eyes blinked as I stroked the outline of her face and softly touched her hair. Tiny eyelids became far too heavy, and when she gave in to her struggle, she drifted into a sound, tranquil sleep. I stood watching her breathe peacefully, her tiny chest moving up and down in a soft, lazy rhythm. Silently I leaned over, kissed her goodnight, and smelled the sweet, peaceful, childlike scent.

With Leslie tucked in, I went to our bedroom and found Barbara in bed asleep. I lay beside my beautiful wife who carried our unborn child inside her tiny, restless body. My mind raced with excitement and joy, but also fear and apprehension.

An apartment door closed somewhere along the outside hallway, then footsteps of a neighbor walking toward the parking lot. Barbara turned onto her side, trying to find a comfortable position, and after a few moments her breathing became more rhythmic. I marveled at how worried, yet attractive my wife appeared—even in sleep.

"Good night," I whispered, kissing her softly on the cheek, then pulling the soft cotton blanket up to her shoulders. She snuggled into the covers and gently touched my hand.

***

As Marve grew older, he would often watch his parents drink themselves into a stupor. After all the abuse, the lonely nights on a tear-stained pillow, and neglected childhood, the young teen figured out how to even the playing field.

Most weekends his parents passed out in their bedroom with music blaring from a record player. He knew that they were completely out when the needle made that irritating scratching noise as it hit the end of the record, over and over. On this night, that loud, continuous noise was Marve's signal.

Now, at fourteen years old, and slowly growing taller, the frightened teenager walked carefully down the dark hallway. He passed a vast collection of framed black-and-white photos of his father during his glorious boxing days. Marve knocked softly on the bedroom door, knowing that if anyone answered, he would simply ask them politely to turn down the music. But if no one answered, he would open the door and carefully enter the disheveled bedroom. He often found them under the covers asleep, and a few times they were spread out across the bed. On the worst nights, he discovered one of them on the floor partially clothed or naked. A hideous, embarrassing scene for anyone to witness, but for a young and abused teenage boy, it justified satisfying his own desires.

When he first started these visits, Marve would stand alone in the dark, thinking. Looking down at them with contempt. Sometimes he stole something small, something he knew his father wouldn't give him under normal conditions: a few dollars out of his dad's wallet, three of four cigarettes from an open package, or several quarters out of his mother's purse.

It started as minor pilfering, a way to get back at a drunk, violent father, but soon it escalated. After a few months, he wasn't satisfied with taking the money. He wanted more.

One night in that dark, smoke-filled bedroom, with his parents in a scotch-induced sleep, the needle on the record player scratching monotonously, Marve needed something more exciting than a few dollars. He needed revenge. Glancing toward a dark corner of the bedroom, he saw the outline of a baseball bat. Marve walked silently to the edge of the room and picked up the old Louisville Slugger. The moment he lifted the bat, a strong, powerful feeling came over him. He gripped it tightly with both hands. A rush of excitement now, like he had never felt before. The excited young teenager walked back to the bed and stood there hoping his father wouldn't hear his thunderous, pounding heart. Slowly, he lifted the wooden bat above his head, looked down at his drunk, pitiful father, and thought of all the times the cruel, heartless man had hit him and kicked him and viciously humiliated him. He knew the opportunity of this moment. Marve held the bat in the air, took a deep breath, then noticed something shiny near the bed. Something sparkling, twinkling, and out of place in the dark, repugnant room.

On the end table, along with the empty glasses, overflowing ashtrays, and brown leatherette wallet were the keys to his father's car. He stood there, frozen in fear, stimulated with an unfamiliar power, then felt a rush of adrenaline shoot through him like rocket fuel. He lowered the bat and reached for the keys.

That night, Marve crossed the hazy borders of his conscience into a new world. A magical, stimulating world of his own control, and for first time in his life *he* became the aggressor. He knew that he could either crush his father's skull with the Louisville Slugger or take his father's car for a joyride around Tulsa. Though only fourteen years old and two full years away from getting his license, he quietly slipped the keys into his pocket, turned off the record player, then walked out of the bedroom into his new life.

***

On a restful, pleasant night sleeping beside Barbara, I dreamed of our younger days in Tulsa. In my dream Barbara and I were students again at Will Rogers High School. She wore a soft, white wool sweater that revealed the outline of her breasts, fuller and more pointed than in real life. As we walked down the hallway toward class, all the students spoke to us and waved as if we were the most popular couple in school. Then we stood beside her locker for a moment and I kissed her, pulling her toward me, feeling her body against mine. Suddenly the bell rang for our next class. But it wasn't a normal bell. But more of a disturbing, annoying bell that wouldn't let up. *It was the phone in our bedroom.*

"Can you get the phone?" Barbara said, as she pushed her cold feet against me in bed, ending my wonderful dream. "Hurry, before it wakes Leslie," she urged. I sat up in bed and reached for the phone.

"Sorry to bother you so early," Jack Murphy said.

"That's okay," I replied, glancing at the clock; barely 5:30 in the morning. "What's going on?" I asked.

"You know Brian?" he asked.

"Sure, the pilot who's working on one of the mining contracts."

"That's right," Jack said. "He's got a problem and can't go out on a job tomorrow. I need you to come in today and get checked out on the Bell 47. You'll go on that job for a week or so."

"I'll be there," I said, looking over at Barbara, who had sat up in bed and figured out something was going on. I hung up and put my arm around her, disappointed I wouldn't be able to fly a Jet Ranger, but excited I would be going out on my own for the first time. I felt a bit guilty I would be leaving Barbara and Leslie again, but the truth is, I looked forward to it.

"Where?" she asked, as she looked at me with those sad blue eyes.

"I don't know for sure," I said. "One guy can't go on a contract, and I have to fill in for him for a week. I don't have to go until tomorrow," I said, smiling as if one day at home should make everything rosy.

"You really like it, don't you?" she asked.

"Like what?" I asked innocently.

"You know what I'm talking about. You like being here, you like the country and the people, and you love your stupid helicopters."

"Of course, I do," I said, defensively. "That's why we came here in the first place. We came to see a new country, to make new friends, and to raise our children. You'll like it, too, once you've delivered and things settle down."

"The things you like about it are the very things I hate," she said, almost crying. "I feel lonesome most of the time. You're off somewhere doing something different and I'm stuck alone in this little community where the people look at me like I'm strange."

"Come on," I said, attempting to comfort her. "You're not strange." Then I rubbed her enormous stomach and smiled, "Well, you might be a little strange with this huge tummy. Come on, give this place a chance. People don't know you yet."

Barbara grinned. "Dave, you are coming back for the baby—not like Vietnam?"

"This isn't Vietnam," I said. "I'll be right here," I promised. We held each other for a while and talked of better days in the future.

For the rest of that day, I stayed busy working with Jack, who gave me a hasty checkout on the old Bell 47. There were no helicopter engineers going along on this job, so he taught me how to perform the daily preflight inspection, put oil in the engine and transmission, and take care of the other basic maintenance tasks.

Jack explained what to look for on the tail rotor drive shaft when it needed grease and how to properly lubricate it. He demonstrated the art of pumping air into the oversized floats, which, he explained, were known for leaking overnight. It would be my first time on a helicopter project without a maintenance person to rely on, so I listened carefully.

Later, Jack and I flew the little Bell 47 to Gander Lake, where he went over the basics of flying on fixed flotation gear. The aircraft had dual controls, so either of us could fly. Several times during a critical phase of the takeoff or landing, Jack would twist the throttle off, simulating an engine failure. Suddenly, the helicopter fell like a rock, straight toward the water. But I had expected this since all helicopter training included simulated engine failures.

To recover from an engine failure, the pilot must execute what is called an autorotation.

"A pilot must react instantly," Jack said, as he circled the lake again. "You should react the same way as you do when you sneeze. You don't think about that, do you? You quickly put your hand over your mouth."

He now had the helicopter pointed into a steady wind and continued to talk me through the procedure. "If you lose an engine, don't sit around thinking, just shove the collective down," which he did, "and line up into the wind," as we were. "Get your airspeed back, pick your landing zone, get ready to level out," he continued.

Thus far in my flying career I had never experienced an actual engine failure, but I understood the importance of the procedure and appreciated Jack being so thorough. He made each maneuver look effortless. During my turn at the controls, I had a little trouble getting used to the way the aircraft handled on the large black rubber floats. It felt slow, sluggish, and about as aerodynamic as a bathtub. I seemed to be moving backwards down the scale of helicopters, from a beautiful, turbine-powered Bell Huey I had flown in Vietnam to an antique, piston-powered, Korean War–era leftover. A helicopter with wooden main rotor blades. Not what I had in mind when I left Texas. But a helicopter nonetheless, and I had a job.

Chapter Seven

Late at night, the nickel-sized gravel crunched loudly as Marve eased off the hand brake and let his father's black Oldsmobile roll backwards down the driveway. The gravel drive ran down a steep slope onto the street and allowed Marve to move the car without starting it. His heart pounded as he imagined his furious father coming out of the house to break his neck.

Marve glanced at the back porch to see if his father might be coming for him, then, seeing no one there, quickly turned the steering wheel and started the car. The Olds lurched forward several times as Marve worked the clutch clumsily and gradually gained control. The neighborhood's narrow streets were dark and quiet at elven o'clock night. Marve, feeling nervous, drove a few blocks before switching on the headlights.

Moving along a small back street, Marve took a deep breath and turned left on Yale, a large, busy street frequented by Tulsa cops. Five minutes later, he stopped across the street from Pennington's, a popular drive-in restaurant and high school hangout. Hot rods, clunkers, and a few "daddy's cars" were parked in the lot, and high school students milled around drinking cokes and talking loudly. Marve watched them for a moment, jealous of their age and freedom. He longed to be more like other teenagers. But he knew that if he stayed around Pennington's he would be noticed.

He drove a few blocks west and parked behind a pool hall on Admiral, where he hoped to find one of his buddies. Feeling frightened but gratified, he turned off the ignition and headlights.

"Hey, Marve," someone whispered from across the parking lot. "Get over here, man."

Marve looked toward the darkest spot in the parking lot, and there between an old Plymouth and a broken-down wood fence stood Charlie, one of his school buddies.

"Get over here, man," Charlie repeated, as he took a black hose out of the Plymouth's gas tank and motioned for Marve to stay quiet. "Be cool," he said, pointing over his shoulder, "I'm borrowing some gas for my motorcycle."

The other end of the rubber hose drained gasoline into the gas tank of a Triumph Tiger motorcycle.

"It doesn't take much," he said, grinning. Marve relaxed and grinned back at him, nervously. He stared at the cool motorcycle. "I didn't know you had a bike," Marve said.

"Yeah, well, I didn't know you had a car," Charlie replied, giggling, as he rolled up the hose and attached it to the back of the Triumph.

"It's my old man's," Marve said, pulling a cigarette out his pocket and reaching for a match. "Just borrowed it for a couple of hours but didn't have anywhere to go."

Charlie frowned, grabbed Marve's hand, and said, "Shit, man, don't light that thing. You want to go up in flames? There's gas all over the place."

Charlie hopped on the Triumph, jumped up slightly and kicked the starter. The motorcycle's familiar idle sounds, *blop blop blop blop blop*, filled the air and both boys smiled at each other.

"Follow me, man," Charlie said, "I'll park this thing, and we can ride around in your Olds."

Marve stood in the parking lot, worried about his father or the Tulsa police catching up with him, then smiled and decided to go with Charlie. He ran back to the Olds, started it, and looked up to see two older, much larger boys walk out the back door of the pool hall toward the Plymouth. Marve looked closer at the Plymouth and noticed that Charlie, in his rush to leave, had failed to replace the gas cap. The shiny chrome cap lay on the ground in plain sight, and Marve knew they would think he did it. He frantically worked at putting the car into reverse, a gear he had never used.

A few steps into the parking lot, one of the older boys saw the gas cap, the wet ground beside the car, and turned toward Marve, who looked as guilty as a bank robber. The tall boy shouted something to his shorter buddy and sprinted across the lot toward the Olds. Marve gunned the gas pedal, popped the clutch, and the gears screeched into reverse. As he shifted into first gear, the car lurched forward into the street and the two older boys yelled insults as they chased Marve on foot.

"Get back here, you shithead! If I catch you, you're dead."

The tall boy grabbed a rock and hurled it at the Olds, but it missed his target, striking a parked car and shattering its rear window. With the first boy still in pursuit, but losing ground, Marve drove faster along the street. At that moment, Charlie came out of nowhere cruising along on his motorcycle, long sideburns and leather jacket blowing in the wind. Charlie rode beside the fleeing car, smiled at Marve, then turned and flashed his middle finger at the lone, exhausted boy. The sweaty, worn-out teen returned the gesture with both hands, yelled another obscenity, and gave up his chase.

When they were a mile or so away and certain they had lost their pursuers, Marve and Charlie stopped for a moment. Marve did his best to act cool when he told his friend he had to get the car back home, but both boys knew the fear Marve felt.

A few moments later, as he got close to home, Marve searched the streets for police cars. Seeing none, he looked to see if his father might be on the front porch waiting for him, smoking a cigarette, ready to unleash hell.

But that night there were no police cars and no irate father waiting for him. So Marve, still nervous but quiet as a church mouse, parked the car and snuck into the house. He tiptoed carefully down the dark hallway toward his parents' bedroom. Once inside, the familiar smell of stale cigarettes and empty beer cans filled the night air. His parents slept quietly, so he carefully replaced the car keys and snatched a few more cigarettes.

A few moments later, tired but keyed up, Marve lay in his own bed, safe, thoughtfully smiling in the dark. He extended his right hand toward the window and felt the soft cotton fabric at the bottom of his tan window covering. The cloth felt comforting, soothing. He would lay there for another hour with his eyes open, thinking about the smooth, sensual feel of the steering wheel in his hands, the smell of gasoline on the ground, and the flood of unrestricted power he had felt driving along the dark streets of Tulsa.

***

Jack finished my Bell 47 training on Thursday, and on Friday morning, Barbara gave birth to a strong, handsome little boy. Life seemed to be changing quickly.Two days later I said goodbye to everyone, including my mother, who had braved the long, arduous flight from Tulsa to Gander. Thankfully, Mom planned to stay a few more days to help Barbara, who needed her badly. I don't know what we would have done without her.

Barbara drove with me to the hangar so we could have a few minutes alone. I wore a pair of jeans, my old gray-green Army flight jacket, new work boots, and I carried a soft case with a few changes of clothing.

Alone in the car, Barbara and I felt the tension surrounding us like a stranger hiding in the dark. I reached for her hand. She took it, but didn't hold it in the way you do when you share a love song or gaze at the sunset. She held it like someone desperate to be touched.

"Your mother has been wonderful," she said. "She came all this way to help us. She's different when she isn't around your father."

"Are you different when I'm not around?" I asked, smiling.

"I guess I'm about to find out," she said, as I pulled into the parking lot near the hangar.

She squeezed my hand and sighed. "I'm going to try to make it here," she said. "But I don't know how long I can last with you gone and no family around."

She leaned across the seat and hugged me. I held her for a moment and kissed her cheek, tasting the wetness of a fallen tear. With that small, loving gesture she gave me the send-off she knew I needed. It wasn't a pep rally, but she gave what she had to give, her love and her fragile hope I would be safe, and more importantly, that she would be all right, too.

When she drove off, I picked up my case and went into Jack's office to get a briefing. Jack sat in his office, ready to talk.

"One thing I forgot," Jack said, reaching into his desk. "I got you something." He removed a blue hardcover book from the top drawer and handed it to me.

"This is a proper pilot's logbook, and I want you to take it with you and start logging your flight time. Keep it neat and accurate, and in a few years, you'll be amazed at the stories it will tell."

"Thanks, Jack," I said, looking inside the official-looking gift.

I noticed an area called "remarks" and wondered what in the world I would ever write in that space. Sliding the gift into my bag, I smiled at Jack and thanked him again.

Outside, I carried out a preflight inspection of my newly assigned helicopter, a Bell 47 which had the tail number or registration PHG. The engineers jokingly referred to it as PIG. An old helicopter, essentially equipped for bush flying. It had large black rubber floats and a long metal utility rack on top of the floats to tie down tools, cargo, and a fuel pump. It also had a ten-gallon can filled with aviation gas, or Avgas. I tied my case beside a small red toolbox on the tool rack. To my surprise, inside the helicopter's cabin sat a heavyset man with a scruffy, ginger-colored beard. His clothing were filthy, he smelled of cigarettes, and he held a flat cardboard cigarette package in one hand and a ballpoint pen in the other. Without looking up, he continued writing on the Export A cigarette pack.

"Look here," he said. Unless you like wet clothes, I suggest you put your bag in the aircraft. Rain don't care if you're a new pilot or the chief pilot."

I realized this was the legendary Robert Penny, known around the hangar as "Batty Bob." Robert Penny, one of the oldest aircraft engineers in Canada, had worked on bombers during World War II, then transferred to helicopters in the late fifties. "Batty" or not, he had a reputation for solving engine and transmission problems on aircraft simply by listening carefully through a hollow copper tube.

"Hi, I'm Dave," I said, extending my hand and attempting to break the ice. Bob continued to scribble on his package.

"What are you doing?" I asked. And again, no response from Bob. He didn't seem to be interested in conversation, so I went back and unstrapped my case from the luggage rack, placed it in the front passenger seat, and tied it down with the seat belt.

"So, you think you're ready to take on this little helicopter?" he asked, looking toward me for the first time. "I heard tell of your Army flying over to Burma."

"Vietnam," I corrected.

"Vietnam," he grunted. "Army must have had lot of helicopters."

"Hundreds of them," I offered.

"Well, we don't. This one's a damn good machine. Old, like me, but it'll do a job. Treat it like a woman, and don't ever cuss at it—no matter what." He took a cigarette out of his scribbled-up box and put it in his mouth. I could still smell tobacco on his clothing and wondered how many packs he smoked every day. "One other thing," he said, reaching in his pocket for a match. "Listen."

"I *am* listening," I said.

"No, listen, damn it."

"Like I said, I *am* listening."

Somewhat exasperated, he said, "Listen ... to the helicopter. When you start it up or shut it down, that's the time she's talking to you. She'll tell you her problems, just like a woman. She'll tell you about her day, just like a woman. And if you really take the time, she'll warn you before she loses control." He hesitated.

"Just like a woman," I said.

He shook his head in agreement.

After thanking the old guy for his advice, I climbed into the helicopter, which reeked of smoke. I took off and flew to a little town called Badger, in Central Newfoundland. Finally on my way. As I flew along, I thought, "Perhaps Batty Bob was right," so I began to listen. The old battered headset they gave me offered no noise reduction, making it easy to hear the helicopter's moans and groans.

During the next few weeks, I worked on a mining project hauling four university students who spent their summers getting field experience. All four were Newfoundlanders with previous helicopter excursions under their belt, and they seemed comfortable around aircraft.

Every morning, weather permitting, I flew them into the bush and dropped them off one at a time near a creek or river. All day, they walked along a predetermined route collecting rock samples in search of a potential copper or silver mine. In the afternoon, I picked them up and brought them and their rock collections back to camp. During the day, I found things to keep me busy like fly-fishing, reading, or cleaning the aircraft. It seemed like a cakewalk, such an easy assignment. Sometimes, out in the open fields, all alone, I thought about Barbara and my growing family. And often, I thought about my brother.

***

On Sunday nights, people in Marv's neighborhood either watched the *Ed Sullivan Show* or attended the evening service at the White City Baptist Church. Marve had other entertainment ideas. On this night, he and a few of his messed-up buddies roamed the neighborhood, looking for excitement.

The four teenagers wore their hair slicked back in ducktails, feigned toughness, and cared little for studies or organized athletics. This was the late fifties when Elvis Presley rose to fame and James Dean became an icon for any respectable hood. Marve and his greaser buddies loved to smoke, skip school, and steal cars.

That night, they walked through the church parking lot, egging each other on while searching for an older car that would be easy to hot-wire. Then they found something better: a green-and-white Chevy with the keys in the ignition, just begging for someone to take it for a spin.

After looking around to make sure they were alone in the parking lot, the four boys piled in and Charlie, wearing his worn-out black leather jacket, carefully drove the Chevy out of the church lot and onto Yale Avenue. For the next forty-five minutes, the boys took turns driving up and down the side streets between Fourth Street and Admiral.

They passed pretty girls in shorts, kids on bikes, and now and then, someone they knew. They saw a lot of things that night, but they didn't see the man who came out of the church about the time they drove away. The startled owner of the Chevy watched his stolen car as it moved slowly out of the parking lot.

The reckless boys took turns driving, and Marve, the youngest of the group, took his turn last. And when his time finally came, he excitedly jumped behind the steering wheel and tried to drive away before the previous driver could get back in. But the quick-thinking teen jumped through the passenger side window as Marve hit the accelerator.

"Man, you almost had to walk," Charlie shouted from the back seat.

Marve drove away grinning and said, "Never drove a Chevy before. Damn, this feels good."

"Hey, let's drive over to Pennington's," Charlie said. "See if we can spot some cheerleaders." Marve looked over at him and grinned. "Go, Marve, go," Charlie said.

Marve gladly drove past the popular teen hangout, but didn't stop since he knew they might be spotted by the cops. Instead, they drove to Will Rogers High School and took a couple of laps around the front circle.

"Guess we better get back," Charlie said, sounding a bit worried.

"OK," Marve said, then turned east to drive back to the church.

When they arrived, Marve slowly crept back to the original parking place with the headlights switched off. He turned off the engine and stepped into a dark, quiet parking lot.

"Stay right where you are," someone said. "And you, punk, put your hands on the wheel."

Inside the car, the other three boys, normally loud and boisterous, went silent as they saw the two husky cops pointing pistols at them. Marve froze as he stared into the blue barrel of a police revolver.

"Out of the car, boys," the cop on the passenger side said.

As the frightened boys moved, the hefty officer on the driver's side shouted at Marve, "Not you, son! You stay right there."

"Yes, sir," he said, as he watched his frightened buddies get out. In less than a minute, the other boys were out of the car, walking away. Now, Marve became aware of just how large an empty car can feel.

Frightened and confused, Marve watched as one cop took his buddies to the edge of the parking lot, then pointed at the street. His friends were being let go, and he felt abandoned and afraid. Soon they would be home, safe. Home. Even as the thought of his father crossed his mind, his home sounded wonderful at that moment.

In a few minutes, Marve found himself in the backseat of a police car on his way to jail. He watched out the window as they drove along the familiar streets of Tulsa. Upon arrival, he was booked, printed, and charged with auto theft. Being the youngest of the group and driving last turned out to be his downfall. Around 10:30 that night the phone rang, and Marv's father answered.

"Hello. What the hell do you want at this time of night?"

"Sir," the desk officer said. "This is the Tulsa Police Department. I need to inform you that we have just booked your son, Marvin, for auto theft."

"What?" Dad asked in amazement.

"Sir," he said. "You need to come down here. Your son's a juvenile, and we have to book him into the system."

"Did he wreck the damn car?" Dad asked.

"Well, no, he didn't."

"Is he in the hospital?"

"No, he isn't in the hospital."

"Then I'll be down there tomorrow."

"Yes, sir," the officer said.

The desk officer carefully replaced the receiver and shook his head. He glanced across the crowded police station at the young, frightened boy sitting alone. Over the years, he had seen hundreds of mixed-up juveniles like Marve—rebellious, lonely, and horribly confused. Sometimes, going to jail scared them enough to change their life in a good way. And sometimes it didn't. But after speaking with this boy's heartless father, the desk officer knew this kid had a tough road ahead of him. It probably wouldn't be the last time he'd be booked into the city jail.

Chapter Eight

There are two primary methods of transporting cargo with helicopters, but only one of them would be considered enjoyable. The second one also provided some challenges and often a few hard lessons. The most common way to haul cargo is internally: stacking boxes, crates, and other bulky items on the floor or in the rear cargo compartment. The second is more difficult, more dangerous, and much more fun—sling loading. During World War II, the military developed the technique of sling loading when helicopters hauled nets loaded with freight from one ship to another across the choppy waters of the sea.

The methods were improved on and used abundantly during the Korean and Vietnam Wars. While in Vietnam, it wasn't unusual to see a large Chinook helicopter haul ammunition, food, artillery pieces, or even a broken helicopter dangling beneath it. Now the time came for me to do some sling loading, and I looked forward to it. Jack Murphy had gone over the technique during our training in Gander, and he had warned me to be careful.

After the first few weeks of working with the engineering students, we had assembled a large collection of heavy rock samples which would eventually be transported to the mining office in Grand Falls. But for now, we were to move our operation to another camp farther southwest near a place called Round Pond.

The easiest way to move the rock samples, camp gear, and barrels of aviation is to sling it under the helicopter in a cargo net. The engineering students prepared the loads, and Albert, one of the oldest of the boys, stood beneath the helicopter, then connected the cable to the aircraft's cargo hook while I hovered above him five or six feet off the ground.

On Friday morning I flew three of the mining students to the new campsite. Two of them were to prepare the new cabin and hook up the HF radio while two of them worked at the helicopter landing zones, or LZs. As usual, the cabin was located near a lake, and nearby, a small beach, 300 yards from the cabin became our LZ. I would be slinging all the rock samples, food cases, radios, and other supplies from the old camp to the new camp, one load at a time.

Because of the freedom of movement, slinging is enjoyed by most pilots since it provides a radical change from hauling passengers. We made several trips that morning, and on the last flight, as I crossed the lake, then flew over the beach, I glanced at the black net below me. Feeling the bulky net swing beneath me, I smiled, thinking about Jack Murphy and how he had taught me to line up into the wind and use as little power as possible.

"Don't let the net get to swinging back and forth, and don't come in for a landing hot and high," Jack said. "Learn to take it slow and easy," he'd added. "Like kissing a pretty girl."

As I eased toward the beach, I went over all the things Jack had told me. So far, everything went well, even though the wind had died down. The tall trees located a short distance from the beach prevented me from taking off into the wind after dropping my load. Now, like first three trips, I sat the bulky net on the ground, waited for Albert to give me the thumbs-up sign, then released the net. Next, I hovered about five feet off the sandy beach, then backed away, across the water, hovering in a kind of reverse mode. I continued moving slowly backwards, gaining airspeed and climbing higher into the sky, and as I started to turn, … BOOM!

Without the slightest warning, the most deafening explosion rang out behind me. For a split second, I was back in Vietnam being shot at with bright orange machine-gun tracers flying across the sky. I saw glimpses of soldiers running in the tall elephant grass beneath me as they escaped a barrage of gunfire. At that instant, I wasn't sure where I was or what was going on, but I was certain of one thing; I had no control over the aircraft.

Forty feet above the lake, the helicopter pitched nose up into the air then rolled over on its back like a whale in the Pacific Ocean. In slow motion, I saw a shocked look appear on Albert's face, wispy, crème-colored clouds adorning the blue sky, and finally crystal-water directly ahead. An instant later, the disabled helicopter plunged upside down into the lake with a horrifying crash, crushing the top of the fuselage, bashing the main rotor blades into pieces, and sending me, strapped to my seat, straight to the bottom of the lake.

Twenty feet below the surface, upside down in the frigid, murky water, I frantically tried to make sense of my situation. Completely disoriented, I searched for the seat belt release. Now, in what felt like an underwater grave, I lost my sense of balance. As I touched the seat belt release, I realized my full body weight pushed down on the seat belt, preventing it from opening. Dangling helplessly, with my head pressed into the mud, I had to overcome one of the most horrible feelings in the world—disorientation. Desperate for air, I relaxed my body and simultaneously pulled the release. *Snap*, it opened. Falling out of the seat, I landed on my side in the mud and broken Plexiglas.

Now, free from the seat belt, I had to find a way out of the mutilated aircraft. I frantically pulled on one of the doors, but it wouldn't budge. I moved to the other side of the cabin, only to find the second door crumpled and useless. The doors were jammed, the Plexiglas roof of the cabin rested against the bottom of the lake, and I had no escape route. In that instant, I knew I must make my own route or die trying.

Feeling around the floor above me, I touched the soft leather cover of the emergency axe fastened against the floor as part of the emergency equipment. I quickly removed the axe, thrust its heavy steel head upward into the Plexiglas, and tried desperately to break the chin bubble. The first blow glanced off the Plexiglas, doing little more than scratching it. Then I struck the second time, putting all my strength, desperation, and fear into one thunderous blow. The Plexiglas shattered, and somehow I managed to squeeze through the tiny chin bubble and rise to the surface of the lake, anxiously gasping for air.

Taking in the fresh, wonderful air, I coughed, treaded water, and looked across the lake. Relief washed over me as the sun warmed my face and glorious oxygen filled my breathless lungs. Someone behind me shouted, "Dave, over here!"

I turned and faced the shoreline. Albert swam toward me. A few seconds later he grabbed me and pulled me toward the beach through the broken Plexiglas, twisted pieces of rotor blade, and oil-stained water. When he dragged me out of the lake, his shirt was covered with bloodstains. I lay in the cool sand, looking into Albert's worried face as he pushed rhythmically against my chest. *What was he worried about*, I wondered. *He* wasn't the one who had crashed a helicopter or promised the chief pilot he wouldn't let him down. And *he* wasn't the one who had told his wife that everything would work out.

I reached up and touched the wet, crimson bloodstain on Albert's shirt.

"Albert," I said, "I think you're bleeding."

He looked down at me as if he couldn't understand my words. Water ran down his face and fear shone in his dark, brown eyes. I tried to speak, to ask him what was wrong, but my voice trailed off to a stubborn silence. I lay there looking into Albert's wet, worried face. My eyes grew heavy, just like the helicopter doors. And, like the doors at the bottom of the lake, my eyes refused to open.

***

I heard the unwelcome ring of a phone but ignored it, pulling a pillow over my head in a futile attempt to cut out the annoying sound. But that made very little difference, so after a while I gave up. Stumbling across the dark hotel room, I picked up the receiver and answered the caller in hushed tones.

"Hello," I said.

"Yank," Big Jim shouted. Loud music blared in the background, loud enough to drown out a normal person, but then Big Jim wasn't a normal person. "What the hell you doin', boy?"

"Not much," I offered. "About to head downstairs to watch TV," I lied.

"Bullshit," he said. "You're sittin' around cryin' in your beer, like all those cowboy songs down in the States. You gonna let a small thing like a helicopter crash get you down? A nice few of us are over to the Albatross. Come over and join us."

"No, man, I can't. I'm hopin' my wife will call tonight."

"Bullshit!" he repeated. "Get your arse out of that hotel room and come over here, or I'll come over and knock your door down." I knew Big Jim would do it. He was that wild. But I also knew that I needed to get out of that room.

"OK, Jim. I'll be over in 20 minutes."

"Good," he said, and hung up.

I switched on the lamp near the phone and looked at my depressing hotel room. The hunter's cabin back at Round Pond looked better than this. I had been lazy and let the small, dreary room get cluttered. Dirty clothes were thrown into piles on the floor, and the stink of leftover food and empty beer cans hung in the air like a hangover.

I thought about Barbara. Maybe she did the right thing, choosing to go back to Oklahoma to live with her parents. But I felt an enormous disappointment when I returned to Gander after the accident only to find out that my wife and children were gone. As soon as possible, I called her from the hospital and told her about the accident. Told her not to worry.

"I'm glad you're okay," she said, her voice sounding strained. "I'm so sorry I can't be with you at the hospital. I had to leave. I couldn't take it by myself in that apartment. I had to get out of there. Little David cries a lot more than Leslie did when she was a baby, and I didn't have any time for Leslie." She paused, then said, "Are you sure you're okay?"

"I'm fine," I said, feeling so homesick for her. Hearing her sweet voice touched me deep inside.

"What if something else happens?" she asked.

"Nothing will happen," I said.

"How do you know nothing will happen? You've only been up there a month, and look at all that's happened already. Can't you come back to Oklahoma and find another job?"

"I want to finish what I started. Please, honey, come back to Gander. I really need you."

"I'm sorry," she said. Then, in the background, I heard the familiar sounds of little David crying, and when Barbara spoke again, her voice sounded even more strained. "I've got to go," she said. "He's hungry again."

We ended the conversation at that point with neither of us ready to change our mind. I didn't know what would become of our marriage. Her parents and sisters were terrific at helping her. The same way they did while I was in Vietnam. But I missed Barbara and wanted her in Newfoundland. One more glance around the messy, depressing motel room and I knew Big Jim said it right; I needed to get out of this place.

***

The Albatross Bar is a well-known watering hole inside the Albatross Hotel. That night the bar had plenty of loud music, blue smoke, and drunk pilots. Young girls seemed to be everywhere, giggling, flirting, and hanging onto every war story the pilots had to offer; a typical Saturday night in Gander.

Big Jim sat in a corner with a couple of fixed-wing pilots drinking Labatt's beer and entertaining three busty locals. The girls were dressed in bell-bottom slacks, hip huggers, and revealing, low-cut sweaters. They were young, pretty, and didn't have a care in the world. A couple of them tapped their feet and tried to sing along to Neil Diamonds' *Sweet Caroline*, blaring on the loudspeaker. The girls fumbled the lyrics and chuckled, knowing they were all mixed up. That's when Jim saw me.

"Yank," he shouted. "What the hell took you so long? I told these girls all about you." With a cigarette in one hand and a beer bottle in the other, he pointed at me and spoke to the girls. "This is him, that crazy American I told you about. In Vietnam he puts helicopters in the jungle, in Newfoundland he puts them upside down in the lake. Here you go, Yank!"

Jim passed me a beer, and I took a long slug of it immediately. The girls looked me over and giggled, and by the looks of it, they were doing their best to keep up with Jim's drinking campaign.

One of the girls, a tall blond, exhaled a large puff of smoke, frowned, and said, "We don't like the Vietnam War. Everyone knows they kill babies over there, and we don't believe in killing babies." She took a long drink of her beer. Now, proud of her little rant, her cynical expression revealed her gratification.

"That's good news," I said, casually. "Then I guess you don't believe in abortion."

Jim and his buddies grinned, along with the other two girls, but the tall girl didn't see the humor. She took another puff on her cigarette, then blew smoke toward me, and turned on her heels. She walked toward the bar, then disappeared into the crowd. I felt glad to see her go, but since I had skipped supper, I felt the warm, calming effects of the alcohol faster than normal.

"Don't worry about Cindy," one of the two remaining girls offered. "She doesn't mean anything." She smiled and pushed her long brown hair off her shoulder. It surprised me how good her smile felt.

I slipped my left hand into the pocket of my jeans, hiding my wedding band as a trace of guilt surfaced within me. But in an instant, the guilt got drowned out by something much stronger. Lust. She looked at me with dark, deep-set eyes, and let her hair cascade across her face. That small gesture, which I believed to be intentional, added to her amazing sex appeal.

"Hey, I'm Clara," she said, extending her hand.

"I'm Dave," I replied, trying to be cool. As she took my hand, I felt the soft, tender skin of her palm. She squeezed my hand gently, with a hint of something more than simply saying hello. Her silky fingers caused my heart to race and I could feel my face flush.

"I like your accent," she said. "Where are you from, California?"

"No, I'm from Oklahoma," I said, feeling a little drunk from the combination of strong beer and dark eyes.

"Oklahoma," I said again, "where men are men and women are proud of it."

Jim slapped me on the back and snickered. Clara grinned, stepped around from behind her friend, and came a bit closer, near enough that I could smell her perfume. I reached behind her and touched the wide white belt looped through her hip huggers. Her jeans were so tight she must have struggled to get them on, but they were worth the effort.

"I like your belt," I said, making an excuse to touch her. "You know, you could get by for a California girl."

She smiled and leaned in as a slow, romantic tune played in the crowded bar. Guilty thoughts of Barbara rushed through my mind, but I quickly hid those thoughts like I hid my wedding band. Until that moment, looking into Clara's eyes, I hadn't realized just how lonesome I felt. And besides that, my wife deserted me, not the other way around. A little flirting won't hurt anything.

Jim grabbed several of the empty beer bottles, and he and his buddies walked toward the bar to fetch another round. Clara's friend chatted with a guy at the next table, leaving Clara and me on our own.

"Do you really think I look like a California girl?" she asked, biting her lip slightly.

"Sure," I lied, tugging gently on her belt. It put her close enough that I could smell beer on her breath and the lusty aroma of her citrus perfume mixed with a hint of female perspiration. All of which I found intoxicating.

With her left hand she casually tugged at her sweater, and I could see that she wasn't wearing a bra. She stretched the sweater tight across her supple breasts and I watched, captivated with the attention she offered. I felt as excited as a drowning man reaching for a life raft.

"You know what," I said, purposely dragging out my American accent, "you would look fabulous in one of those beach movies or walking along Sunset Boulevard. No shit, if you were in Hollywood looking like you do right now, they would sign you up in a minute."

She smiled, knowing a lie when she one, but I could tell she loved it. We continued to flirt as the beer and loneliness took me down an exciting, unfamiliar path. A path I willingly explored. Then I heard the soft sound of Kris Kristofferson' singing *Help me Make it Through The Night.*

For a moment I blocked out all my troubles, pushing them back and storing them neatly in a little box at the back of my mind, along with every trace of guilt. At that moment I didn't care about anything—not my wife, my job, or my future. I only cared about being with this beautiful woman and forgetting everything else.

She looked at me with a slight grin, the room seemed to pause for a split second, and Kris Kristofferson sang more of his sexually honest ballad right at me. His deep rich voice spoke into my troubled soul and took away any doubt. I wanted this woman to help me make it through this night.

Chapter Nine

On Easter weekend during my sophomore year at Will Rogers High School, I drove from Tulsa, Oklahoma, down to the Texarkana Prison to visit my brother. Marve and another teenager had escaped from a juvenile facility in eastern Oklahoma, stolen a car, and driven it across the state line into Missouri. They were caught, tried, and found guilty of transporting stolen property across the state line, a federal offense. It would be my first time to visit him since he was sent to prison, and it is scared the hell out of me.

Saturday night I worked a full shift at the grocery store, then left town around 10 o'clock. A few miles south of Tulsa, the highway ahead of me appeared as dark as the inside of a tunnel. Glancing into the rearview mirror, I saw the beautiful lights from the buildings in downtown Tulsa, and the suburban lights of houses and shopping centers spread out along the edge of town. I had never driven out of town alone. Now, fear worked its way into my head, along with fear's hostile twin brother—uncertainty.

Ahead, past the headlights of my old Plymouth, I stared into a pitch-black night with the occasional white lines along a narrow, two-lane highway. There wasn't a town, filling station, automobile, or so much as a light bulb from a farmhouse to be seen. The total darkness outside a city took me by surprise. *Perhaps music will help.* Switching on the radio, I quickly turned to KAKC, one of Tulsa's most popular stations, known for playing the top rock-and-roll hits. My favorite DJ, Dick Schmitz, was on the air, doing his thing.

"Here's a new song from Dee Clark," he said in his deep radio voice. "This one is called *Raindrops* and it's for all you guys who don't have a date tonight."

That's just great, I thought. Now I feel even lonelier. "Guess what?" I said to the radio. "I'm one of those guys you're talking about, a loser without a date on Saturday night."

I kept driving and got used to the long stretches of black highway. Around 1 a.m. I pulled into a little town called Hugo. An old-fashioned country town, Hugo has a city hall and police department near the town square. Since I didn't have enough money for a motel, I parked my car in a safe place, right across the street from the police station. I crawled into the back seat and slept the rest of the night.

The next morning, I drove the few hours to Texarkana, Texas, and the drive gave me a chance to work up my nerve to walk into a federal prison. Near the main building, I drove along "Prison Road" and saw, in the distance, the large, imposing white structure, then noticed men working in the fields nearby. The well-cultivated land north of the prison resembled a large farm with evenly spaced rows of cotton. Sun-baked prisoners, both black and white, wore sweat-stained white uniforms and worked in tight-knit groups. A few prisoners held hoes or picks, and some carried brown burlap bags. Near the prisoners, there were several guards. Wearing large cowboy hats, the guards carried lever-action .30/30 rifles and rode horseback, carefully watching their inmates. I drove slowly and searched for Marve but didn't see him. Several prisoners looked my way, but I quickly looked away, intimidated by their forlorn stares.

Turning off the road into the visitors' parking lot, I got my first close-up look at the prison. The main building, with its enormous white portico, numerous guard towers, and manicured lawn looked every bit as ominous as I had expected. I walked slowly toward the visitors' entrance as the hot April sun bore down on me, and I wondered how prison life had changed my brother. In a few minutes I would find out.

Once inside the prison, they had me sign in, then a guard searched me. After that, I followed another visitor to an outdoor, open area where visitors sat around wooden picnic tables playing with children and waiting for their loved ones to arrive. I watched for my brother and noticed that the other visitors seemed more comfortable about being there.

Fortunately, it wasn't long before Marve appeared at the gate, and what an impressive sight. Now a towering six feet, four inches tall, in spotless prison whites, Marve was tanned, slim, and solid with a smile as big as a hood ornament. He wore his thick, jet-black hair combed neatly in ducktails and he walked confidently, practically strutting as he passed the other visitors and inmates.

I relaxed then, seeing his signature grin, knowing it pleased him to see me. Marve gave me a big brother hug and called me Hot Rod like he always had, and I felt the rigid muscles of his broad shoulders. He wasn't the skinny, freckle-faced boy who had lost fights back in our neighborhood and had cried when our father had beat him. My brother, behind those prison walls, had become a man. A man to be reckoned with.

His first question didn't surprise me. "How's Mom?" he asked. "Why didn't you bring her?"

"She had to work two split shifts this weekend," I lied. "She even has to work tomorrow."

Marve frowned while he thought it over. "She's been working at Southwestern Bell for over twenty years and those assholes won't even let her off on Easter Sunday. She's been there long enough to be a manager, but they treat her like shit."

He frowned again, his face showing his distrust. "Listen to me," he said. "Mom works her ass off and always has. She calls in sick once in a while, because she drank too much the night before. So what? They forget about all the times when she went to work on her day off because somebody else called in sick."

I didn't want to tell Marve that Mom called in sick more often these days, so I changed the subject, "You're right, Marve. You're right. But, tell me about this fancy hotel here. What's it like, do they have room service?"

Marve giggled, and we sat down. It broke my heart to see him standing there grinning at me while the whole world passed by outside those prison walls. But he seemed glad that I asked, so he explained his duties: cleaning floors, working in the laundry, and sometimes getting the opportunity to work outside.

"You tend to forget a lot of bad shit in here," he said. "You forget the fights with Dad, the drinking and all that. You try and think about the good stuff. About home and everything you miss. And hey, I got lots of good to think about: Mom's brown beans and cornbread, Suzie dressed in her blue jeans, excited about going out with Billy on Saturday night. And remember Dad playing football with Tommy Harris and all of us trying to tackle him in the front yard?"

Then Marve looked over at me with a more serious look in his eyes. "And you and I exploring that little creek that runs through the cemetery up on Admiral. Remember that?"

"You mean when we used to catch crawdads in the creek?" I asked.

"That's right," he said. "In those days we thought we were real explorers. Remember, we'd sneak into the graveyard and walk along the creek, inside the tree line where no one could see us, and after a short walk, we'd come out all the way on the other end of the cemetery."

"Sure, I remember," I said, watching his eyes, wondering what he must going through.

"Sometimes," he said. "When I need to think my way out of this place, I remember back when we were kids, coming out of that creek, past the trees and walking to that nice, peaceful open area. It was our secret, wasn't it? It had big ole cottonwood trees, nice grass, and no graves or headstones. Guess it was a place they hadn't used yet. I remember we'd sit in the shade and talk, not wanting to go home 'cause Daddy was drunk, swinging at anything that moved. But that little spot in the cemetery seemed like a private heaven, where we could relax and forget all about the problems at home."

"Sure, I remember," I said. "I never figured out why they hadn't buried anyone over there."

Marve shook his head and looked up into the sky. We talked a while longer, and he told me about some of his buddies inside. I kept expecting him to tell me how he hatted being locked up, but he never did. He never griped about any of it.

I didn't realize it then, but Marve had adapted to prison life, and in a way, he started to feel at home. We talked for a couple of hours, and toward the end it wasn't easy to think of something to say. We both knew I could only stay until 11, the end of visiting hours. Just before the appointed time, a surly guard walked toward us and immediately Marve's posture changed. No longer the fun-loving eighteen-year-old big brother, he was Marvin, the young, hard-ass con, who knew it all and stood ready to take on anyone.

Marve tossed his cigarette into a large red tin can, then stood up tall and strong. The time had come to say goodbye, and say all the things we meant, as well as the things we didn't.

"I'll write more," I said. "And I'll bring Mom down as soon as I can. I love you, Marve."

"I love you too, you little shit," he said. "And tell Mom and Dad I love them, and I'll try to stay out of solitary."

One of the guards walked around the edge of the visiting area, joined by a couple of other guards. Marve hugged me again, then went through the gate without looking back at me. I don't know if he didn't want to look at me or if maybe looking back might make him cry. But watching him walk away, past the last guard and back into that hopeless, dreary prison, brought tears to my eyes.

I felt emotional going into the prison, but now I felt heartbroken walking out. I wanted to take him back home with me and worried about him going back to his cell. He must be feeling lonesome and depressed. He must be fighting off homesickness. I wondered how many times he will be forced to fight his way out of trouble in that vast inescapable prison.

I sat in my car, looking up at the nearby tower where a uniformed prison guard held a scoped rifle as he peered down into the prison yard below him. Did he gaze down at Marve walking back to his cell? Did he realize that my brother is a great guy? I held my hand over my face as I sat in the car and cried, wanting so badly to hug Marve one more time.

On the drive back to Tulsa, with a heavy heart, I remembered it was Easter Sunday. There were people in the little towns dressed in their Sunday clothes, coming and going from churches and cafés. In one small town I drove near a Baptist church where several Negro families walked along the sidewalk, apparently on their way home from an Easter service.

The men were dressed in clean, well-worn brown suits with bright white shirts and thick, dark ties. The ladies wore colorful dresses and pretty hats, and the children were proudly dressed: boys with pressed slacks and white shirts, girls with starched dresses and black shoes. These people, though poor, were proud to be in church on Easter Sunday.

Along the sidewalk, a beautiful young girl, no more than three years old, skipped along with her family. She dropped her Easter basket and started to cry, but instantly her father scooped her up and retrieved the basket and kept walking. She smiled at her father, secure in his arms as he kissed her on the forehead.

I thought of all the boycotts, freedom marches, and daily images on TV lately which showed cruel cops beating up Negroes. Then I wondered how anyone could drive by and not see the precious love this modest family had for each other. It made me think of Marve and something he and the rest of us have in common with the little girl. Like that sweet little black child on the sidewalk, all of us, at some point in our life, need our father to reach down and take us into his strong, loving arms. And if he doesn't, something important, something vital will be missing.

Chapter Ten

One Monday morning in Gander, I awoke to someone knocking on the door of my hotel room. I glanced at my watch. "Hell," I said, "it's already 9:30?" I jumped out of bed, trying to remember what time I needed to be at the hangar. I wiped my hand through my sleep-mussed hair and opened the door. Jack Murphy stood there with a folder in his hand. "Big weekend?" he asked, leaning against the door frame.

"Good morning, Jack," I replied, sheepishly. "Guess I overslept. What's goin' on?" I hated to think what might be in that folder. I worried it might be the results of the accident investigation. Jack looked at my room and shook his head.

"Why don't we talk downstairs in the restaurant," he said. "Looks like you're not quite ready to entertain guests."

"Sounds good," I said, embarrassed.

After cleaning up, I went downstairs and found Jack sitting alone at a table that seemed to be as far from the other customers as possible. I sat across from him, thinking that he may have picked this place in order to fire me. Or worse, maybe the folder contained a stack of invoices for the mutilated helicopter.

Jack sipped his coffee and glanced at me with his poker face. I tried to glean any traces of information from the look on his face, but it was a lost cause. He could be holding a straight flush or a pair of fives and have that same nonchalant expression.

"You need to see this," he said, finally handing me the papers from his folder.

I took the report from him, but couldn't understand the format.

"Jack, I've never read a report like this. It's much different than what I've seen in the Army. For that matter, it's different than anything on the safety bulletin boards at the hangar."

"OK," he said, taking the report back. "This is a government document and strictly preliminary in its scope. That means there will be a more formal conclusion later, but this one gives us the main points."

I worried the report would be stating a cause of pilot error. We were taught in the Army that 90 percent of all accidents were caused by pilot error.

"Dave, there is a lot of information here, and we can go over it in more detail later. There are metallurgy tests that have to be done on the mainland which will tell us more about the engine and transmission. But it appears that at the time of the accident the engine functioned normally, providing power at the time of impact."

"That's good," I said, not sure of what it meant. Jack glanced up at me and continued, "Yes, the engine checked out, but here's the crux of the report: the transmission failed on that helicopter, and it failed at the worst possible moment. You were flying over water, hovering backwards, and the transmission caused the explosion you heard."

His words sent relief through me like water flowing through a desert gulch, but I could tell he wasn't finished.

"You mean I didn't do it?" I asked.

"It means there were complications from a maintenance issue," he said cryptically.

"Say again, Jack."

"It means you won't get a black mark on your flight record," he confirmed.

At that point I was elated and felt a major load being lifted off my back. I wanted to jump up, but I knew this wasn't the time. Anyway, I could tell Jack had more information.

"The investigator," he said, "had a lot to say about your flight scenario at the time of the transmission failure, and he recommended more training—a recommendation I agree with completely."

At that point Jack gave me a stern look, which made me think I really preferred his poker face after all.

"This afternoon we will spend more time untraining you from your Army flight techniques. We'll work for a couple of days here in Gander, and when were finished, you're going back in the field. Maybe the mining job or maybe something else. We need a good pilot, but we don't need a cowboy, you understand?"

"Yes, sir," I said, humbly, still wanting to ask questions about the transmission but thinking this might not be a good time. Jack put the accident report back into the file folder, and I was about to ask him what time to meet at the hangar. Without warning, I felt a pair of small, smooth hands around my neck.

"Guess who?" Clara asked as she stood behind me. Jack looked up at Clara, and the passive look on his face changed to deep concern. He couldn't have looked any more surprised if he had seen the queen of England standing behind me.

***

During the next two days, the hungry hordes of large black flies around Gander must have loved the heat, because they never let up. But neither did Jack Murphy. He demonstrated and redemonstrated every flight maneuver and safety feature. We performed at least thirty auto-rotations, which is a fancy name for recovering from an engine failure. We also did more sling loading, water landings, and water takeoffs. He taught and retaught me all the safety briefings and passenger procedures. During this whole exercise, Jack was all business, offering little or no chitchat, even while flying from point to point with time to kill. Around seven p.m. one night, we sat in Jack's office while he documented the training. The room seemed unusually quiet as tension lingered between us. Jack's placid temperament had bothered me during the flight training, and I had a fairly good idea what caused him to act this way.

"So, I head out tomorrow morning," I said, trying to engage him. He finished signing my logbook and shook his head, but he said nothing. For two days he had given me the cold shoulder, and I had enough of it.

"Jack, what's the problem? You've been acting like I robbed a bank or something."

His piercing blue eyes drove right through me, like a father looking at a wayward son. He stopped working and sat back in his chair.

"You remember our discussion about hovering backwards," he asked.

"Yes, sir," I said, guessing he was still upset about the accident.

"When you step outside your marriage, you might as well be hovering backwards. You might as well look for a place to crash, because you *will* crash."

"Wait a minute, Jack," I said. He put his hand up for me to keep quiet, and I did.

"That girl in the restaurant, that's what I'm talking about. You're going into isolated country where no one will know how you fly and no one will know how you live. But it doesn't mean you don't have to answer to anyone."

"Hold on, Jack," I said, trying to interrupt him. But once he started, he wouldn't let up.

"You hold on," he said, with more anger in his voice than I had ever heard. "You don't realize now, but the person you have to answer to is *you*."

This wasn't right. He has not right talking to me like this. "Who do you think you are, lecturing me about my private life? Do you give this lecture to all the pilots and engineers, or just to the new guys?"

Jack leaned across the desk, his face resuming his standard passive look. I had no idea what he might be thinking.

"Well, maybe you're right," he said, in a more composed tone. "It's pretty common around here for guys to have something going on outside marriage. We've had pilots fly in the worst snowstorm you've ever seen, trying to get to a village or town where they know a girl." Now Jack's face grew sad, almost gloomy. "They forget their wife and kids once they go into the field."

"Jack, I'm not going be like that," I said, still sore about the lecture.

"Dave, I've been doing this a long time, and I see things from a different perspective than you. You may not think so, but I'm trying to help you."

"You mean like when you let me go up to Labrador with street shoes. Let me go into the bush with snow up to my ass and didn't warn me."

Jack waited a moment before he answered, surprised at my anger.

"That's right," he said, with no sign of an apology in his voice. "There are two kinds of mistakes: the ones that make you and the ones that break you. Some are things you need to learn the hard way, and the other things you need to avoid altogether. Let's say you're out in the field and forget to bring your sleeping bag. You get fogged in or have mechanical problems with your helicopter and need to spend the night in the helicopter. After freezing your butt all night, you'll never forget your sleeping bag again, will you? Boots and heavy socks, that's the same kind of thing. On that first trip up to Labrador, you learned a lot."

"I get it," I said.

"But the other kind of lesson is this: Let's say you make a habit of stretching each tank of fuel in your helicopter. Trying to squeeze a bit more time out of your fuel. Then one day you run out of fuel and crash. You won't be able to live long enough to learn from that mistake. So, stretching a tank of fuel is a mistake you're better off avoiding altogether."

"I understand," I said, looking at Jack and waiting for him to make the connection to my weekend in Gander.

"All right, if you understand those principles in flying, then the same thing goes for romance. Let's say you go out to supper with your wife and a pretty girl walks by. You take a good look, and your wife sees you and she gets upset. Next time a pretty girl walks by, you want to look but you don't, because you've learned from your mistake.

"On the other hand, think about this—you're working out in the field and meet this young, pretty Newfoundland girl. She's starving for attention, and the next thing you know she's ready for a sleepover in your motel room. One night when you're back home with your family, the doorbell rings. Guess who's there with her big brother? That's right, the pretty girl from the village. You stand in the doorway looking at your visitors when your wife shouts 'Who is it?' That's like running out of fuel; it will break you."

"I get it, Jack. I get it." I understood his point, but I didn't need this lecture. Jack relaxed a bit, looked over at the window, then back at me. His face was sincere, his eyes gentle. "More important than any of those reasons," he said. "You sat right here and told me what a wonderful woman your wife is. You told me about how she waited for you to come home from Vietnam, and how she believed in you and came three thousand miles so you could become a bush pilot. If you want her to believe in you, find something else to do when you're away from home . . . books or music, whatever you like."

At that point, my feeling of anger evaporated, replaced by remorse and regret.

"Thank you, Jack," I said. I'm sure he could tell from my face that I took his comments seriously. With nothing else to say, I grabbed the maps, logbooks, and flight report books that he had prepared. Jack shook my hand, and I thought I saw the faintest hint of a smile. I don't know what he was thinking, but I do know he had delivered his message and it had hit me right in the heart.

***

Compared with my first month in Newfoundland, the rest of the summer seemed calm. Oh, there were weather issues and maintenance problems, of course, but things settled down to a kind of normalcy, if you could call it that. My assignments took me from south coast villages all the way back up to Labrador, and during those weeks I began to feel comfortable flying the Bell 47, finally understanding its capabilities. Soon I recognized weather patterns, what to expect, and most of all—what to avoid.

One beautiful summer day I flew alone across the south coast of Newfoundland on my way to a village called Burgeo. I went there to pick up the manager of a mining project and spend the day with him in that area. That morning the weather was clear and the wind calm, but soon the fog rolled in from the Atlantic, covering the hills and bogs in a gloomy gray blanket.

As I flew along the shoreline toward Burgeo, fog shrouded the Atlantic and loomed larger than life. An endless barrier that rode atop the massive ocean like a wall. Flying over the water now, on my left, the rocky coastal cliffs jutted out at me, at times no more than fifty feet away from the tips of my spinning rotor blades. The fog pushed me closer and closer to the shore, but I had no place to land.

Ten minutes later, I could see the outline of two or three colorful houses and a small dock. I quickly turned toward what appeared to be a tiny village, or what Newfoundlanders call an "outport."

There was a grass-covered clearing near an old, two-story wooden church, and I landed there. I shut off the engine, and as the wooden rotor blades whirled above me, I looked toward the church to see if the curious people from the outport would be approaching the helicopter. I wanted to make sure that no one walked down the hill into the spinning rotor blades.

The vast, silent fog continued to spread from the ocean, past the dock, and now covered the tiny fishing village. It spread like a massive wave overpowering a sandcastle on a beach. One moment I could make out a few shabby wooden houses, but soon the fog obscured everything except the blue frame of the church. But still, no people anywhere. *They must be frightened*, I thought. There were stories about helicopters going into remote villages and outports like this for the first time, and how the residents, being shy and fearful, remained in their homes.

I walked toward the houses, which were colorful, square structures, some on stilts, and a few sitting right on the massive bedrock. Nearby, a large, two-story house with small square windows faced the bay. Quickly I walked over to it and knocked on the door loudly, but no one came to the door. I knocked again, and only silence. Stepping to the house next door, I knocked harder, as I felt irritability claw at me like a nervous cat. *Where's that famous Newfoundland hospitality I heard so much about?* In the still, foggy air, the village remained silent, somewhat eerie, except for the lonesome sound of a loon crying across the bay.

Retracing my steps across the wooden platform, I decided to find out what why no people were around. I stood at the edge of the dock, faced the houses, and yelled into the air, "Hello!" No one answered. Then I thought of something. I yelled, this time louder, "Hello, I'm not a

Canadian Mounted Police Officer. I'm not a Mountie."
Silence, again.

I went to the door of the two-story house and knocked, then opened it slightly. "Hello," I said. "Is anyone home?"

Carefully I stepped inside, taking a moment to let my eyes adjust to the gloomy interior. My heart beat faster as I waited for someone to show themselves and order me to leave. Not a sound could be heard, not even the loon's complaint. "Hello in the house," I said. "Anybody home?"

I walked quietly, expecting at any moment someone would jump out of a closet or come running out of the bathroom. My eyes slowly adjusted to the natural light, and I could see a clean interior with simple, handcrafted furniture. A few pieces made from what appeared to be barn wood or barrel wood. Thick wooden steps led to the second floor, and I walked up slowly, only to find another room full of old furniture. A beautiful, handwoven bedspread lay across a child-sized bed with a well-worn teddy bear propped against the pillow. The abused bear seemed to be made from strips of old shirts, pieces of gabardine, and had little rubber boots made from tiny sections of discarded hip waders.

"But where are the children?" I wondered aloud. Not a sound, nor a movement of any kind, and like *Goldilocks and the Three Bears*—these people had gone out and left their home unlocked.

It felt strange, being in what appeared to be an abandoned village. I ran outside, down a small gravel pathway to a little house built on planks above the water. It seemed solid enough, but crude in its design and structure. This time I banged hard on the door and the door swung open as I struck it.

Walking into the house, I stooped to cross under the short, narrow doorway, feeling as though walking back in time. Like the other, this tiny house had the same rough furniture in the hallway and kitchen. There was a simple pinewood table and chairs, but no sink. A homemade bookshelf, and something I had never seen before outside a museum . . . a perfectly good, full-sized spinning wheel. A rare, lovely antique.

Then I looked closer and noticed an old oil lamp atop the bookshelf. It had a chimney stained black from use, and brass fixtures which were dulled but usable. Its green porcelain base seemed to be in perfect condition. The brand name of the lamp was Aladdin. Then it hit me, this village has no electricity and no running water.

At that point I relaxed and enjoyed looking through the house. Each room had worn but well-maintained furniture, antiques, rugs made of rags, rugs made from flour bags, Aladdin oil lamps and hand-sewn bedcovers. I noticed a small stack of wood near a stove in the kitchen, so I helped myself and made a fire. I sat in one of the kitchen chairs, smelling the aroma of the sweet burning wood, listening to the crackling of the kindling, and felt warmer and more relaxed. Outside, the solitary loon called for his lover, and a second later it disappeared, hidden once more in the capricious fog.

Leaning back in the chair, the soothing warmth of the fire felt wonderful. Stripped of all worries and concerns, I looked around the room. In that quiet moment I let my mind stray to the things and the people I cared about. What were Barbara and the kids doing at that moment . . . My parents? My sister? And, of course, my brother?

Chapter Eleven

In a small, two-man cell, deep in the bowels of the Oklahoma State Prison, inmate number 71907, Marve Eagleston, lay on his bunk, carefully watching the open door for unwanted visitors: sadistic men, looking anywhere for a fight, or someone to maul. He occupied the bottom bunk, which offered less light for reading, but as the new guy, he kept his mouth shut and took the lower bed without a word.

The prison, known as Big Mac due to its proximity to McAlester, Oklahoma, held over 2,000 inmates when Marve arrived in 1965. They had transported him, along with six other new fish, to the prison in a white bus. The driver stopped in a small spot off the highway, right before they entered the prison gate. He parked in a position which afforded the new prisoners a good view. A look at the massive death-gray building which would, in a few minutes, become their home. The somber men sat quietly in the bus looking across the open fields at the prison's main building and were justifiably intimidated. The driver glanced at the pale faces of his passengers, knowing he had accomplished his goal, then crept back onto the road and drove the next half mile to the prison.

As the surly bus driver brought them closer, the fearful new prisoners watched two chain gangs working in the prison farm, south of the main building. Marve watched poker-faced as striped uniforms labored in the hot afternoon sun. He had heard about Big Mac and knew that it would be a hellhole compared with the snug cells at Texarkana. He had never worked on a chain gang before, but as he watched the men struggle, he told himself he would figure out a way to get through this.

***

In his cell, the constant noise and incredible heat seemed unbearable. Temperatures in the rotunda often climbed well above 90 degrees, and the thought of air-conditioning was only a dream. One of nine hundred inmates in the east cell house, main rotunda, Marve did his hard time with thieves, rapists, child molesters, and murderers. Regardless of their crime or propensity for violence, they were housed together.

The guards, or keymen, as the prisoners called them, were paid around $300 a month to risk their lives twelve hours a day and worked mandatory overtime due to understaffing. With their long hours, poor pay, and dangerous duty, it wasn't unusual for a guard to take a bribe or do a favor for an inmate.

Given their inability to enforce even the most basic of rules, the guards encouraged a system where prisoners were self-policed. Each cell section had a "straw boss" who intimidated, managed, and often beat his fellow prisoners. The boss was either the toughest con in the group or had the ability to manage several of the most dangerous prisoners. Those who kept him in power acquired authority and privilege for themselves.

When a guard needed a group of inmates for a work detail, say ten men for the mess hall or twenty for the corn crop, he asked the boss. The straw boss selected the men, and they reported for duty without hesitation. The system worked because anyone who didn't follow orders paid a violent price while the guards looked the other way.

While many of the prisoners were confined to their cells when they weren't on a work detail, the straw boss roamed the rotunda freely. He often became so close with a guard that he strolled into a guard's office, had coffee, and helped plan the day's activities.

Because Warden Ray Page had a goal for the prison to be self-sufficient, its built-in free labor produced everything they needed to eat: cattle, swine, eggs, milk, corn, beans, and several other crops. So organized, it produced more than necessary and often sold excess produce to local schools. Along with the farm work, inmates could be sent for inside duties like the prison furniture factory, license tag section, and cannery. Prisoners knew they were going to work somewhere, so they needed be in good with the straw boss and get an assignment to one of the best work gangs.

But the worst work detail, the place to be avoided at all costs was the brickyard—a large, dusty, open area where bricks were manufactured and heated in a giant kiln. A place where treacherous men labored in horrible conditions, making and stacking bricks. A guard tower next to the brickyard provided the guards an excellent view of prisoners working below, and there were a few guards on the ground to try and maintain order. But the tower guards didn't worry about the inmates around the brickyard, because they were the most dangerous and unruly. The worst of the worse. It wasn't uncommon for an inmate to crush a fellow inmate's skull or even attack an unsuspecting guard with a brick. The brickyard would be the deadliest of all work assignments.

At twenty-two years old, Marve was one of the youngest men in the massive, overcrowded prison. He worked hard at staying alive and trying to stay out of the straw boss's way. Like most inmates, he stayed in contact with the outside world through the letters he wrote and received. During those early days in Big Mac, his thoughts normally turned to girls.

Somewhere between his easy stretch in Texarkana and his current prison sentence, Marv met and married Donna, an alluring young girl who had recently graduated from high school. Barely eighteen and running with a fast crowd in the various Tulsa bars and nightclubs, she met Marve on a Saturday night and fell for him on the spot.

When she saw the six-foot-four bouncer, with thick, wavy black hair, rock-solid prison-buffed body, and brooding dark eyes, she might have thought he looked like a TV star. Perhaps he seemed worldly compared to the younger people she knew. Whatever it was, from that moment on, he made her life more exciting. They frequented the Tulsa night spots and ran with Marve's ex-con buddies, and at some point, they were married.

In those days, Marve worked as a bouncer at a well-known Tulsa night club and spent many of his off-duty hours skirting the outer limits of the law. He carried a pistol most of the time and pulled off a few minor-league crimes, and it eventually led him back to prison. Donna had been young and hopeful, but the relationship didn't last long. Her hopes and dreams of a normal marriage never had a chance. They were divorced in less than a year.

Now Marve wrote cute and charming letters to other girls he had met, and occasionally wrote his mother. Of course, by this time his mother had become accustomed to it all. She had sat alone and humiliated on the hardwood benches of several Tulsa courtrooms, faithfully and grudgingly attended her son's hearings and trials, and spent her own hard-earned money to pay his lawyers and court fees.

She had been raised by her widowed mother during the depression in a father-less family that had survived on government assistance and the meager income from her two older brothers. Growing up in the tiny boom towns around the Eagle Picher mines in Eastern Oklahoma, his mother had respected hard work and obeyed the police. She now worked as a telephone operator.

His mother couldn't imagine that one of her own sons would ever spend time in prison, and it took her several years and a full head of premature gray hair to get over the realization that her sweet, handsome Marve was becoming something most people only whispered about and her friends never mentioned—a criminal.

It tore her up inside to see him sitting in court and to hear his name read aloud from the police records. Of course, she also felt a mother's private guilt for the mistakes she might have made which caused him to be there, and the never-ending public shame. So a liquid escape became an essential part of her life. If she had craved alcohol before her son's legal battles, now she demanded it.

During those years, if her son was on parole or out of jail awaiting a court appearance, she couldn't relax because she knew the phone would ring at any moment. She knew they would inform her when he went to jail, or wound up in the hospital, drunk tank, or worse. But deep in her soul, so deep she wouldn't admit it to anyone, not even herself, she knew that she would only be able to stop worrying when he went back in prison. So, she pushed those thoughts even farther back in her mind, because thinking such cruel and callous thoughts made her feel even more guilty and made her crave that alluring liquid escape even more.

***

"Wake up," someone said. In a sleepy daze, I glanced around the kitchen in that abandoned Newfoundland house and saw two men gawking at me. They wore tall rubber boots, well-worn, warm clothing, and appeared to be fishermen. The eldest, in his seventies or eighties, stood a bit taller than his young friend and had a scruffy white beard and a full head of silver hair. The younger man, shy, reserved, in his early twenties, kept his distance.

They were an odd pair, tanned and trim, but otherwise complete opposites as far as features, age, and mannerisms. Where the older man had a friendly and outgoing personality, the young fisherman seemed quiet, somewhat suspicious of me. Both men squinted, as if their eyes were adjusting to the indoor light, then glanced at each other before the older man finally broke the silence.

"Are you a Mounty?" he asked.

"No, I'm not. I'm a helicopter pilot."

"Are you a wildlife officer?" the old man asked.

"No, sir."

The old man took off his hat, scratched his head and asked, "Then are you here on any government business whatsoever?"

"No, sir. I'm here because I got trapped by the fog. I had to land somewhere, so I put my helicopter over there by that church. I went around to talk to the people that live here, but I couldn't find anyone."

"I'm Robert Hearn," he said, "And this be my grandson, Ralph." They relaxed then, relieved to know I wasn't a Canadian Mounted Policeman.

"We live in Western Newfoundland during the winter and come back here each summer," he said. "This is Petites; it's one of many outports that got caught up in that *Newfoundland Resettlement Program*."

"The what?" I asked.

"Resettlement program," he said. "See, there are no roads to this place and very little coastal transportation. It cost the government a lot of money to subsidize food shipments and send medical people every month. And, like a lot of other places along the south coast, you can only get in and out of here by boat. Completely isolated. A few years ago, the Newfoundland government decided to uproot hundreds of families along the south coast, including all the families from here, and pay to have them move to regular towns and cities in Newfoundland. That left tiny settlements like this totally abandoned. Ghost towns, my son. That's what they are."

At that point Ralph filled in the rest of the story, "Grandpa and I fought tooth and nail to try and stay on. Didn't we, Grandpa?"

"That's right, Ralph," the old man said, smiling a bit, letting Ralph continue.

"Begged our relatives not to go. But after a while, like everyone else, we up and moved away."

"Joey Smallwood," Mr. Hearn said. "Joey done this."

"The premier?" I asked.

"That's right, b'y," he said, shaking his head. "He done it, and he don't care what happens to the likes of us. But we sneak back here come spring and go out for cod."

"Sometimes," Ralph said. He foolishly looked around the room to make sure we were alone. "We put out a thousand hooks, bait them with herring, then takes a boatload o' cod down to Burgeo."

"A thousand hooks?" I said. "That's a lot."

Old Mr. Hearn winked at me, and I took it as a subtle sign that his grandson might be exaggerating . . . just a bit. A peculiar young man with a muscular body and a thin, rugged face. But somehow the combination seemed a bit odd. His hair, dark and dirty, rather long, and when he smiled, I noticed several teeth were missing. He seemed to think hard before he spoke, carefully releasing his sentences, words that weren't quite ready to escape. But he showed great respect to his grandfather and spoke politely and cautiously to a stranger.

"Yes, boy," Mr. Hearn said. "That Joey Smallwood changed all this," he said as he pointed to the empty room. "And he's like a god to some, the ones who think he can do no wrong. You may not believe this, but ten years back if you visited a house like this, people only had three pictures on the wall: the pope, the queen, and Joey Smallwood."

"He's right," Ralph said, excited about the discussion.

"And something else," Mr. Hearn said. "People used to be so crazy about Joey Smallwood that when they died, they was buried with a picture of Joey in their coffin."

"My gosh," I said.

Out of the blue Ralph asked, "Where are you headed?"

"I'm trying to get to Burgeo. Been waiting for the fog to let up."

"Yes," Ralph agreed. "Fog's wonderful t'ick this morning. It's going to take some time for the fog to burn off." Then with a bit of Newfoundland charisma, "So, come on now, boys, let's have a cup of tea and a biscuit."

Ralph seemed to know his way around the house, even though it wasn't their house, and since I had a fire going, they suggested we stay right here. Ralph ran off for a few minutes and returned with tea bags and a package of stale cookies, happy to share what little they had.

We relaxed and enjoyed the tea and cookies as they explained that the house we were in belonged to one of their friends, Albert Brown. They told me he too returned to Petites for a few weeks every summer.

"So, the guy who owns this house is coming back here?" I asked.

"Yes," Ralph said, "he'll be here, won't he, Grandpa?"

"Yes," Mr. Hearn confirmed, smiling at his grandson, pleased to see the young man engaged in conversation.

"Good," I said. "He has something in the closet I would like to buy from him." I walked over to the closet, opened the door and brought out a large, antique, double-barreled shotgun with the longest barrel I had ever seen. The stock was hard wood, possibly walnut, and sturdy as a rock. The muzzle and barrel steel were well worn and slightly rusty, but the gun appeared to be in good condition considering it might be over a hundred years old. It didn't take an expert on flintlock or percussion shotguns to know that I held true collector's item.

I waited as the two of them muttered something, conferring, and perhaps arguing on a price. I expected them to mention a $500 price tag that would be so far out of my league it might as well be a million.

"Well," the old fisherman said, "that ole thing is only good for shooting ducks, and time back then we shot twenty or thirty ducks at once with it. But it's good no longer. Take it with you, sure. Albert won't care."

"Yes, sure, take the old thing," young Ralph said, smiling as if he had been the owner. It surprised me that they didn't ask for money, because it was obviously a rare and valuable antique shotgun. I felt a strong temptation to follow their advice, but then I thought of something else. With a pen that I removed from my flight jacket, I wrote to Albert Brown on my small notepad. The note included my name and phone number.

The two fishermen gave up their efforts to try and convince me to take it, but they seemed pleased with the idea of leaving a note for Mr. Brown. The matter was settled. Then, just to pass some time on a foggy morning, I asked Mr. Hearn to tell me a bit more about his background and how long he had been a fisherman.

"Grandpa, tell him about killing swiles," his grandson said excitedly.

"What are swiles?" I asked, but quickly remembered the old skipper telling me about seals the day we got off the ferry.

"Boy, you got lots to learn about this hard country," Mr. Hearn said. "Swiles is seals, and each spring the seals come down from the Arctic on the ice. Newfoundlanders have been going out and killing swiles for more than a hundred years, and I done it five years in a row when I was young."

"Grandpa, tell about the *Newfoundland* and ole Captain Kean," Ralph said, excitedly.

"Yes b'y, yes," his grandfather agreed, his kind, wrinkled face turning from a smile to a look of stern concentration. As he gathered his thoughts, his grandson took a deep breath and watched closely with admiring eyes.

"Well, that year, already eighteen years old, I set to go on my first seal hunt. My two friends and I had everything planned. Between us, we had enough money to get to St. John's and planned to sign on with any ship that would take us." Then his face looked sad for the first time as the twinkle left his blue eyes. "But me mother, fearful I'd be killed, got me drunk with rum and locked me in the basement, so I missed the boat to St. John's."

"So you went the next year?" I asked, trying to understand why he looked so disappointed.

"Tell him, Grandpa," the eager young man said. His grandfather sighed, collecting his thoughts.

"It was March of 1914," he said. "My two chums made it to St. John's, where they signed on with an old sailing ship after failing to get on a steamer. Young and inexperienced, they were lucky to get on at all, sure. Now in those days, the hardest, most famous ship captain was Captain Abe Kean. A living legend, feared by every man on every ship, regardless of their position. His word was law.

"And that year one of Captain Kean's sons commanded an old wooden ship, the SS *Newfoundland*. After sailing through rough ice all the way from St. John's up to the Gulf of St. Lawrence, the ships spread out along the pack ice in search of seals. The sea was covered with ice making for slow progress. When the first ship spotted the swiles, the captain yelled, 'Over the side, lads,' and the men went onto the ice, never knowing how far they would walk or when they would return."

For a moment the old man seemed stuck inside his memories, so I glanced at Ralph, who quietly waited for his grandfather to continue. The old man picked up a cookie, but then changed his mind and put it back on the table. Finally, he turned toward the window and spoke softly, "Later that day, all through the northern peninsula and Labrador, it come a terrible storm, it did, and the men from many a ship walking out on that ice got caught in it. Most of them made it back to their ships or to another ship before nightfall, but some of the old wooden-hulled ships got stuck in the ice and couldn't fetch their men.

"The SS *Newfoundland* was one of those stuck in the ice. A large group of exhausted, hungry sealers from the *Newfoundland* walked all day and made it to Captain Abe Kean's ship, the *Stephano*. They thought they had been saved and figured he would let them spend the night on that wonderful steel-hulled ship. But no, he didn't let them stay. He gave them a mug of tea then put them right back onto the ice. Cruelly ordered them to walk back to their own ship.

"The deadly storm got wonderful strong, and a few hundred men spent the night out on that barren ice field. Some were already wet from falling in the water, and they were all out of food, bitter cold, and bone-weary.

"The freezing winds howled all night long, and ice covered the men's faces and hands. In those days they didn't have proper gloves or winter clothes. Some of those men and boys gave in to it and lay down on the ice to sleep and to die. But some fought bravely and somehow survived one of the worst winter storms in history. Those poor devils suffered through it for two days and two long nights on the wide-open ice packs at the edge of the Atlantic Ocean.

"The morning when the storm finally let up, the steel ships were able to break through the ice and search for the lost men of the *Newfoundland*. They found them, and it was a tragic sight they seen. So tragic and appalling, it broke the hearts of the hardest, toughest men among them. More than one hundred men from the *Newfoundland* had gone onto the ice two days before, and what remained was a silent death camp where men and boys littered the ice, frozen where they slept or where they fell.

"Ice-covered bodies, scattered in bunches. Some found flat on their back looking up toward the sky as if they had seen a friend or a vision of their wife right before they gave up. Many were found huddled together with their friends, arms around each other in a vain attempt for community heat. In a few grotesque locations, men had made wind barriers or walls by stacking the frozen bodies of their fallen friends to protect themselves from the furious winds. But, Dave, the most heartbreaking sight of all was an ice-covered man, frozen solid, sitting between his two sons, with his arms around them in his last gesture of fatherhood. These men were left to die by the heartless captains who only had money on their mind." [1]

"That's horrible," I said. "Didn't the government put the captains in jail? Weren't they responsible?"

"No, b'y," the grandson answered. "They had an investigation, sure. A big government query, or something. But they did nothing. Nothing."

"Inquiry," the old man said, gently correcting his grandson. Then he looked back to me, "You know my two friends, the lads I told you about, who had never been to the ice before? They were there, and they helped carry some of the bodies and even fetched one poor soul who survived."

"Did they meet Captain Kean?" I asked.

"No, they didn't see Abe Kean."

"Well, what about the ole captain?" I asked. "Did they force him out?"

"No," Mr. Hearn said. "They puts a lot o' pressure on'm, but he didn't flinch during the inquiry and came out of it without a scratch."

"And what about your two buddies, Mr. Hearn? Did they go back to the ice, or did they quit after such a dreadful experience?"

"They didn't quit. They went with me for the next five years, and when we were on those ships, Frank told and retold the story of the *Newfoundland* to anyone who would listen. Many a time, as we drank a mug of tea or cleaned seal pelts on deck, with wide-eyed young men listening, Frank told that tragic story and always ended it the same way:

"'Two of us went on the ice that fateful year of 1914. Risking life and limb, we did. Enduring one of the hardest starms in these parts, looking death right in the eye. Right in the eye. Yes b'y. Yes, we did.'

"Frank looked over at me, as his listeners followed his lead, 'But during that horrible winter storm,' he said. 'Only one of us sat in his mother's warm basement. As we risk life and limb, he risk tea and crackers. As we looked death in the eye, he looked his dog Willy in the eye.'

"At that point, the entire assembly would shriek like a bunch of wild animals, while I turned as red as Santa's suit. 'Damn you,' I'd say, then throw anything I could get my hands on—a bloody seal pelt, a flagpole—and a few times I would chase Frank around the deck, ready to kill him if I could."

"I'm glad you didn't go that year, Grandpa," Ralph said, admiring his grandfather. "You might have been one of the poor souls that didn't come back."

"What an experience," I said. "Thank you for telling me."

Looking past the two men, through the kitchen window, I could finally see the sun's bright light. The fog had finally cleared, and I would be able to leave soon. After thanking my two new friends for sharing their hospitality and wonderful stories, we walked to the helicopter, bade farewell, and I took off, then circled low over Petites.

Soon, the sky became a rich, lush blue, as clear and calm as the water at the edge of the village. Now in the open sky, I could finally see what the fog had hidden: the colorful abandoned community of Petites.

The short flight to Burgeo gave me time to think about Old Man Hearn, his loving grandson, and his exciting past. I could still picture him in the kitchen of that small, dimly lit house as he smiled and looked at me with his sad, knowing eyes. I could see his robust, wrinkled face, saltwater-cured by years of exposure in open boats, and his hands: tough as leather. He had lived a full, exciting life, and even though he had missed that famous adventure, he lived life his own way—sometimes on the water, but always *near* the water.

Chapter Twelve

By his second week at the Oklahoma State Prison, after five fights and being jumped from behind twice, Marve was ready to fight anyone. No more crap from the other prisoners and he didn't care about the punishment, either. He'd had enough.

He expected a certain amount of trouble because of being new. But several times now he got tripped while moving in or out of the cell blocks and shoved five or six times. The first time, a burly, unshaven prisoner called Pickens had pushed Marve as they went out the west door into the exercise yard. Marve fell face down onto the pavement and got up feeling blood run down his face. But blood wasn't the worst of it; he also heard the laughter of a dozen other prisoners nearby who had witnessed the incident.

Another time, while they were leaving their cells and walking through the rotunda, Pickens struck again.

The OSP rotunda, a large, domed circular room three stories high, was located in the center of the prison and had three cell blocks running in separate straight lines from it. Six guards stood watch at all three levels above the prisoners, alert for trouble with their rifles continually aimed toward the prisoners below.

From the rotunda, three cell blocks housed between 300 and 900 prisoners each. Prisoners walked single file around the outside perimeter of the rotunda between yellow lines on the floor. If they stepped over the yellow line for any reason, they were shot.

One morning when he glanced up he noticed something unusual: a guard walking along the elevated steel walkway between the second floor perimeter and the middle guard cage. It surprised him to see the guard out in the open, and he let his gaze linger for a split second longer than usual.

And that's when it happened: all at once he felt his feet go out from under him, his head strike the polished cement floor, and the jolt to his ribs as someone kicked him hard in his side.

The well-timed attack took place right below the second-floor catwalk. That meant the upper guards couldn't see it, and the floor guard had been looking the other way. One prisoner had tripped Marve, and Pickens, the next in line, delivered a couple of hard kicks the second Marve hit the floor. Guards were unable to identify the attacker, but they heard the commotion and fired warning shots immediately. In an instant, all the prisoners were flat on their bellies between the yellow lines as the guards assessed the situation and shouted for order.

Twenty minutes later, after the rotunda was cleared, they carried Marve to the infirmary. He offered no explanation as to how he wound up on the floor with a broken rib and a sliced bleeding eye. A quiet and sympathetic trustee taped his ribs and put stitches in his right eye. He waited for the day-shift guard supervisor to leave. Only when they were alone did the older prisoner begin to speak.

"Son," he said. "Someone is always trying to make a name for his self in here. They try to get noticed by the straw boss or need to show everyone how they can hurt a person. You can fight 'em or you can be their girlfriend, but you can't ignore them."

Marve glanced at the older prisoner, who seemed sincere, but at that point he didn't trust anyone. During the next week Marve drew a variety of work details and carefully watched everyone around him, while waiting for the next attack to come. His wounds were healing slowly, his ribs were sore, and he felt a sharp pain each time he lifted anything.

One day while he worked in the furniture factory, two of the prisoners near him were discussing various sports, including boxing. Before he knew it, Marve was drawn into their conversation and he surprisingly found himself talking about his father.

"Yeah, my old man was a professional fighter," he said. "Fought Golden Gloves, then turned pro before the war."

"No shit?" one of the prisoners asked.

"Yeah, pretty good, too," Marve said. "He fought in Madison Square Garden."

"What was it, 'punk' day in New York?" someone behind him said. Marve turned and saw Pickens and three other men in the hallway. Pickens, the largest of the four, stepped toward Marve, and the two men talking to Marve slowly moved out of the way.

Pickens moved closer, "Look here, Peckerwood. I'll bet your old man couldn't spell Madison Square Garden." Half smiling, he glanced confidently at his three buddies.

Marve knew he was outnumbered and would be getting his face smashed again, but he wouldn't be the only victim. As the bulky, overbearing prisoner came closer, Marve swung at him with his right hand, and Pickens, expecting the blow, raised both hands to block the punch.

Marve stepped into him with his full weight and landed a left hook to the bully's side. Pickens stepped back, feeling the pain in his kidneys, and Marve charged him with a series of blows to the face and midsection. Pickens, stunned by the lightning-fast blows, seemed shocked for an instant, and Marve felt as though he might win this one. But then two of the men in the hall rushed forward, getting into the fray, swinging at Marve from either side.

Marve got off a solid punch at one of them as the other man grabbed his arms and tried to hold him from behind. Pickens and the third prisoner landed several jabs while Marve's hands were behind him. Somehow Marve pushed backward, throwing the prisoner behind him against the wall. For a second, Marve's hands were free, and he took full advantage of it. He broke away from the three attackers, grabbed a broom, broke it in two, and threw the large end away. In a blind rage, he ran at the three men using the sharp end of the broomstick as a knife. Within seconds he had successfully driven the broomstick into all three men and was about to stab Pickens again when a fourth prisoner grabbed his arm.

"That's enough, Ace," he said. "That's enough." It was Ben, his straw boss.

Ben held Marve's arm with his left hand and waved his right hand at the three prisoners. "Back off," he said firmly. And they did. A guard ran in, and seeing Ben in the room, immediately relaxed.

"Just horsing around a bit, Jack," Ben said. "Everything's hunky-dory."

"Okay, Ben," the guard said, but then he looked down at the broomstick in Marve's hand. "What's that?"

"Here, you take it," Ben said. "About time the state bought some decent brooms. It's the second one that broke this week."

The guard took the broken stick from Marve and walked past the three tough-looking prisoners in the hallway. They managed to hide their wounds and pretended nothing had happened. The guard knew he'd missed a good fight, but he seemed satisfied with how Ben had handled the situation. No one got killed on his watch, so he didn't care what else he had missed.

"Heard you talking about boxing," Ben said.

Marve, unsure what to say, shook his head.

"You know, boxing is all about money, and money is all about odds," Ben said, as Marve looked at the other three men, ready in case they resumed their attack. Marve was silent and Ben continued; "Your odds in here aren't very good, but I can tell you know how to even the score."

"I'm not sleeping with anyone," Marve said defiantly, ready to fight again. "Bring 'em back in here if you think I'm somebody's punk."

"Listen, kid. I'm not talking about bunking down. I'm talking 'bout you working for me. That is, if you can get smart. Your fighting skills impressed me, but your thinking skills need some work. You did some good with Pickens and the boys, but you gotta think smart or you'll wind up in the ground over at Peckerwood Hill."

"What you need me to do?" Marve asked.

"Keep your eyes and ears open. Report back to me what you hear around. I'll send you on various work details, and you let me know what's going on. If things go right and you're a good listener, I'll bring you in to work for me all the time, like Pickens."

"And what's coming my way?" Marve asked, wiping blood off his face with his shirtsleeve. Ben grinned, walked to the doorway, and turned back toward Marve. "It's what's not coming your way, Ace."

The large, overweight straw boss strolled down the hallway, escorted by two of his three bodyguards. Pickens, still brooding over his defeat, glared at Marve, then joined Ben's group.

That night, lying on his bunk in the darkened cell block, Marve felt he had done the right thing by joining up with Ben. He was surprised at how well he had fought against such terrible odds at the furniture factory, and surprised that Ben had asked him to be part of his group. But the biggest surprise of the day had to do with the anger he felt when Pickens made fun of his father. It amazed him to think that he would ever fight for his father, the man who had beaten him, demoralized him, and the one person that he blamed for his being in prison in the first place. It had been a day filled with surprises.

***

In early August, I received another surprising phone call from Jack Murphy. Sounding unusually chipper, Jack said something that didn't sound quite right, so I switched off the TV and asked Jack to repeat what he had said.

"Dave, we need you to take that aircraft to PEI," he said.

"You mean Prince Edward Island?" I asked, amazed.

"Yes," he confirmed. "Got a new job for you and need you to get there as soon as you can. This will be much different than anything you've done for us so far. It's an offshore job in support of Hudson's Bay, a Canadian oil company that's drilling offshore, north of PEI. Think you can handle it?"

"Yes, sir," I said, wondering how in the world I was going to land on an oil rig. I had never seen one, much less landed on one. *Why did they pick me?* I wondered.

"I'll drive to Deer Lake tomorrow morning and give you a full briefing," Jack said. "Give you some cash, phone numbers, and everything you might need. An engineer will meet you in PEI and he has a small life raft, life jackets, and other safety gear for offshore flights. He'll take the time to install a different type of radio, especially for that job. This will be Universal's first chance at working on an oil rig, and we need you to give it your best."

"Yes, sir," I said.

"You're probably wondering why we chose you," Jack said.

"Well, yes, sir, I am."

"OK, I'll tell you. Partly because a couple of pilots quit this summer, and it put us in a bind. Plus the fact that I've been getting good reports from your customers. You seem to get along with tough clients, and they like you for some crazy reason. Pleasing clients isn't as important as safety, eh, but it's pretty important. The PEI job won't get you a lot of flight time, but we need it to go smoothly. In addition, I have a hunch they will move up to a Jet Ranger if they trust you. This might be your chance to get back to turbine helicopters."

"Man, that is the best news I've heard in a long time," I said, barely able to contain my excitement.

"Well, there's something else," Jack said. "You're going to be there several months, and I thought you might want to ask your wife to move up from the States. Prince Edward Island is a beautiful place in the fall, and she might find it a lot more like home than Newfoundland."

"I'll talk her into it," I said, getting even more excited. "Thanks a lot, Jack."

I couldn't believe it! New contract, the possibility of transitioning into a Jet Ranger, and an opportunity to bring my family back together. It had come so abruptly, like a bolt of lightning on a clear day. After I hung up, I thought of calling Barbara, but decided against it. I wanted to make sure this was really happening. I decided to wait until I was safely across the water and working on the little island of PEI before telling her the big news.

Jack's briefing the next day covered everything I needed to know, but he couldn't simulate taking off or landing on an oil rig. He told me to approach the helideck slow and easy, the same as the final approach to a hill or pinnacle. That made sense to me, but I still wished we could land on a real oil rig.

Later that morning, I flew solo over Port aux Basques, the place where our ferry had docked a few months before. One last affectionate glance at Newfoundland, then I looked ahead at the seemingly endless body of water in front of me. Flying to Prince Edward Island from the south tip of Newfoundland required a sixty-five-mile flight over water to the north tip of Nova Scotia, then south across Cape Breton Island, and last, a forty-five-mile flight over water to the east side of PEI.

Now I flew over the rugged, choppy waters of the Atlantic Ocean with its dark blue, bottomless water visible in each direction. The wind skipped across the waves, making a white-plumed spray and propelling my aircraft from behind. The wind, that magical, elusive component of nature, seemed to be my friend at that moment, but unfortunately a friend I couldn't trust. Unaccustomed to flying over water, I scanned the horizon for a glimpse of land. Yet nothing was visible—not a ferry, small boat, island, or anything else to navigate by. Just water and miles and miles of more open water.

Glancing at my map and the notes I had made, I knew that crossing the Cabot Strait should take a little more than an hour. Back in the hotel room, one hour didn't sound like a long time. But at 6,000 feet, alone in a small helicopter with nothing to navigate by except for a small magnetic compass, sixty minutes of ocean can be nerve-racking. Even considering that there were large black floats attached to my helicopter, which would allow me to land on the water and float for a few minutes. To add more anxiety to my already nervous state, I thought about the transmission failure a few months earlier. What if something like that happened again? Or perhaps something less dramatic like a clogged fuel filter or a spark plug blowing?

The feeling of isolation gave me a few brief thoughts of returning to the safety of land. Then I thought of Charles Lindbergh flying solo all the way across the Atlantic Ocean. All alone in his little aircraft for more than thirty hours. He must have had a heart as big as the Atlantic Ocean itself. He would laugh at this little water crossing facing me.

Where, I wondered, was *my* Lindbergh heart?

Surrounded by water in an old helicopter manufactured during the Korean War, I tried to keep a steady hand on the controls while anxiously searching for my first glimpse of land. Glancing at my ten-dollar magnetic compass as it bounced around in its black liquid, I thought of all the navigation equipment in my Army days and realized I had never fully appreciated it.

Fifty minutes into my flight, I figured I should have already been over land. Instead I could only see water and low cloud cover in three directions. I decided to turn forty-five degrees right and try to track southeast. Making a mental note of the time, I pulled a little more power and searched for land, feeling nervous again.

Now the cloud formation in front of me grew darker, more solid like a thunderstorm, so I glanced at the outside temperature gauge, and sure enough, it was much warmer. While I carefully checked my other instruments, I ran smack into a squall line, shocked into alertness as rain splattered against the helicopter bubble, sounding like a thousand plastic bullets. For a split second I couldn't see the horizon or even the water below, so I made a split-second decision and used the only visual aid I had in the helicopter for orientation. This "tool" was a heavy two-inch fishhook that dangled from my instrument panel on the end of a piece of nylon fishing line. I had used this crude method before in the bush when I had run into fog momentarily, or when I had found myself caught between cloud layers.

In the pounding rain I watched the hook closely. As I banked the aircraft, the fishhook moved in the opposite direction, showing me that the aircraft turned on its side. I made slight corrections, leveling out and centering the fishhook. This was, of course, the crudest method of orientation known to aviation, but since the only other instrument in my helicopter was an altimeter, I used what I could. I had to stay upright and get through the pounding rain.

A long two minutes after I ran into the squall line, I came out on the other side. There in front me, no more than two miles away, in a clear sky, I gazed at a most beautiful sight: the northeastern tip of Cape Breton Island. What a welcome sight, Cape Breton with its rocky shoreline, rich green forest, and a cluster of small communities. There were a few sandy beaches and numerous small boats anchored near an isolated harbor. Past the shoreline I could see hiking trails and a multitude of lakes and ponds. Feeling such relief, I watched as the sun shone on lush green trees, soaked from a summer rain. I felt relief and thought, *Lucky Lindy, thanks for the encouragement.*

Across the narrow, scenic peninsula, I flew past what looked like a large spacious national park, and it took me less than fifteen minutes to reach the western coastline. There I spotted an excellent place to land near a beautiful coastal village called Inverness. After making sure that I wasn't landing in a government park, or near homes or log cabins, I put the helicopter down in a magnificent open space a few yards from a picturesque river. A beautiful, serene setting. A stark contrast to the hour-long flight over the edge of the Atlantic.

Fishing would have been fun, but I had work to do. I removed my shoes, rolled up my jeans, and for the next half hour scrubbed my dirty helicopter in the pristine waters of a crystal clear river. Using a bucket, a sponge, and some utility soap, I cleaned the aircraft and dried off the bubble with a borrowed hotel towel.

Next, I put the contents of the two ten-gallon cans of Avgas into the helicopter's fuel tanks and stored all the utility equipment as neatly as possible. I took out the clean shirt and slacks I had hung in the helicopter and changed into my fresh clothing. Flying my shiny-clean helicopter, dressed in my flared tan slacks and blue short-sleeved shirt,

I felt ready to make my entrance at Georgetown, Prince Edward Island.

Compared with crossing the Cabot Strait, the short hop from Inverness to Prince Edward Island was more fun than work. There is something calming about being able to see your destination regardless of its distance from you. In this case, my destination was a lovely island with windswept shores, tiny villages, and a veritable rainbow of colors. From my perspective, PEI resembled the world's largest, most panoramic golf course.

As I flew closer, I could see rolling hills and rich red and brown soil. A little more than a hundred and forty miles long and forty miles wide in parts, the island looks as though it had been created with the same love and craftsmanship you would expect to find in a picturesque sculpture or colorful, luminous painting.

After an enjoyable twenty-minute flight, I found it easy to distinguish the outline of the little village of Georgetown on the east coast of PEI. I flew a slow circle around Georgetown, taking in the various features like a sawmill, an active shipyard, a couple of tugboats, and several freshly painted older homes, with neatly trimmed yards and abundant flower gardens. Then I saw the white-and-blue house trailer with a forty-foot radio tower beside it, which Jack Murphy had told me to look for. In a small place like Georgetown, it didn't take long to find that red-and-white tower.

Trying my best to avoid flying directly over the village, I made my approach to the small field near the trailer and landed on a makeshift landing pad made of thick wood planks. As the blades whooshed overhead, I noticed three men standing nearby. One of them looked like the helicopter engineer assigned to work with me, and the other two, I assumed, were from the oil company.

Before I could get out, the helicopter engineer opened the door with a fake smile pasted on his face and said, "I'm Paul. We can talk later, but I want to warn you; don't tell anyone you've never landed on an oil rig before. Got it?"

"Ah . . . yeah, I got it," I stuttered, returning the phony smile as the two oil company men looked on. *Good Lord*, I thought, *this customer thinks I know what I'm doing.*

Chapter Thirteen

Several months had passed since Ben had invited Marve into his prison serfdom. The rugged straw boss had seen to it that his youngest "soldier" found the time to lift weights and exercise, and the results were impressive. Marve grew stronger, tougher, and wiser, and under Ben's guidance, got the best work details. Often, this meant working on the farm.

Marve had kept his end of the bargain by providing his boss with information about guards, prisoners, and contraband. A few times they called on Marve to apply a bit of muscle on Ben's behalf, but that didn't happen often because most prisoners knew the score and avoided physical confrontation.

Most of the time, being part of the inner circle, Marve chose his work details, preferring animal feeding or barn cleaning over field work or the furniture shop. He wasn't sure where his love of animals came from because he had never been around horses or cattle before. But it didn't matter, because somehow, he had found something in that harsh, corrupt environment that he truly enjoyed.

Marve quickly worked his way up the ladder in Ben's organization and even the guards took notice, giving him a bit more latitude, allowing him more time with the animals.

"Don't forget to brush that mangy horse before chow call," said Bill, a chubby-faced older guard. Leaning on a door post with his carbine, Bill peeked into the barn where Marve kept busy stacking bales of hay. "You'll lose this duty if you don't take good care of these animals."

"Yes, sir," Marve answered, grinning. "I'll have him looking good."

The stout guard glanced outside, then turned back to Marve again. He watched this tall inmate, knowing his connection to Ben's crew, and for some reason, he slowly started to like him.

Bill had worked at OSP for twenty years and had seen hundreds of men come and go. He saw many of them return to serve a second or third sentence. And tragically, he had watched a few prisoners die. A few were buried up at Peckerwood Hill, the lonely cemetery where deceased convicts wound up if they went unclaimed by family or friends.

Bill purposely worked at not getting close to the prisoners and always kept his distance both physically and spiritually. He chose to stay clean and refused to take a bribe because he knew he would have to give up his self-respect in the bargain. He would quit before doing that. As his tall prisoner brushed a black gelding, Bill spoke again, allowing himself a faint smile.

"Marvin, you done any riding before you came here?" Bill asked.

"No, sir," Marve replied, stroking the neck of his beautiful workhorse. The gentle animal shifted slightly as Marve worked from his neck to his midsection.

"I'm a city boy," Marve said. "Grew up in Tulsa and never been around animals much before I got here six months ago."

"Well, you seem pretty comfortable with them, anyways."

"Yes, sir. I guess they know who cares and who don't, just like people."

"Boy, you said that right," Bill replied with a slight chuckle. Then, after a long silence, "Marvin, you hear about the prison rodeo?"

"Yes, sir. I can't wait to see it if I'm allowed."

"It's a humdinger," Bill said. "Twenty thousand people come here to watch prisoners ride bulls, wrestle steers, and do about anything you ever heard of at a rodeo, plus a hell of a lot more."

"Yes, sir. I can't wait to see it," Marve repeated.

Bill waited a few minutes, expecting Marve to speak, but when he didn't, the old guard asked the essential question, heavy on his mind.

"Ever given any thought to being in a rodeo?"

***

As I stepped out of the helicopter, Paul grabbed the tie-down to secure the main rotor blade. The men standing near the office wandered over to the helipad and introduced themselves. They were friendly enough, but seemed a bit reserved. Employees of our client, Hudson's Bay Oil and Gas Company, the men were locals except for one man. Standing alone, the guy looked annoyed at something or someone. I found out later he was the rig boss from Edmonton, Alberta.

The group walked around the helicopter and took a close look, which included examining the cockpit. Good thing I had stopped near the river to give the chopper a bath. One of the men, well dressed in slacks and an open-collared sports shirt, looked inside the aircraft at its simple, practically bare instrument panel.

"This thing doesn't have a lot of instruments, does it?" he asked.

"I get by okay," I said, a bit too defensively.

The man reached over and touched the fish hook. "What's this for?" he asked.

Paul, standing beside me, leaned in and replied, "Fred, Dave here's been working in the bush over in Newfoundland for the past few months. You must have heard of all the fantastic fishing over there. Isn't that right, Dave?"

"Some of the best fishing in the world," I replied, catching on. "I've got a telescopic fly rod right there in my toolbox." The well-dressed man seemed pleased, but he still looked unimpressed with the instrument panel.

I closed the door on my side and walked in front of the helicopter where the guy from Edmonton stood. Muscular with sun-bleached, close-cropped hair, he wore dark blue coveralls and sturdy work boots. He chomped the last few inches of a soggy cigar butt, looking more like a Marine sergeant than an oil man. Paul and I watched as he strolled around the back of the aircraft grumbling something under his breath.

"So you like fishing," Fred said, smiling. "Well, you're going to get a chance to fish on the rig," he said. "Some of the best flat-fishing around. Sometimes halibut, sometimes flounder, which is what they call blackjack around here. But you always latch onto something."

"Sounds good to me," I said, liking this guy already. Then the tough guy came around to my side of the aircraft, and I noticed the others gave him plenty of space.

"My name's Stanislaw Krassman," he said, shaking my hand with a grip strong enough to pull the handle off of a car door. "Roughnecks call me Stan," he added. "I'm the tool pusher on our rig, the Wodeco II." I had the feeling the roughnecks might call him a few other things, but I didn't mention it.

"What's your experience flying offshore?" he asked. I glanced at Paul and tried to think of how I could dodge the question. Fortunately, Paul must have had the same thought.

"Dave, I need to call Gander and report your arrival," Paul said, interrupting Stan. "I need your exact arrival time. Better yet, I'll take you to the boarding house so you can call them yourself. The chief pilot will be some mad if we don't call right away."

Stan looked carefully at Paul, his black beady eyes missing nothing. "Well, go on then," Stan said, "but be ready anytime, in case we need the chopper. That's what we're paying you for."

I wasn't sure what to say.

Then Fred spoke up, his gentle approach in stark contrast to the tool pusher's drill sergeant style, "Dave," he said, "why don't you get settled in at the boarding house? Get to know the place a little, but like Stan said, have your chopper ready to go in case of an emergency on the rig."

I smiled. Fred had said about the same thing Stan had told us but managed to say it without the attitude.

"Sure," I replied, taking my case out of the helicopter and helping Paul get the equipment unloaded. After a moment or two, the company people went back into the office, leaving Paul and me alone for the first time. I felt a sense of relief.

We stacked the equipment beside the far end of the trailer and chatted. When Paul walked a bit closer, I asked him, "What's wrong with that Stan guy?"

Paul grinned and said, "Didn't you ever hear the rule: 'a slob on every job'?"

We both giggled. About that time, out of nowhere, Stan stepped around the corner with his permanent scowl. "Guess I missed the big joke," he said.

I looked at Paul and had to think fast. "Paul asked me if I knew a guy in Gander they call Bob ... from the Mob." Stan gave Paul a suspicious look, but he wasn't sure if he had caught us at something or not. He decided to let it go.

"Yeah, OK," Stan said. "I forgot to tell you something. I know Paul's heard about this, but I want to make sure you've got it crystal clear." He puffed on his cigar butt and pointed toward the coast. "There's a barge that sank off to the north a few days ago. Did ya hear 'bout it?"

"No, I haven't heard anything," I said.

"You haven't heard about the Irving Whale?" he asked, as if someone from Canada had landed on the moon. "What the hell. Don't any of those Newfies own a television set?"

"Sure, they have television," I said, trying to avoid an argument. "But I haven't seen anything about the barge. Does it belong to Hudson's Bay or something?"

"Shit, no," he said, "but it's a hell of a problem right now. All over the news. The Irving Whale is a commercial barge that they were towing out in the Cabot Strait, north of PEI. A few days ago some asshole screwed up, and it broke away from the tug that was towing it. A day later it broke up and sank. Damn thing carried four million gallons of oil, and now the people around PEI are going nuts over the pollution. They're driving us crazy thinking our rig might be polluting the waters, too. Local idiots are worried about the damage to fishing and tourism. Screw them, that's what I say."

"It's been all over the news around here," Paul said, trying to calm things down. "And even on CBC."

Then Stan continued his impassioned rant. "Now, here we are trying to drill an oil well thirty miles east of a sunken barge, and people are worried we might be the next company to pollute the waters around PEI. So, you two guys listen up. Hudson's Bay is being extra cautious right now with all this shit going on, so keep your mouth shut about the drilling operation. Don't make any statements to the press, and *don't* tell stories around town on what Hudson's Bay is doing. We got a company spokesperson takes care of this kind of horse shit. You guys stay out of it!"

"Don't worry," I said. "I get your point."

He grunted and started to walk away, which gave me another moment of relief, but it was short-lived. He stopped and turned back.

"One more thing," he said. "The president of Hudson's Bay is coming out here from Calgary in two days, so you be ready to fly him to the rig."

"We're always ready," Paul said.

Stan, with his gruff poker face, looked at Paul as though trying to choose the right insult. Fortunately, he turned and walked back to the trailer, grunting something to himself along the way. When we were sure Stan had gone inside, we walked over to the helicopter, where Paul wiped grease off the tail boom. I stood beside him trying to choose my words carefully and glanced behind me to make sure we were alone.

"Paul, who in the world told those guys I have experience on oil rigs?"

Paul turned to me with his sly grin, "Who do you think? Gary Fields, of course."

I hadn't thought of Gary Fields in over two months. Gary had convinced me to drive to Newfoundland in the first place and told me Americans wouldn't have to pay Canadian taxes.

"Really," I said. "I want to meet Gary Fields someday."

Paul stopped cleaning and turned toward me with a big grin.

"Yeah, I'll bet you do," he said. "I'll bet you do."

***

The rest of that day Paul and I prepared the aircraft for work. I found out that Paul, like me, had never worked on an offshore oil project. But Paul *did* know how to act around difficult customers, and he passed along some helpful advice. As he drove to the boarding house, I took in my first glimpse of Georgetown from ground level.

A clean and wholesome little town, Georgetown had tall, healthy oak trees, freshly painted cottages, and a perfect view of the harbor. A working-class community filled with common people who clearly had a connection with the sea. I felt certain Barbara would like it.

That evening Paul and I drank several Labatt beers and got to know each other a little more. Naturally, the TV in the bar was tuned to a hockey game, but the bartender got upset about his team "playing like a bunch of girls." As he mumbled something, he switched the channel to a familiar scene in Archie Bunker's living room.

Archie argued with his wife . . . again.

"Stifle yourself, Edith," he said, and quickly the bartender switched channels once again. This time he changed it to a report on the Calgary Stampede. Paul and I glanced at the TV screen from time to time while chatting, and soon I noticed a sequence on bull riding. As the camera followed a rugged cowboy coming out of the chute atop one of the meanest-looking bulls I'd ever seen, a rodeo clown ran toward the bull waving his arms. The bull dipped his head, hooked his horns into the clown's body, and tossed the helpless clown into the air.

"Yes, boy," Paul said in his Newfie accent, "now there's a hard way to make a living."

"You're right about that," I agreed. The TV screen showed the rodeo clown being carried away, and I thought of another rodeo, one that had fences to keep the animals in, and forty-foot concrete walls to hold the cowboys. In that rodeo, cowboys wore black-and-white striped uniforms, because they were the inmates at the Oklahoma State Penitentiary in McAlester. One of the wildest, most dangerous rodeos in the world.

***

When I returned to the States from Vietnam and could arrange things with the commanding officer of my unit, I traveled from Fort Wolters, Texas, to McAlester, Oklahoma, to see my brother. Marve had written a few letters to me in Vietnam and had recently written and asked me to come to visit during the prison rodeo. He said he would be working at the rodeo, and it would mean a lot to him for me to be there. I had no idea what he would be doing, since we were both city boys. Maybe he would be working in the grandstands or helping with the animals. It didn't matter, because it seemed to be important to him and I hadn't seen him for a long time.

On Friday night I drove to Oklahoma with one of my fellow warrant officers, Bruce Jenson, who seemed upbeat and somewhat overcurious about visiting a prison. Pleased to have him with me since I needed company on the drive, despite the fact that Bruce's morbid curiosity about a prison seemed obvious.

"I'd love to go," he said, childlike wonder showing in his eyes. "I've never been to a prison before. Maybe we will see someone famous like Al Capone."

"That's cute, Bruce. I'm afraid we're twenty years late for that."

"Okay, how about that guy Cool Hand Luke?"

"A movie, Bruce. Only a movie."

"I'm just pullin' your leg," he said.

After leaving work early in the afternoon, Bruce and I changed into civilian clothes and then made the 260-mile trip to McAlester, Oklahoma, arriving shortly before the rodeo started. The parking lot outside the rodeo grounds held some four or five hundred cars that night, and the enormous rodeo arena was located inside the giant prison walls. Bruce's mood and facial expression changed immediately as we walked through the imposing main gate, past a barbed-wire fence and through a wide corridor leading to the stadium. No longer my jovial, wisecracking buddy, this slightly overweight soldier quickly turned serious. I glanced at him as we walked along the restricted corridors, and I could see the rising fear in his beady black eyes.

The night was warm, and the smell of dirt, horse manure, and cigarette smoke filled the air as we walked into the well-lit outdoor arena. I felt an overwhelming mixture of excitement and fear as the familiar sounds of Johnny Cash singing "*I Got Stripes*" played loudly over the PA system. The oval-shaped arena, fenced in all the way around, had a thick floor of wet black dirt. On one end of the arena, there were large steel gates and chutes to corral the animals before they were released. On that same end a booth held the rodeo officials and the amusing announcer. On the other end was a large gate that opened to allow animals to escape into the outside holding pens after their events.

On both sides of the arena, pockets of prisoners sat along the fence dressed in large black-and-white striped prison uniforms, cowboy hats, and little numbers on their chests. Prisoners kept a close watch on the guards, and guards kept a close eye on the prisoners. Some of the inmates scanned the vast audience, perhaps looking for a family member, or enjoying their proximity to the outside world, or more likely searching for a pretty girl.

Beyond the arena on the north end a large white concrete wall rose higher than the top seating of the rodeo grounds. There were six guard towers at strategic locations around the wall with armed guards clearly visible on every wall, a stark reminder that regardless of how much this might seem like a rodeo, it was a prison. The jovial men in front of us were hardened criminals whose crimes included everything from theft to manslaughter.

"Hey, Dave, do you see him?" Bruce asked, interrupting my thoughts.

"Well, I don't see him yet," I replied, glancing over at Bruce, who now looked even more concerned.

"Beautiful night for a rodeo, isn't it?" I asked, trying to lighten the mood.

Sweat dripped from Bruce's chin onto his shirt, and he looked at me, a terrified look on his chubby face. "Let's find your brother," he said. "We may need to head back pretty soon."

"OK," I agreed, seeing he wasn't doing well. "First, let's try and find a place to get a Coke or something."

"Coke, my ass," he said, wiping his face. "I need a beer!"

As we stood up to find a cold drink, the music softened and the announcer welcomed everyone to the "McAlester Prison Rodeo."

Worried that I might miss Marve as things got started, I looked frantically across the arena and throughout the stands but couldn't see him. I reached into my wallet, got a dollar bill, and handed it to Bruce.

"Why don't you find someplace to get us a cold drink, and I'll stay here to look for my brother?" Bruce stood for a moment as the music played over the loudspeaker, his plump face red and moist. He glanced down at the prisoners directly in front of us as one of them, a large man with a depraved look on his tanned, scarred face, grabbed his crotch and grinned at Bruce.

Immediately Bruce sat back down. "I can wait," he said, sliding closer to me. "I can wait."

During the next hour or so we watched one event after another. Prisoners competed in roping competition, bareback riding, bronco busting, and calf tying. The announcer kept the evening moving by mixing his event recaps with personal tidbits about the prisoners. He wouldn't hesitate to mention a prisoner's name as well as their crime, and the smiling prisoners seemed to enjoy their moment in the spotlight.

"That was Billy Harding doing his best to stay on Wanderlust," the announcer said, as a prisoner, after being thrown off an unhappy bull, got up and dusted himself off, then limped carefully to the fence. "Billy is our guest for five to fifteen years for armed robbery, but it looks like Wanderlust is the thief tonight after he stole Billy's chances to win a prize. Let's hear it for Billy." The audience laughed and applauded sparingly as a near-crippled Billy climbed up on the fence, joining the other prisoners.

"Folks," the announcer said, "I know a lot of you have traveled a long way to be here tonight, and I'd like to find out just how far you came. So, who is here from Oklahoma City?" A large group from the audience applauded loudly. "Great, now who is here from Kansas?" he asked, as another smaller group applauded. "Terrific, how about Missouri?" Then the same thing, as 30 or 40 people applauded and yelled.

"Folks, that's terrific, and I want to hear from the other places in a moment. But now we're ready, and I hope you are, too," the announcer said excitedly. "It's time for one of the most dangerous events you will ever see at a rodeo." His voice grew louder. "You don't want to miss this one, so everyone saddle up and hunker down and get ready for . . . MONEY THE HARD WAY."

For the first time that night the audience stood up and applauded, and even though I didn't know what was coming, I stood with them, knowing we were about to see something special.

From the north gate, four mounted prisoners rode into the arena and spread out evenly facing the chutes, keeping their horses calm and carefully monitoring the sudden, loud activity taking place at the business end of the rodeo. At first, I couldn't see the cause for the commotion in the chutes, but then a large Brahman bull jumped high enough for me to see its massive size as the prisoners near it leaped out of its way.

"Folks, that bull is mad," the announcer said jokingly. "And I wouldn't want to be close to him right now, would you? But that's what these prisoners have got to do tonight. They'll be trying to steal a small red bag tied around that bull's head. The little red bag has a one hundred dollar bill in it, and anyone who can steal it from the bull without gettin' killed gets to keep the money. I'd say he's gonna earn it, wouldn't you?"

"Yes!" the audience yelled, followed by more applause.

"Now let's meet our brave cowboys," he said, as eight prisoners ran into the arena.

They were various shapes, ages, and sizes, and as they lined up for their names to be read, I saw him right in the middle of them all. My brother wasn't dressed in prison stripes. He and one other inmate wore rodeo clown outfits, and now he stood in front of the gate, right where the bull would be coming out. Since the other inmate was short, the two clowns made an amusing pair. Marve looked over at me and waved. No doubt in my mind; it was him.

"See that tall clown right there," I said. "That's my brother. That's him."

"Great," Bruce said. "Can we go now?"

Chapter Fourteen

Paul and I spent the rest of the evening in that Georgetown bar discussing helicopters, girls, and music. It seemed like the only thing we had in common was helicopters. The two of us couldn't have been any more opposite: I enjoyed the easygoing sounds of Glen Campbell or the Carpenters, and Paul dug the heavy tones of the Who or the Rolling Stones, and he could have easily passed for one of the long-haired rock singers in the band Three Dog Night.

"By the way," Paul said, downing another half a bottle of beer in one gulp. "You said your wife is gonna be here soon? Our landlord has a nice cabin out west of town."

"Great," I said. "Let's go see it tomorrow morning. I need to call my wife tonight and talk her into coming up here. I want to set things up in the cabin and try to make up for the months we've been separated."

"No sweat," he said with confidence. "Your wife will love that little place."

The next morning, we stopped by the cabin and had a quick look on the way to the Hudson's Bay office. The rustic log cabin sat near a forested area along a small road northwest of Georgetown. It wasn't fancy, but it had a built-in stove, several pieces of furniture, and one more valuable thing from my perspective—privacy. There were no other houses or cabins within a half mile.

"Barbara's gonna love this place," I said, as we drove back into town.

"What did I tell ya?" Paul said with grin.

That morning I flew my first trip to the rig. After taking off from Georgetown, I headed northeast along the coast of PEI, enjoying the beautiful scenery near Souris and Red Point while keeping watch ahead for the rig.

I cruised past a charming, brightly colored lighthouse near East Point, and after heading out to sea, it wasn't long before I spotted the Wodeco II drilling rig, a giant piece of steel jutting up out of the water. I flew directly to the rig, feeling a slight headwind over the water. When I reached the rig, I circled overhead looking at the wind sock and helideck. The vast blue water surrounding the oil rig appeared clean and pure, like a giant swimming pool. I set up my approach to the landing area, keeping my airspeed slow and holding in the aircraft's power. I thought about what Jack had told me,

"Land into the wind, me boy," he had said. "The same way you would on a pinnacle, stay high and keep plenty of power for the last segment. Now, when you cross the threshold of the helideck, if you have too much speed, execute a go-around, make a circle, and do it again."

Jack would have been proud of me on that first approach. The wind was right on my nose as I crossed the helideck, and touching down on the sturdy steel deck, I relaxed and let the collective down, gently allowing the helicopter's weight to settle on the flat steel structure. It felt wonderful. Glancing at the enormous structure on my right, I had my first close-up look at an offshore oil rig.

I stood on the helideck taking in the unusual sights and sounds and enjoyed the excitement of being there. The combination of the large motors running constantly and the giant sections of drill pipe being slammed into place made it clamorous and noisy. I thought of how unusual it felt to be thirty miles from land in open water, and for a brief moment I felt an unusual sense of adventure.

But soon that moment of peace evaporated, as I saw Stan walking toward my helicopter with his permanent scowl and his ever-present cigar. Stan had a man with him as they walked right up to the helicopter and untied my cargo without a word. The rig hand put the cargo up on his shoulder and walked away, leaving Stan and me alone on the deck.

Without so much as a "hello" or "glad you made it out here today," Stan said, "Got another flight." He didn't say it, but growled it.

"OK," I said. "How many passengers and what time?"

"It's not to this rig," he replied. "Mr. Barnett is coming in from Calgary tomorrow, and you gotta pick him up in Charlottetown and take him out to see the oil spill. Find out where the Irving Whale went aground and fly him out there to look around and take some pictures. You can manage that, can't you?"

"Yes, sir."

"All right then. Fred will give you the flight details. Mr. Barnett might want you to bring him out here after you see the Irving Whale, and he might just fly back to Calgary. Don't know, don't care. Be there to pick him up and do whatever he wants. You got it?" he growled.

"Yes, sir, I will." But as I said it, I realized that Barbara and the kids were flying in from Oklahoma the next day. I felt disappointment and couldn't hide it from Stan.

He frowned and asked, "What's wrong? You don't like to fly two days in a row?"

"No, sir," I lied. "I'll be ready, and I'll take him wherever he needs to go."

As Stan walked back to the derrick and disappeared, I thought about the situation. Mr. Barnett, the president of Hudson's Bay, couldn't have picked a worse day to come to PEI. But what could I do? I had to take him. This would be an important flight.

While thinking about my predicament and how disappointed Barbara would be, I took a quick look around the rig and met a few of the rig hands. My first trip to an oil rig was mostly uneventful, and I had a good feeling about it all. I couldn't figure out why people worried and fussed about flying offshore.

That night I called Barbara and explained that I would be flying a VIP. I explained that I would pick her and the kids up at the Charlottetown Airport as soon as I finished my flight. She sounded disappointed I wouldn't be there when they arrived, but she didn't press the point. She sounded joyful but apprehensive about coming back to Canada. The kids were noisy in the background when she tried to talk, so we didn't stay on the phone long.

"Don't worry about anything," I said. "I have a nice place for us to live. Not like that little apartment in Gander either." I wanted to reassure her. "By this time tomorrow night, we'll be all set up."

"OK," she said. "I can't wait to see you."

"Leave it all up to me," I said. The line went dead, and I held the phone for a moment before walking back into the bar to join Paul for one more beer. Her words were still fresh in my head, "I can't wait to see you." That's all I needed to keep me going.

***

The exuberant audience at the prison rodeo came to life as they watched the large arena floor. The two clowns and six mounted inmates waited for the angry Brahman bull to be released. The announcer read each contestant's name, and then it was Marve's turn. He looked my way and smiled.

"Our tall clown is Marvin Eagleston," he announced. "Looks like he's big enough to jump on that bull, but I don't think he's gonna be doing that tonight, do you?"

For a second Marve grinned like the star of a Broadway play, but his moment was interrupted by a ruckus at the end of the arena. A loud, giant bull tried desperately to break down the gate and the cowboys looking after the animal scattered once again. I looked back at Marve, standing a short ten yards from the gate, as confident as a Marine at the White House. If he felt any trace of fear, he didn't show it.

After the eight prisoners were introduced, the announcer set up the event, "Now, folks, this is how it works," he explained. "Our friend Major Dan is about the meanest bull in Oklahoma, and he will try his best to run over as many cowboys as he can. These eight crazy inmates will do their best to stay out of the way, but they gotta get close enough to Major Dan to grab that red bag. If they get it, they get to keep the money. If they don't, they get to go to the hospital. Now, folks, if any of you are a bit squeamish, this is a good time to go buy some popcorn or to go and see a man about a dog. Because, most likely a few of these men won't walk out of here tonight. Are you ready?" The crowd cheered wildly. "Here we go."

As he said the word "go," the cowboys released the lever on the gate, and Major Dan came out of the chute jumping and running, all muscle, spit, and speed. The enormous humpback animal raced wildly across the arena in ankle-thick mud as the mad scramble commenced.

One frightened inmate, struggling to free his right foot from the mud, had barely started to run as the giant bull closed in on him. Despite the efforts of the two clowns, the massive animal put his head down, rammed the fleeing cowboy, and tossed the screaming inmate ten feet into the air. As the man fell flat on his back in the mud, Major Dan stepped on the crumpled body with his monstrous hooves, then turned and chased the other frightened runners.

The remarkably large and vicious bull had taken complete control of the arena. The prisoners, who a few minutes before had stood with their hands on their hips in kind of posed, tough-guy fashion, were now frantically running for their lives. One short, stocky inmate, void of even the slightest trace of bravado, ran a zigzag pattern for a few steps, then gave that up as the furious bull ran dangerously close to him. The inmates were on the bull's turf, and he wasn't happy about it.

One small but speedy runner raced toward the fence and slipped in the mud right before he jumped up and grabbed the fence railing. That split-second fall was all his pursuer needed to get close enough to put one large horn into the inmate's right leg. As the bull turned and ran along the fence, the small prisoner fell into the mud holding his bloody leg, writhing in pain.

The snarling bull ran toward the center of the arena and made a small circle, digging one hoof into the deep black dirt, watching, waiting, and apparently trying to decide where he would strike next. Behind him, near the fence, the two injured prisoners were carted out of the arena on stretchers. Marve and the other rodeo clown stood near the announcer's booth and waved at the bull, then Marve bent forward and pretended to be a bull. He made horns with his hands, holding them against his head, and pawed at the mud with his foot. The audience loved it and the bull took the bait.

As the animal drew closer to the fence, both clowns jumped onto the fence, and it appeared that Marve and the other clown would climb a few rungs higher to elude the bull. But Marve stayed on the lower part of the fence, eye level with the charging bull. When the animal got to the fence and turned right, horns barely missing Marve's torso, Marve jumped left, cutting it so close that one of the deadly horns tore his shirt.

I could see the rip in his shirt, but I couldn't tell if he was cut. At that point the bull ran away looking for easier prey, and Marve ran into the center of the arena. Suddenly the audience rose to their feet in a roar of applause. They saw it before I did . . . the red money bag that Marve held in his right hand. With the bull at the other end of the arena, the audience and other inmates cheering him on, Marve stood in the mud, his shirt ripped and bloody, waving into the grandstand, slowly turning until he faced me.

The announcer could barely be heard through the cheering and yelling in the packed arena. "Folks, that's why they call it MONEY THE HARD WAY!"

Marve brought his hands together, pointed toward me, then tipped his head forward and stood tall and proud in the spotlight. Inmates tossed their hats into the air, and several jumped off the fence and ran through the mud to congratulate their tall fellow prisoner. Music and applause thundered as ecstatic inmates banged on the fence so hard that a few fell off on the audience side, alarming the guards. As several seasoned guards clutched their rifles and took a few steps toward the inmates, the two men quickly hopped back to their rightful place on the fence. But not before one flirtatious inmate, who had landed ten feet from a beautiful blond, blew her a kiss, then slowly eased up on the rails facing her with a sly grin on his weathered face.

Marve took it all in, relishing the unforgettable moment, enjoying his precious window of freedom. He had always longed to be a hero in his little brother's eyes. And I had always longed to see him achieve something truly special. That night, both of us got our wish.

Chapter Fifteen

The next day the thought of seeing Barbara arrive in Prince Edward Island consumed all my thoughts. Several months had passed since I had seen my wife and kids, and I tried to imagine how much the children might have grown. But first, I had to find the Irving Whale and fly over Canada's largest oil spill.

After finding out all I could about the location of the Irving Whale, I arrived early at the Charlottetown Airport, refueled the helicopter, and filled a ten-gallon can with Avgas. I wiped the Plexiglas window with a towel and prepared the aircraft for my special passenger, Mr. Barnett, who arrived right on schedule.

Mr. Barnett was a middle-aged businessman, medium build and short gray hair. That morning he wore khaki slacks and a black waist-length jacket. He had an air of confidence about him, but he seemed a bit worried about the helicopter. He introduced himself and handed me his leather briefcase. I placed his case on the seat in the middle of the helicopter where he would have access to it and helped him into the aircraft. After a short safety briefing and discussion about the flight, we were on our way, flying across the northwest arm of Prince Edward Island.

It provided a wonderful opportunity to see the beautiful island, and I enjoyed the scenery while chatting with Mr. Barnett through the headsets. There were narrow highways winding through central and western Prince Edward Island, as well as tree-lined hills, rolling pastures, and quaint farmhouses.

We passed tourist cabins, clean, picturesque farms, and it wasn't long until we crossed the crimson, sandy beaches east of Tignish.

I made a mental note of the time as I steered northwest across the open waters of the Gulf of St. Lawrence. I wanted to keep an accurate track of our fuel consumption. We were already twenty minutes into the full tank I had taken on back at the airport. Now, we were flying across a vast area of water, and as I worked the cyclic control, I felt moisture on my palm. My heading was an estimate, because I had no way of knowing the exact location of the barge. Then, as I watched the waves below us, I allowed for a slight correction due to a cross wind. So far it appeared to be an easy mission, and Mr. Barnett turned out to be a friendly enough person to have on board.

"Have you ever seen an oil spill before?" Mr. Barnett asked, reaching into his briefcase and removing a camera.

"No, sir, I haven't."

"I'm sure you know, from all the local and national publicity, this ship is the Irving Whale. It sank while being towed from Halifax, Nova Scotia, to Bathurst, New Brunswick. When it sank with over four thousand tons of Bunker C crude oil. Not gallons, but four thousand *tons* of crude. It went down a week ago, about thirty or forty miles from here. We might be able to see it or it might be so deep we won't, but from all the reports we'll see the oil, you can be sure of that."

He removed his camera from its case and held it in front of him, adjusting the lens, preparing to take photos. I had heard about the oil spill on the radio, and everyone around PEI seemed to be talking about it. They weren't sure what to make of it and didn't trust the announcements. The ones that stated that the beaches of PEI would be spared the sludge and slime coming from the sunken ship.

After fifteen minutes we spotted several ships off to our right, about four or five miles away. Two of them appeared to be red-and-white Canadian Coast Guard ships, working around the spill. I corrected my heading, and soon we were directly over the three ships. The ships were in the middle of a dark, shiny oil scum covering several miles of water. The smaller vessel had a line of rubber or plastic booms in the water, conducting some type of oil removal. The larger Canadian Coast Guard ships were separated about a mile apart, apparently anchored, monitoring the situation. I circled the perimeter of the area the ships were working in and searched for any sign of the sunken ship, but I saw nothing but dark gray residue with silver traces. We had flown over miles and miles of pristine environment, but now we were looking at an environment totally violated.

A massive blotch of Bunker C oil sat on the water's surface without pattern or shape, as if it were refusing to sink. The tarry unwelcome guest carried with it an abundance of toxic chemicals deadly to fish, seabirds, and other creatures. Its shiny substance frightened me as I considered the fact that we could only see a minute portion of the actual spill and what it could be doing to the marine ecosystem.

I glanced at Mr. Barnett, who shot one photo after another. He stopped to look carefully at the giant mess below us and held his camera in his lap. His weary face clearly revealing the concern for the situation.

"Have you seen a spill like this before?" I asked.

"No, I haven't," he said, "Don't think there's been one like this before in Canada. This is our worst fear—that we might experience something like this on one of our rigs." His face had a look of determination and strength as he brought his camera up, ready to record the evidence of the spill. "Say, can you circle the other direction and let me face the oil spill?" His request seemed logical enough, so I switched directions, and in doing so, placed him on the inside of the turn so that he faced the spill and all the activity around it.

"This is better." he said. "Can you slow down a bit and maybe get down lower?"

"Yes, sir," I said, now circling into the wind, reducing our speed, and lowering our altitude to 100 feet above the water. At that altitude we were able to see better, but I wasn't comfortable staying that low for any length of time. He took one shot after another and quickly reloaded his camera as I tried to keep the helicopter stable. The wind increased in strength, and soon we were fighting turbulence.

"Lower?" he asked, a bit more forceful this time. "Can we get lower so I can get to another angle?"

"We'd be smoother at higher altitude, sir," I offered. "Much smoother."

"Take it down more, take it down," he said.

Reluctantly I lowered the collective slightly, trying my best to keep the helicopter into the wind and out of the water. It was a tricky bit of maneuvering since the large, bulky floats were blown sideways each time we were cross wind.

"That's good right there," he said, taking several shots of the work ship lowering large rubber objects into the water. "Those are booms," he said. "They are used to catch the oil and try to contain it, but they need a hundred times more than they have."

"I see what you mean," I replied, not sure of how they could ever have enough booms to contain all that oil. We were so close to the slimy oil that I could clearly smell the putrid, foul odor from it. The thought of crashing into the thick crude oil scared me enough to speak up.

"Mr. Barnett, we've been out for one hour, sir. We should be starting back because of our fuel situation. I'm going to climb back to a better altitude, so hold on for a moment."

"OK, Dave," he said, continuing to work. "I only need a few more shots. Can you put me over there behind the Coast Guard ships and let me take a shot back this way? I need a few shots from there."

I wasn't sure how to handle this. He had made his request in such a kind way I couldn't refuse. He glanced over at me, and I shook my head affirming his request.

Soon I had him in the position he wanted, south of the oil spill with the sun behind us, and the massive black and gray petroleum waste floating atop the sea with the three ships rolling softly in the waves. "Yes!" he said, excitedly, "This is good!"

He was the big boss, and I wanted to please him. But I started worrying about my fuel situation. I could feel a deep pain in the pit of my stomach, and before I knew it we had added ten more minutes to our time offshore. That meant I had less than thirty minutes of fuel in the tanks.

"Sir, we have got to go," I said, with more authority in my voice.

He turned, looked at me and understood completely. "OK, let's go," he agreed.

I turned toward Prince Edward Island and realized the wind had increased during our flight. Now we were heading right into the wind, which meant my ground speed became even slower than the usual sixty-five knots. Searching the horizon, I could only see water. No sign of land.

Using my best guess based on the magnetic compass and the wind, I steered east-southeast and searched frantically for land. Looking down at the waves confirmed my concern that our ground speed had fallen to horribly slow 50 or 55 miles per hour.

After ten minutes, I could finally make out the island ahead of us and guessed our distance. I glanced at the fuel gauge and the clock and knew we were in trouble. At that moment my thoughts rambled in all directions. Maybe I'd get fired for running out of gas. Maybe I would drown along with my first offshore passenger. Perhaps

Barbara, upon arriving that afternoon, would be told her husband had crashed offshore and there was a massive search and rescue operation underway.

Shifting gears mentally, I wondered how reliable the fuel gauges were and if I had remembered correctly the various times I had calculated during our flight. Out of the corner of my right eye I noticed Mr. Barnett looking over at me suspiciously.

"Are we okay?" he asked, quietly. I didn't answer.

"Are we okay?" Mr. Burnett asked again, sounding more concerned.

"Sure," I lied. "The wind is just a bit stronger than I expected, so we won't have enough gas to make it to Charlottetown. But that's not a problem, we will need to set down on the beach somewhere and put in the Avgas I brought along. You know, just to be on the safe side."

"I see," he said, looking at me suspiciously. Fearing that my eyes would give me away, I avoided looking directly at him. But I sensed his fear.

As we got closer, the island ahead of us grew larger, but it seemed as if each hard won mile took ten minutes. I flew as low as possible, hoping to cut down on the cruel headwind, knowing our situation grew more critical by the minute. Once again, I wondered, *How did I get into this mess?*

The white lines running along the waves confirmed that we were flying dead into the wind, and I went over everything Jack had taught me about recovering from an engine failure. There was more than a good chance that my engine would soon quit due to fuel starvation.

"Steer into the wind, bring your airspeed back to about forty knots, and look for a place to land," Jack had said. I went over it a hundred times as the miles crept by—miles that took forever.

Then, as I felt the sun's heat beating down on my face and sweat trickling down my side, we flew the last and longest mile to the lovely beaches of PEI. Each agonizing second of that final five thousand two hundred and eighty feet, I listened for total silence when the Lycoming engine sucked up its last drop of fuel and shut down. The thundering silence which meant fuel starvation.

Along the beach there were several open areas to choose from, but I took no chances. I flew directly toward the nearest piece of sandy real estate and picked an open spot close to vacationing families with their blankets spread out and their children digging in the reddish sand.

Keeping a safe, but frighteningly close distance from the tourists, I quickly set the aircraft on the sandy surface. Relief swept over me like morphine, and in that instant our situation changed dramatically, spared from the dreadful and potentially deadly experience of an emergency landing in the ocean. Looking toward the beach, I noticed children running up to the helicopter, their parents in tow, trying to keep up with them. I jumped out quickly and stopped the spinning rotor blades. Soon, we were surrounded by families, some who were excited and curious, and some who were upset a helicopter landing dangerously close to them. I felt so relieved to be on solid ground that it didn't matter. But I realized I should handle the situation carefully.

"Sorry to land so close," I said, loud enough for everyone to hear, and adding a bit of drama to the apology. "We've been offshore inspecting the Irving Whale oil spill."

"Wow!" one of the kids said. "Did you see the whale?"

I grinned at the little girl as Mr. Barnett came around the helicopter, joining me to face the gathering crowd. I pointed to him and said, "This man right here can tell you all about it. I have some work to do."

All at once the crowd's attention switched to Mr. Barnett, and it caught him by surprise. While he tried to answer their questions, I quickly untied the ten-gallon fuel can. Climbing onto the storage rack, I removed the metal cap from one of the helicopter's two fuel tanks. I looked inside the tank. Normally you could see the fuel level in the long, deep container, but this time, there wasn't a drop of fuel. Not a trace, not an ounce.

The fuel line that goes from the tank to the engine appeared to be empty, and my guess is, we were within a few seconds of having a devastating engine failure. Once again, I stared into the empty tank, knowing how lucky I was to be alive. Mr. Barnett turned from his growing crowd of onlookers and noticed the concern on my face.

"How did we do, son?" he asked.

"Guess we could have made it to the airport after all," I lied. "But since we landed, I'll put this fuel in and be on our way."

With several children and adults gathered around him, the oil company president and my first offshore passenger looked up at me with a familiar hint of suspicion.

While I pumped the fuel into the two tanks with my handpump, Mr. Barnett finished his unexpected speech, telling the onlookers about the Coast Guard ships and the oil slick, while reassuring them that everything would be controlled by the Government.

He looked relieved when I told him to get back into the helicopter, and the crowd seemed disappointed to see that all the excitement had come to an end. When they were a safe distance from the helicopter, I started the engine and took off into the wind. As we crossed the bay, I made a slow circle back around the beach, as Mr. Barnett and I waved at the people below. They returned our gesture while walking back to their blankets and sand castles. I called the tower at Charlottetown Airport and let them know our position.

Mr. Barnett keyed his mike and said, in a serious tone, "I only have one question."

Here it comes, I thought. *He knows we almost ran out of gas.* "Yes, sir," I replied.

"Do you think you could fly past Green Gables on the way to the airport and let me take a picture for my wife? That's all she can talk about anytime we discuss our drilling program in Prince Edward Island. *Anne of Green Gables. Anne of Green Gables.*"

"Yes, sir," I said, as relief swept over me again. I felt giddy with relief and welcomed the opportunity to please the man. "Yes, sir, we should be going right by it in about five minutes."

As I guided the small helicopter into the sky over the villages and farms along the northern coast of the lovely island, I felt calm and peaceful for a moment. As if our brush with death had never really happened. As if the first passenger I had ever flown offshore had not suspected our dilemma. As if I actually knew what I was doing.

***

The strain showed in Barbara's beautiful face as I ran into the Charlottetown Airport, two hours late. Leslie, our tired little angel, stood beside her mommy clutching her favorite blanket while watching passengers walk through the terminal. Barbara smiled as I approached them. When Leslie spotted me, she dropped her blanket and ran as fast as she could, jumping into my arms. I hugged her, then carried her back to her mother and held her as I kissed Barbara and looked at our son. He had grown so much more than I had expected.

"I'm sorry I'm late," I offered. "The flight this morning took more time than expected. I wish I could have been here to see you walk off the plane. I'm really sorry."

"That's okay," she said, bravely. "We're all right." She looked down at David Jr. lying in his little plastic baby bed. "What do you think of your son?"

"I can't believe it's the same kid. They didn't mix them up on the airplane or anything, did they?" I looked at Leslie and said, "That happens sometimes, you know."

Leslie looked at her mom, then got the joke. "Daddy."

"Don't worry," Barbara said, grinning. "He hasn't been switched." She lifted our son out of his bed and handed him to me, and I knew it was him. I hugged Barbara again, amazed at how beautiful she looked after such a long trip. I thought about how wonderful it felt to hold her again.

"Okay, everyone," I said, "Let's go and see Prince Edward Island, our new home."

"Okay!" Leslie shouted as she tugged at her mom's dress. "Let's go, Mommy!"

I loaded the generous assortment of luggage into our Pontiac, and we headed for the eastern edge of PEI. As we drove along the beautiful highway toward Georgetown, Barbara filled me in on the latest news from home.

First, she told me all about her mother and father and how things were going with them. How her brother and sisters were so helpful while she lived in Oklahoma. As she told me one story after another, Leslie listened attentively while enjoying the ever-changing scenery. The drive took us past the western edge of Hillsborough Bay with its marshes and bogs, past several charming villages and farms. Leslie seemed to enjoy every moment of the drive. She had improved her speaking skills and could form sentences. She had learned a lot being around Barbara's family.

"There's a big cow, Daddy," Leslie said, pointing to a group of cattle chomping away at their meal.

"Yes," I said, with serious tone, "several of them live around here."

Barbara became more relaxed as we drove east past Cherry Valley, and you could tell she was taken in by the captivating charm of Prince Edward Island. Her tension slowly evaporated as she realized I had been truthful in my description of the island.

"I didn't expect it to be this beautiful," she said. "Why didn't you tell me?"

"I did tell you."

"But I didn't believe you. I thought you were only trying to get me to come here and be with you."

"You're right about that. But I told you the truth when I said that PEI is fantastic."

For a moment Barbara seemed content that we were to be a family again. But she had news to tell about Oklahoma. "I saw your brother," she said.

"What did you say?" I asked.

"I saw Marve," she repeated. "He's out on parole again."

"I hope he can stay out," I said. "Last time he got out, his freedom almost killed him. Remember that?"

"Yes I do," she said, gazing off in the distance.

***

In a small apartment complex located in an impoverished North Tulsa neighborhood, several occupants had complained about the constant noise coming from apartment 210. Mrs. Arnold, an elderly lady with a smoker's cough and a voice as deep and gravelly as the Arkansas River, called the police several times, but had yet to see a police car. On that sultry Saturday night in August, when the temperature refused to go below eighty degrees, the heat and noise were more than she could bear. After her fourth call that night, the desk sergeant, either because he wanted to do the right thing or because he wanted to get the old lady off his back, finally dispatched an officer to the apartment complex.

When the officer arrived, he climbed the stairs to the second floor and stepped carefully around a garbage pile to avoid rats in the dimly lit stairwell. He heard loud music before leaving the stairwell, and grinned as he thought of his cranky desk sergeant.

"Get over to that shithole," Sergeant Lucas said, "and put a .38 round in that guy's ghetto blaster. Then go and find that ole bitch and tell her to quit callin' me, for cryin' out loud. Hell, I'm off shift in an hour, and we got real crimes to worry about."

In the stairway shadows, the young cop smiled as he opened the door to the second-floor hallway and recognized *The Doors* singing *Light My Fire*, one of his favorite songs. *At least these guys appreciate Jim Morrison*, he thought. He walked along the hallway and noticed the open door to apartment 210. The security chain was loosely fastened from the deeply scratched door post, leaving a six-inch opening, which allowed the music to escape loudly into the hallway. He stepped closer to the door, put his fist up to knock, then peered in. It wasn't what he expected. As he looked closer, the seductive music mixed with the super-sweet scent of marijuana.

Inside the dark, dingy apartment, four people sat around a table listening to music, smoking pot, and playing cards. Two familiar-looking hookers along with a couple of seedy men sat at a table filled with beer bottles and cigarette butts. Through the hazy and faintly acrid smoke, the officer could make out a bottle of scotch, several bottles of beer, and a couple of plastic bags, which appeared to contain pot or other more potent drugs.

The largest of the two men sang loudly and put a rubber strap around his arm in preparation for shooting up. The worried officer watched carefully, assuming he had happened on some sort of drug house. He wasn't sure if he should go back to the car and call it in or handle the situation on his own.

"You runnin' tomorrow, Marve?" the smaller man asked.

"I said I would, didn't I?" the taller guy replied, unhappy with the question.

"Sorry, man," the little guy offered, and then wisecracked, "I thought you liked that highway down to McAlester."

The tall guy chuckled, then spoke in a more charming, boastful tone, to the woman next to him. She smiled, then gently placed her left hand behind his head and massaged his neck. The big guy said, "Ever since I got out, I have never failed to help Ben when he needs a package. I'm like that, you know." He leaned in and looked closer at the hooker. "I help people when they help me." Then he turned to the little guy and said, "Let's forget about that shit right now, Randy. Hand me that pig sticker before I use it on you."

The young cop, growing more frightened by the second, understood he had his hands full. Yet he knew he had the element of surprise on his side. He didn't want to wait until the big guy shot up with cocaine or anything else. Last year in a sleazy bar, he and his police partner had fought a short, thin guy high on cocaine. His partner had tried to cuff the guy from behind, but the drug-crazed idiot had incredible strength and proved impossible to bring down. So his partner, forced to use his night stick almost broke the guy's skull.

Now, as the frightened cop looked through the narrow door opening, he knew he didn't want any part of a fight once the huge guy got high on cocaine. And now, to make matters worse, the big guy asked for a knife.
The anxious officer, with his pistol drawn, thought again of returning to his car to call for backup, but feared he would lose his jump on them. Music swelled in the room. The young cop needed to act fast.

"Police!" yelled the cop. Immediately, the people in the room went ballistic. Both women screamed, the short guy fell out of his chair, and Marve stood, pistol in hand.

The cop, amazed to see a pistol appear out of nowhere, realized the situation had escalated to dangerous proportions.

Thirty seconds before, the officer had thought of getting backup and now wished he had trusted his instincts. But it was too late. With the music blaring, two drunk girls screaming, and one man on the floor searching for a weapon, the officer had the presence of mind to focus on the pistol pointed directly at him. In less than a second the cop squeezed off two rounds, slammed his shoulder against the door, then ran into the room.

"Get on the floor, now!" he yelled, as the terrified hookers screamed hysterically and Marve fell heavily onto the floor, dropping his pistol.

The officer quickly grabbed the discarded gun and yelled a warning at the short guy. Marve lay on the floor, wounded, gasping for breath, blood covering his T-shirt. In a room that had spun out of control, the petrified hookers yelled, and Jim Morrison sang the final bars of *Light My Fire*. A red stream of blood ran across the grayish-brown wood floor toward the officer's shoe, as Marve lost consciousness.

"Marve!" his buddy yelled. "Marve, you're bleedin', man!"

The officer shivered slightly as adrenaline surged through his frightened body. Standing in the hallway, looking into the apartment, stood an old woman in a scruffy pink housecoat. She had her right hand over her mouth as she stood wide-eyed, shocked at the horrific scene before her. Seeing her, the officer reached across the filthy table with his left hand and gently switched off the ghetto blaster. Jim Morrison immediately went silent, and now, except for the hushed tones of two sobbing hookers, apartment 210 finally became quiet.

Chapter Sixteen

Holding my wife's smooth, tiny hand, I turned off the main highway right before reaching Georgetown, Prince Edward Island. A small dirt road took us northeast, into the countryside, thick with trees and thickets. After only five minutes, I pulled into an area cleared of trees, with a small wooden cabin near the road. Feeling the excitement of having my family with me again, I parked in front of the cabin and Leslie woke in the back seat looking sleepy-eyed. A worried look came across Barbara's face.

"Okay, everybody," I said. "Here we are. This is our new home."

Leslie crawled out of the car on my side and ran up to the front porch and waited there. "Mommy, come," she said. "Mommy, Daddy!"

Barbara got out of the car slowly, somewhat reluctantly. She held the baby in her arms and walked toward the front porch. Knowing she loved plants, I expected her to comment on the shrubs and mossy plants along the side of the cabin, but she said nothing. From the guarded expression on her face, I got that nagging, fearful feeling. Like earlier that day when I came horribly close to running out of Avgas. Barbara looked around. There were no other houses or cabins in sight, and it seemed unusually quiet as she stood there in thought.

"It needs a little paint here and there, but it will be great," I said. "You'll make it look like new once you have a chance to decorate a bit." I bent down to Leslie and said, "There are all kinds of birds and animals around here that we can watch and feed. I even saw an old barn owl over there in those trees the other day." I pointed toward the woods near the house and Leslie looked in that direction for a moment.

"Where, Daddy? Where? Let's go see."

Barbara's face told me I had better get them inside. "We can go later, Pumpkin," I said. I opened the front door, switched on the overhead light, and took a step back as I made a wide, sweeping gesture with my arms to welcome them in. "Come into my castle!" I said bravely.

Leslie went in, playing along happily. As she did, I noticed a musty smell in the front room. Her mother entered next, more cautiously, moving slowly around the room, holding the baby, and looking at everything from a woman's perspective.

Just an old-fashioned summer cabin with a tiny living area that held a well-used chair and loveseat which didn't match. The living room opened into a small kitchen area with several wood cabinets, easily accessible since they had no solid wood doors. Instead of wood, the doors were covered with chicken wire. I had seen the same type of chicken-wire doors in many of the camps in Newfoundland to keep the animals out. So I thought nothing of it, but now with Barbara staring up at them, I wasn't sure.

"Like, Daddy!" Leslie said. "I like this."

"Good girl," I encouraged. "I'm glad you like it."

Barbara ignored our exchange and continued looking suspiciously at the primitive kitchen. The floor, made of wide wooden planks needed a good cleaning. She examined the cabinet doors and looked at the small board running along the edge of the cabinet, put there as a meat block or bread kneading board. It was rough and certainly well-used by the previous tenants through the years.

The floor creaked as she walked across the room to inspect the stove. With the baby in her arms, Barbara leaned down, careful not to touch the iron structure.

"What is this?"

"This is a potbelly oil-burning stove," I said, joining her and quickly removing the cast iron cover. Pointing into the deep dark stove I said, "When you turn the oil on, it drips down into the stove. You light it, and it makes heat for you to cook with, and heat to warm the house in the winter."

Unimpressed, Barbara walked back toward the cabinets. "What's this?" she asked.

"Oh, that's the sink," I said.

"Where's the faucet?" she asked, looking under the sink.

"There is no faucet, because there's no running water. But the neat thing is, there's a well in the back, and the water is crystal clear." I pointed to the hand pump next to the sink. "See, you'll get the hang of it."

That comment did nothing to change Barbara's stoic appearance. But at least little Leslie enjoyed the cabin. Barbara stared at the antique stove, then back at the sink, and without looking at me, she asked her next question.

"What about the bathroom?" she asked, sounding even more worried.

"It's right over here," I said, walking across the room, hoping to change the way things were going. I stood by the door as Barbara and Leslie watched carefully. With a forced smile on my face, I brought the door toward me a few inches, then felt a solid bump as a small animal darted out of the bathroom. It ran between us, its feet clacking on the wood floor, then scampered across the living room and out the front door.

"Daddy!" Leslie screeched. Barbara screamed, clutching the baby even tighter.

"Don't worry. Don't worry," I said. "That's just a little ole raccoon. Now that we live here, they won't bother us anymore."

Barbara shook her head, looking grim-faced.

"Come on, don't let something like that bother you," I said.

Leslie looked at her mother with such worry that it now appeared I lost my only supporter. After a moment, when no other animals were discovered, Barbara worked up the courage to walk to the bedroom. Standing in the middle of the dark, dusty room, she took a deep breath and stared at the old-fashioned metal spring bed with a worn-out, filthy mattress across it. I had planned to get sheets and blankets and make up the bed before she arrived, but somehow forgot. The old striped mattress had dark stains as well as a few rips which exposed filthy cotton stuffing.

Barbara walked carefully around the room, looking for something else.

"Well, what about a closet?" she asked.

"I don't think they have a closet," I admitted. "But there are lots of nails in the walls, and we can put in as many more as we need."

Barbara walked to the tattered bed and stood beside it for a moment, as the last drops of hope drained from her weary face. Leslie, knowing her mother so well, stepped across the room and gently touched her mom's hand. Barbara sat on the bed, holding the baby with her left hand, clutching Leslie with her right. She tried, but she couldn't stop the small, silent tears that appeared below her lovely blue eyes. Beside her, even Leslie knew. Even my little daughter knew what I should have known. What everyone in the family now knew.

Don't ever let Daddy pick out the house.

***

That night I gave up the old cabin and took my family to a motel. In the Hudson's Bay office the next day, one of the ladies told me about some new tourist cabins being built along the coast near Montague. I had explained to her the disappointing results of the old cabin in the woods, and that's when she grinned and said something I'll never forget.

"There are two important rules all married men should know before looking for a new place to live. Number one: never pick out a house without your wife. Number two: never forget rule number one."

"Don't worry," I said, grinning at her gentle rebuke. "I've learned my lesson."

We stayed in a small motel for a few nights and searched the area for the best housing within our budget. Then one afternoon we drove over to Montague, a small village ten miles from Georgetown. The Montague River, with its clear, fresh water ran right through the middle of town, and there was a lovely park along the river with foot trails into the north woods. Several privately-owned pleasure boats were anchored on the river and a picturesque bridge crossed over the river to Main Street. It's a lovely place where the Brudenell, Cardigan, and Montague Rivers wind past towns and villages and drain into Cardigan Bay. The area is sometimes known as the Three Rivers section of eastern Prince Edward Island.

We loved Montague immediately. A mile or so past town, we drove through a smaller settlement called Lower Montague. Located across the harbor from Georgetown, the lovely country setting offered trees and a sandy beach nearby. It was remote but not isolated like the old cabin. Without delay, we made a deal with the landlord to occupy the only finished cottage. It had running water, a new fridge and stove, and came completely furnished with basic furniture, silverware, dishes, and bedding.

Later that day while we were moving in, the construction manager came over and introduced himself. Mr. MacLean was a large, rugged Scotsman in his '60s. He had kind, clear blue eyes, graying hair, and a quiet, unassuming manner. Gentle around us, but not at all shy or tender supervising his men.

While talking to us that afternoon, he turned occasionally, shouting at his men, barking orders at them as they worked on the unfinished cottage nearest to ours. There were five or six young carpenters working for him, and they showed the greatest respect for Mr. MacLean.

The Scottish foreman wasn't mean or forceful, but firm and direct. A tall man with wide shoulders and a thin waistline, more fit than most men in their thirties, much less sixties. I suspected from his tanned, wrinkled face he may have been a fisherman at one point in his life. But, regardless of his background, he had a ready smile and a gentleness in stark contrast with his rugged occupation. Every bit the grandpa type, he obviously loved children and enjoyed playing with Leslie, letting her hold his carpenter's tools and sometimes lifting her over his head.

In a short time, Barbara transformed our little cottage into a home. We had a few things to decorate the house, and she purchased a few more in Montague. Soon we felt right at home. While I flew during the day, she would take the kids on long walks along the beach, and when I returned in the evening, we would head off discovering the island and finding new places to visit.

Sometimes Barbara would show me a flower she had cut and put in water or plant cuttings that Mr. MacLean had shown her. He knew the names of all the plants and Barbara wrote them down, making a list of the ones she enjoyed the most. Soon she could point to nearly any shrub or flower on our evening outings. She showed us holly, wild roses, choke cherry, and during one of our drives, she pointed out witch hazel and dogwood. She loved the abundance and variety of native flowers and shrubs in Prince Edward Island.

As summer turned to fall, the colors of the trees and bushes along the east coast of our beautiful island changed rapidly—almost magically. On my daily trips to the oil rig, I flew low above flaming red spruce trees and obscure, shallow swamps. I enjoyed seeing a variety of rich autumn colors like the gold leaves of the elm tree and the beet-red chokeberry bushes, heavy with edible fruit. There were lush forests, picturesque farms, and rich fir thickets beside wetlands. And adding to the allure, there were lovely ponds, streams, and beaches, which created a panoramic view as alluring as any pilot has ever had the pleasure of flying over. I looked forward to every flight to the rig, and each night I had something new that I had seen that I could share with my family.

While Barbara and the kids enjoyed the days along the beach, I became more accustomed to flying to the oil rig, despite Stan the tool pusher's filthy mouth and never-ending criticism. By ignoring his constant gripes, I was able to build a relationship with the managers and oil field workers. Each day as the drilling program progressed, the company used the helicopter a bit more; then, around the middle of October, Hudson's Bay Oil and Gas agreed to upgrade to a larger, more modern model: a turbine-powered Bell 206 Jet Ranger. Finally, I would be entering a new phase of my commercial flying career.

***

Bill, one of the oldest guards at the Oklahoma State Prison, stood outside of the west cellblock, enjoying the fresh air as he chatted with one of his fellow workers. The two guards watched as a group of new inmates walked from a white bus across the cracked pavement on their way to get processed. As usual, there were several whites, a few Indians, one Mexican, a few blacks, and one tall prisoner with a familiar face. Unfortunately, the old guard's prediction had come true: Marve had returned to Big Mac.

Bill felt a surge of disappointment watching the young man, but after seeing hundreds of return customers, nothing surprised him. As the new inmates walked toward the door, Bill, feeling a combination of disappointment and anger, started one of his lectures about the drawbacks of their unappreciated occupation, "Things have sure changed since I started here," Bill said.

"I know," the young guard offered, knowing where the conversation was going.

Bill shook his head and said, "I had one the other day that was hard to cuff."

"So how'd you cuff him?" the young guard asked.

"I knocked his ass out. When he woke up, he was ready to go."

"You can't keep doin' that, Bill," the guard said. "Like you say, things are changing."

The older guard smiled, exposing a crooked line of nicotine-stained teeth. He took one step toward the door that led back to the cellblock and turned to argue his case.

"I'll tell you one thing," he said, looking around at their little open space and enjoying the fresh air. "If I couldn't come out here once in a while, I'd go nuts."

"What?" the young man asked, unable to see the connection.

"Never mind," Bill said. "Things might be changing on how to handle prisoners, but then again, they might not. But if I walk along checking the cells and one of those peckerwoods throws shit on me, I'm gonna whup his ass."

Bill noticed the serious look on his fellow guard's young face. "Sure," Bill said, "I'll counsel him, just like the new state guidelines tell us to do." Now in slow motion, one short word at a time, he pretended to counsel a prisoner: "Don't ... do ... that ... no ... more!" Bill's face darkened. His tone more authoritative, he said, "Then I'll take him to the hard end, and when I'm done, I'll go to the house." The other guard shook his head but said nothing.

Bill continued, "I don't take nothin' in there that I don't take out on the streets. And I don't take *nothin'* out on the streets."

"Yeah, I know, Bill," the guard said, glancing at his watch. "We better get over to the captain's office for that meeting."

The two guards stamped out their cigarettes and walked back into the west cell house. Bill held the door open, allowing the younger man to go first. Before he stepped into the hottest, loudest section of the prison, he looked up at the sky, appreciating the peacefulness, and noticed an unusual cloud pattern forming. When he closed the door behind him, the noise inside the massive cell house was practically unbearable. His body grew rigid, his senses sharpened, his peripheral vision focused. He became mentally aware of everything going on around him. Internally, he snapped to attention. Without looking down, he touch-inventoried his weapons and considered his best method for drawing them if needed. Bill may have been old-fashioned in the way he treated hard-to-deal-with prisoners, but he knew without a doubt the prisoners still considered him The Man.

Chapter Seventeen

When Bob Brough, one of the senior pilots, brought the Jet Ranger to Georgetown, I was so visibly excited that he took one look at me and told me to calm down. The sleek, swift Jet Ranger represented a major leap in technology from the Bell 47, and I felt nervous thinking about its power.

I had flown Hueys in Vietnam. The Bell 204 and 205 "Hueys" were the backbone of the US Army's helicopter fleet. The Jet Ranger was a smaller, commercial helicopter with two seats in front and three seats in the rear cabin. It will cruise around 110 miles per hour, which is a great deal faster than the 60 or 70 miles per hour in the Bell 47.

"You think you can handle her?" Bob asked, looking across the front seat with his poker face. It had been a one-day checkout including, among other things, a trip to the rig.

"Yes, sir," I replied, grinning. "I'll go over the flight manual again while I'm sitting on the rig."

"Well, all right," he said in his now familiar Newfoundland accent. "You're doin' good with her. Remember, with three or four people on board, it will be limited on power. Better to hold it to three passengers. Yeah, and another thing. If you get downwind, you're in trouble. Stay into the wind, keep your power up, and you'll be fine."

We walked over to the older, steel-framed Bell 47. Next to the Jet Ranger, the 47 looked like a Model A Ford. Bob put his headset in the seat and checked the equipment tied to the outside cargo rack. I could tell he was anxious to get going.

"Gonna head toward Port aux Basques," he said. "Should make it an hour or so before dark." Then he exhaled. "Keep it down to three people, and you'll do good."

He started the helicopter, hovered for a moment, checked the controls carefully, and took off slowly and gracefully toward the east.

Watching Bob's smooth-as-silk takeoff, I felt like a rank amateur. He had a gentle touch that allowed the aircraft to find its own way through the air. I stood in silent admiration, watching a true expert fly east across the village of Georgetown into a cloudless sky.

That afternoon I made one more flight out to the Wodeco II carrying my first two Jet Ranger passengers. It was a fast, straightforward flight with lovely, sunny weather. The aircraft felt easy to control, and the exhilarating power of the turbine engine seemed rich and smooth as we skirted low across the blue water toward the giant steel structure. I circled the rig, pulled back gently on the cyclic, and made a slow hover onto the helideck. The large black rubber floats touched silently on the hot steel deck, and we were down without so much as a hiccup.

After shutting down on the heliport, I stood nearby and admired my shiny green-and-white helicopter. Like the Bell 47, it had large black floats on either side of the cabin, cumbersome and anything but aerodynamic.

As I stood on the rig with the backdrop of the blue water of the Gulf of St. Lawrence, the freshly painted green-and-white helicopter gave me a deep sense of pride.

But then, like being aroused from a Marilyn Monroe dream, Stan walked across the heliport, stern-faced, chewing his nasty cigar. The magic moment quickly evaporated.

"Eagleston, you're damn lucky there are no other helicopter companies around here," he said, pointing his half-chewed cigar toward the aircraft, "or your ass would be back in Newfoundland raising turnips."

Without waiting for a reply, the grumpy Polish rig boss spun around and walked toward the worried tool pusher who saw him coming and forced a smile. I felt like shoving him off the heliport. But I said nothing and waited for instructions to return to the shore base back in Georgetown. Hopefully alone.

But that didn't happen. While I stood in the rig's radio room, Stan came in and announced he planned to fly back to Georgetown. As the bad news soaked in, he picked up his clipboard and stepped closer. "Eagleston, what are you doin' sittin' around here? This ain't the US Army."

"I'm ready when you are," I said, feeling my face flush with anger. Without another word, I left the radio room and went to the heliport. Soon both of us were in the aircraft together, side by side and far too close for comfort.

On the flight to Georgetown I tried to ignore Stan, but he wouldn't sit back and enjoy a quiet flight. The aircraft had a headset for the front-seat passenger, and at that moment I wished it didn't work. After my initial takeoff call to Georgetown, giving my time off and ETA, it was quiet for five minutes or so, before Stan broke the silence.

"So Eagleson, admit it. You've never flown this helicopter before now, have you?"

"Stan, there's a 'T' in my name. It's Eagleston, not Eagleson," I said, reminding him again. "But to answer your question, yesterday was the first time I flew this aircraft."

"So, Hudson's Bay is basically paying for your training, aren't we?" he asked, with a look of satisfaction on his unpleasant face.

"Our chief pilot gave me a proper endorsement for this aircraft and went over all the emergency procedures. So I wouldn't call this flight a training flight."

"Bullshit! A couple of hours on the ground and forty-five minutes of flight training. That ain't what I call a proper endorsement."

"Stan," I said, growing more irritated. "I have eight hundred hours on larger turbine helicopters, so it didn't take much to do a transition into the Jet Ranger. I believe our company complies with Department of Transport regulations."

"I'm sure you're a real ace," he said, sarcastically. "I guess the eight hundred hours were over in Vietnam shootin' children. Bet you're a regular Lieutenant Calley," he said, referring to the My Lai Massacre.

"Mainly I flew soldiers out to the jungle," I said, thinking how I'd like to fly him out to a jungle and leave him there.

"So you didn't shoot anyone?"

"Didn't say that."

"So did ya?" he asked, trying harder to bait me into a quarrel.

"I also flew gunships for several months. Of course, my job included the use of firepower."

"I thought so," he said, giggling under his breath. "Bet you shot the shit out of those villages just like they show on TV. Bet you didn't care how old those poor people were, you shot them and loved it."

I did my best to ignore him the rest of the flight. When we finally arrived at Georgetown, I wanted him out of that helicopter so badly I couldn't land fast enough. I wanted to say a lot of things, but I had to stay cool. My pulse raced when we landed, and his insults hung in the air like the putrid smell of Bunker C oil. After we landed and I shut the engine off, I then reached up to turn off the battery.

"Just a minute," he said.

"What?" I asked, glancing over at him.

"Why don't you go back to the States?" he sneered. "We don't need baby killers in Canada." Then he took his headset off, flung it to the floor, and got out and stomped to the office. My fist tightened, wanting so badly to slug the bastard. The thrill of flying a new helicopter completely evaporated, replaced by humiliation. In this new world I lived in, the world of commercial aviation, I couldn't fight a client or return his insults, no matter how much he deserved it. I had to sit and take it or lose my job.

"What in the world was that all about?" Paul asked as I got out of the helicopter. "Looks like someone's ready to play Mr. Scrooge tonight for Halloween," he said with a broad grin on his face. "Dave, me son, don't let that asshole bother you."

"Halloween," I said. "I forgot all about that. Man, I better get home after we put this gem away for the night. Where's the logbook?"

"Yes, boy, don't worry about that tonight," Paul said. "Go home and get away from Stan while you have the chance. If that little shit gets cranky, I'll give him a taste of Muhammad Ali," he said, dragging the name out, sounding like Howard Cosell. "That's right," he said. "MOOO-Hammmid-Alliii." I couldn't keep from laughing. Paul stood like a long-haired, dazed boxer, his two fists up and ready to fight.

"Thanks, Paul," I said, then took his advice and drove home, the anger, like an unwanted passenger, riding with me in the car.

***

In his cell, Marve thought of how it all seemed so familiar: stuffy, cramped quarters, constant noise from nine hundred inmates, and the lonesome, familiar faces. With few exceptions, the same dangerous cons were still in power. Oh, there were a few new faces, but mostly the same messed-up people. Like Ben, whose unit Marve would be working in once again. After all, Marve had kept the overweight straw boss supplied with meth and cocaine during Marve's brief visit to the real world.

Still sore from his gunshot wounds, Marve lay on his bed and mentally tuned out the cell block noise by focusing on thoughts of his second wife. He smiled, fantasizing about her soft, sexy skin and long brown hair. Sweeter by far, than his first wife, and she knew how to party.

They had married in mid-February in Eastern Oklahoma, and since Marve needed cash, he quietly pulled off a couple of small jobs without her knowing. In the evening, after telling his bride that he went out for a walk or a game of pool, he broke into a house or store. She never suspected her tall, handsome husband would be doing anything other than playing pool, and the extra money he brought home wasn't at all suspicious to her.

One evening, feeling confident and slightly high, Marve broke into a local clothing store in a small town called Idabel. Since he drank often during the past two days, he made a series of mistakes which led to his arrest. Later that night, when his bride visited him in the Idabel jail, the look of disbelief on her young, innocent face caused Marve to have a moment of remorse. Of course, that quickly evaporated when the older deputy sheriff, standing near Marve's young wife, ogled lustfully, and explained the serious charges against her husband, then offered to drive her back to the hotel.

She declined his flirtatious advances and looked at her husband. She felt deceived and betrayed, and fully realized at that moment that she had made an incredible mistake. Reluctantly, she made a few calls for Marve and helped him make bail. But she also called her father and tearfully admitted that he had been right about her husband.

When she visited Marve the next day, her father, a husky Korean War vet escorted her. Furious over his daughter's heartbreak and disgrace, her father gave the deputy a stern look as he walked down the corridor toward the holding cell. Marve lay sleeping on the floor of the dusty cell.

"Eagleston, get up," the deputy shouted. "You have a visitor." Marve woke slowly, brushed hair out of his eyes, and squinted, trying to figure out who his visitor might be. He stood up and felt the first traces of a hangover coming on. His father-in-law looked through the bars of the jail at the man who had somehow managed to both win and break his daughter's heart in less than a month.

"Are you my lawyer?" Marve asked.

"No, I'm not. I'm Linda's father, and I'm here to take her home." Marve smiled slightly and offered his hand, but the man didn't shake it. Marve's smile faded as he withdrew his hand.

Not sure what to say, Marve looked down at the floor for a moment, then spoke in hushed tones, "Sir, I had too much to drink last night and wound up in that store. I thought I was going into the back of the pool hall." Linda's father, stoic, stern-faced, said, "Really?"

Marve, sensing a slight trace of empathy, continued along the same deceitful path,

"Sir, I feel terrible about this," he said, doing his best impression of an innocent man. "I would never risk hurting your daughter, and I promise I'll never hurt her like this again."

Linda's father, composed and silent up to now, reached in to take Marve's hand, and it appeared he had changed his mind about the handshake. Marve stepped forward, offered his hand, and a few seconds later regretted it. What Marve didn't know is that Linda's father had already spoken with the sheriff and had learned about the stolen jewelry found in the accused's pockets, and the cardboard boxes found in the trunk of his car, stuffed with stolen clothing.

The deputy watched carefully and would later tell people that he had never seen anything like it. "This little guy, who was pretty darn mad, but never showed it, reached through the bars and shook hands with my prisoner. The prisoner stood about six-four and weighed a couple of hundred pounds. Once the little guy had the prisoner's hand, he squeezed it so hard the big guy turned red, fell to his knees, and practically passed out. I found out later, his father-in-law, had been a Marine during the Korean War and now rode bareback in a bunch of rodeos in Oklahoma and Texas. Damn guy had the largest wrist I'd ever seen."

When Linda's father let go of Marve's hand, he leaned in and said, "One thing you said is true. You will never hurt my daughter again. This marriage will be annulled tomorrow, and she will never speak to you again. If you call her, write her, or try to visit, I'll come after you with one of the many military weapons I've collected over the years. They range anywhere from World War II Nazi bayonets to US Army flamethrowers. I don't care what authorities do to me afterward or what law I break finding you. But I do care about Linda, and I *will* find you, son."

Marve, now standing, looked at the man and wondered how the little guy could ever be so strong. He rubbed his hands together, hoping the pain would go away soon and carefully considered what to say. Obviously, Linda's father saw though his lies, so Marve knew he must be careful here.

"Sir," he mumbled. "I believe you. I think you would come after me."

"So?" the father said.

"So what?" Marve asked humbly.

"So, you understand and agree to what I've said?"

"Yes, sir," Marve said. "I promise not to call, write, or visit Linda."

"OK then," Linda's father said as he turned to leave. Marve relaxed for a second, then tensed again when Linda's father turned back toward the cell. The rugged visitor stuck his hand between the bars and said, "Then let's shake on it, son!"

Chapter Eighteen

It was a beautiful fall afternoon as I drove along the tree-lined road trying my best to enjoy the fall colors and forget Stan's insults. My job would be perfect except for having a horrible boss like Stan. Try as I could, I couldn't find a way to win him over. But it was Halloween and I had promised to take Leslie out for her first trick or treats.

Getting closer to our little group of cottages, I noticed something going on near our home. There were several people congregated near our parking space: five or six men, including Mr. MacLean, were on their hands and knees on the ground. Barbara stood nearby watching the men with a worried look on her face. As I drove closer, I could see Leslie kneeling on the ground, too, and that bothered me.

I hurried along the dirt drive, trying not to panic. After parking quickly, I jumped out and ran to Barbara to find out what was happening. "Hi, Dave," Barbara said, casually.

"Hi, Dave," Mr. MacLean offered, looking up briefly from his crawling activities. "Right there, fellas," he said, pointing to something on the ground. The other men moved in the direction he indicated. "Try there," he said. I walked closer to Barbara, and she smiled that goofy smile of hers. Sometimes an adorable smile, but sometimes aggravating, and this time the latter.

"What are they doing down there?" I asked in frustration. Barbara looked toward me and started to speak, but she was interrupted by Mr. MacLean.

"Found it, boys, I found it!" he said, standing up and dusting off his pants legs. "Is this it, sweetheart?" he asked. He leaned down toward Leslie, who I noticed, wore the most unusual Halloween costume.

"Mine!" she said. "Ring, mine," she said excitedly, as she took a small toy ring out of Mr. MacLean's tough old hands. He smiled broadly as he picked Leslie up, and she clutched the plastic ring tightly and gave him a hug as his payment for finding her lost treasure. The four men who worked for Mr. MacLean got up slowly, with far less enthusiasm than he had shown. They continued to stand there for a moment, ill at ease.

"All right, fellas," Mr. MacLean said in his stern, Scottish voice. "Fun's over. Let's get crackin'! There's boards to nail and not much light left in the day." He looked back at the cute little girl in his arms, and any trace of authority on his wrinkled face evaporated.

Barbara explained that while Leslie played outside, she lost her little plastic ring. We had given it to her a few days before, and it had only cost fifty cents. But that didn't matter to Mr. MacLean when he heard Leslie crying and saw her and her mother searching for it. He had stopped all construction activity while he and his men searched frantically, on their hands and knees, for the fifty-cent ring.

"Thank you, Mr. MacLean," I said. As far as I could tell, the great ring hunt had cost Mr. MacLean around twenty or thirty dollars in wages, but he didn't seem to mind. I'll bet if he'd had ten men working that day, all of them would be right there on the ground with him, searching in the dirt. I thought of how terrific it would be if Mr. MacLean took over Stan's duties at Hudson's Bay Oil and Gas.

"Yes, thank you so much, Mr. MacLean," Barbara said, still smiling. Then she looked back at me. "Daddy, did you see Leslie's bunny outfit?"

Leslie ran toward me, clutching her toy ring, and I finally figured out what kind of costume she had on. She wore a homemade Halloween outfit that Barbara had fashioned out of Leslie's one-piece pink pajamas. She had drawn little black whiskers on Leslie's face with an eyebrow pencil, and to complete the outfit, Barbara had formed a bunny tail out of a fistful of cotton balls. It was Leslie's first Halloween, and she seemed excited. A sweet, excited little bunny.

A little later, around sunset, we drove to Montague and walked from house to house along Hillcrest and MacDonald Street. We enjoyed a crisp fall night, and the lovely homes with large yards, old-fashioned front porches, and tall birch trees. Barbara held the baby and walked with Leslie and me. After a while, our little son grew tired, so Barbara took him to the car to look after him. Each time Leslie and I passed other children, she stopped, trancelike, to gaze at their colorful costumes.

That night we had only been out an hour or so, but Leslie loved it and beamed each time someone commented about her "cute little bunny outfit." But it was time to be getting home, and I had to break the news to our bunny.

"Okay, Pumpkin," I said. "It's getting late, and I'm afraid it's time for us to go home."

"More!" she said as she looked up at me with her little blue eyes. "One more, Daddy. Please, Daddy," she pleaded.

She looked so adorable I couldn't refuse, although it became the third "one more" I had agreed to. But *this* one would truly be the last one. Barbara was tired, and we needed to get the baby home. It was a beautiful night, and we enjoyed and appreciated how the people of Montague had been treated us.

"OK, Miss Bunny, one more," I said. "Then we're going home."

"Let's go!" she said, scurrying along the sidewalk toward the last house on Belmont.

We waited at the front door of a typical house, and I expected an elderly couple to answer, because many of the people on that block were older, retired residents.

But much to my surprise, a much younger woman greeted us, smoking a cigarette, and yelling over her shoulder at someone inside the house, "I'll get you a beer in a minute," she said in her deep, gravelly voice. She bent down, looking at Leslie, and quickly changed to a more friendly tone, "Oh, hello, cutie."

Leslie looked up at the woman, held out her paper bag, and waited for the candy to be dropped into it. "Treat?" Leslie asked, smiling.

"Well, aren't you the most adorable little thing?" the woman said softly. Then in a louder, less patient voice, she yelled at someone in the house, "Just a damn minute! We have trick-or-treaters on the front porch. Grab that bowl of candy on the table!"

A man in the house yelled back at the lady, "Get your *dupa* off the porch." I didn't know what that meant, but due to his harsh tone, I thought about picking up Leslie and leaving. But the woman obviously enjoyed Leslie, so I didn't want to hurt her feelings. I think she noticed the worry in my face and quickly yelled again, "Hurry up, they have to get this little bunny home before midnight." Then, at the top of her voice, "Get the damn candy."

Now I knew we should go. We were about to witness an all-out domestic dispute. I picked up Leslie and did my best fake smile for the lady and started to leave. But I had waited too long. Beside this boisterous woman with a bowl of candy in his hand and a stubby cigar in his mouth stood Stan. A mixture of nervousness and concern came over me. His beady eyes stared directly at me. His face had that critical, condescending smirk I had seen several times before.

"Shit, you didn't tell me it was our helicopter pilot," he said to the lady. Before she could compose an answer, he said, "So this your little girl, Eagleson? What's her name?"

"That's right," I said, trying keep it nice and hoping he could do the same. "Her name is Leslie."

He bent down, pretending to show Leslie his full attention. "Hi, little girly," he smirked. "You're pretty cute. But ya know somethin'? Leslie's a boy's name." He grinned, then said, "Say, how come you wearing your stupid pajamas on Halloween? Your ole man won't buy you a real costume?" Stan giggled, stood up, and looked at his wife, who didn't find his comments amusing. But that didn't bother him.

I picked up my daughter and stood on his front porch with Leslie in my arms. She frowned, sensing the wrongfulness of this man. Turning quickly, I started down the steps toward our car. Barbara sat in the front seat. She looked at me and smiled. Behind me Stan shouted, "You didn't let her have any candy!"

Of course, Leslie, like any other child, reacted to that, "Candy?" Leslie asked, looking at me with her sweet little bunny eyes. It was, after all, her special night. Back up the steps I went with Leslie holding her bag out for her candy. Stan grinned, cigar sticking out of his piggish face, and I longed to cram it down his throat.

"Now Stan, knock it off," the lady said.

"Knock what off?" he asked. "I'm givin' pajama girl her candy! Here, Chuck, or Leslie, or whatever your name is, take some damn candy. I'm goin' back in the house for a beer." He threw a handful of candy at us. Several pieces went into her bag, but most fell onto the porch. Stan's wife, looking defeated, shrugged her shoulders and closed the door.

Leslie and I picked up the candy that had fallen onto the porch. She started to cry. "Don't worry, Pumpkin," I said, looking at her sweet little face. "I guess that man doesn't like children." Then, to get her back in a fun mood, "But, look at all the candy you have. We had lots of fun tonight, didn't we?"

She shook her little head, and I took her to the car. The night air felt cooler, and it seemed we were the only ones on that street. I put Leslie in the backseat and got into the front with Barbara, who held little David as he slept peacefully. I started the car, looked down the street for a moment, then switched off the ignition.

"Back in a minute," I said. "Forgot something."

"What?" Barbara asked. I ran back up the steps of the porch, knocked on the front door, and the coarse lady answered with a surprised but friendly look on her face. Smoke from their hallway escaped through the screen door. I smiled and said, "Can I speak with Stan a moment?"

"Stan, come here!" she said. Then a little louder, "Come here!" A moment later Stan approached the front door cussing about his beer. When he recognized me, he scowled and spouted, "What the hell do you want now, more candy?" His exasperated wife shook her head again, then disappeared down the hall. More irritated now, Stan said, "I said, what do you want?"

"Oh, I'm sorry to bother you again, Stan. Can you come out here for a minute?" I tried to sound cheerful. "What the hell," he said.

"I need to keep an eye on my family," I said. "They're in the car over there." I pointed to my car, and Stan reluctantly stepped onto the porch, letting the screen door close behind him. As the door slammed shut, I quickly grabbed his shirt right below his neck and pulled him over to the far side of the porch, into the shadows. With one hand clutching his shirt and the other grabbing his belt, I slammed the surprised drunk against the side of the house with all the force I could muster. Now, close enough to him to smell the beer on his breath, I thought of breaking his nose, but knew my wife and daughter were only a few feet away. In the shadows of the porch, I lifted his struggling body and shoved his head against the wooden structure. His black, well-chewed cigar flew out of his mouth, bounced off my shoulder, and hit the floor. Stan tried to yell, but I put my hand over his mouth and squeezed hard.

The rage which consumed me at that moment simmered as I looked into his fear-filled beady eyes. "Don't you ever talk to my little girl like she's dirt," I said. "She's not one of your rig workers or helicopter pilots. She's still young enough to think people are good. She's too young to know that there are assholes like you in the world."

I relaxed my grip on his mouth and Stan started to say something, then I pushed again, forcing him to moan. "The thing is," I said. "You treat everyone like they're scum, when it's you that's scum. You may know everything about oil rigs, but you don't know shit about people."

"Wait," he said, whimpering. I released my grip on his face and mouth and let him move. "If you ever speak to my daughter again or even refer to her at work, I'll find you one night in town. Don't worry, I'll find you."

Stan mumbled something that I couldn't understand. Looking at him, whimpering, red-faced, pressed against the wall, I could see that all along, he had been able to hide the fact that he was just a shallow, pathetic coward. A man filled with nothing but vile speech and hate. And in that moment, my anger turned to pity.

"And one more thing," I said. "In case you're thinking about telling anyone about this or trying to find a way to run me off—forget it. Mr. Barnett warned me about you two months ago and gave me his phone number in Calgary. Make something out of this and it'll be you that gets run off."

Stan leaned against the house as I walked away. In the car, Barbara had a look of concern on her face, but said nothing as we drove away. Later that night, after we put the kids to bed, we lay next to each other in the dark. "What happened tonight at that last house?" Barbara asked. "I know that guy," I said, stroking her face with my fingers.

"That was Stan, the jerk I've told you about at Hudson's Bay."

I felt her body grow tense, and she started to ask another question. I put my finger on her lips. "Don't worry," I said, reassuring her. "We worked everything out."

"Are you sure?" she mumbled.

"Oh, yes, I'm very sure," I said, leaning over and kissing her full on the mouth. She felt tense for another moment, but soon she relaxed and pulled me closer. It was a long, sweet kiss, wet and generous, a kiss that brought our bodies closer and kept the world far away.

Chapter Nineteen

In a sweltering, foul-smelling cell, Ben, the straw boss, and Pickens, his ruthless bodyguard, chatted with Marve about Marve's return to prison. Ben seemed friendly enough, but Marve knew the man could get violent at a moment's notice, so he listened apprehensively while watching his bodyguard.

"Did they patch you up good in Tulsa?" Ben asked.

"Not bad," Marve said, listening to Ben, while watching Pickens suspiciously.

"How were the nurses?" Ben asked, grinning.

"I got some good stories about that if you got a couple hours to spare?" Marve joked.

"That's all good, Ace," Ben said, standing up and stretching his arms. His eyes narrowed, "But we got something else to talk about."

"What's that?" Marve asked, worry showing in his eyes. Now Ben stood directly in front of Marve as the tall prisoner took a step back, his head touching the wall behind him. Ben stepped even closer. "You weren't out of this hole a year, and you got arrested twice and shot once. From what I hear, you were using more drugs than you were selling." He poked his finger into Marv's chest. "You're about the dumbest asshole ever did a stretch in this circus."

"Hang on, man," Marve said, but Ben interrupted him. "Hang on? *You* hang on!" Ben said, annoyed. "I set you up with an apartment and the right contacts, and you couldn't even run some shit down here once a week. You get married to someone you just met, and while you're on your honeymoon, you knock over a five-and-dime and get your ass arrested by the town clown. My boys bail your ass out, then you and two streetwalkers get stoned, while some old bitch down the hall goes crazy from the noise and calls the cops."

"I told you he's nothing but trouble, Ben," Pickens growled. "Let me talk to him."

"Wait a second, man," Marve says, trying to speak. "Shut up," Pickens shouted, making a fist with his right hand, ready to swing on Ben's command. Marve looked down, sullen-faced, knowing Ben was right, but worried about what came next.

"To top it all off," Ben continued. "Some pig fresh out of the pig academy shoots your ass through the front door because you left it open far enough for the whole world to see in. You pull a piece on the cop, but you're blazed and don't know which end is up."

"Wait," Pickens said softly, as a guard walked slowly past the cell. The conversation stopped abruptly. Bill, the older guard strolled quietly along the corridor, making his rounds.

Ben's face relaxed slightly while the old guard passed. Another moment, then Bill's footsteps faded. "OK," Pickens said. Ben continued in a hushed, astringent tone. "Let me tell you somethin', dummy. There is only one reason you're here right now and not over at the brickyard getting your head smashed in: you kept your mouth shut in the Tulsa lockup. If you'd said anything in there, I would have heard about it the same day."

Marve remained silent. He knew he had screwed up, so he kept his mouth shut while Ben continued to ramble, blowing off steam. A few minutes later, when he felt certain Ben was finished, Marve promised to be a loyal, hardworking soldier.

"Get your ass out of my cell," Ben said. Marve took the few steps to the open cell door, turned and said, "Thanks, man. I owe you." Pickens sneered, "You heard the man, get out of his cell." Marve walked along the corridor toward his own cell and grinned slightly, relieved that it hadn't gotten physical with Pickens. He knew Ben liked him, but he also knew that it would take a while to get back to the status he had previously enjoyed. He wanted Ben to trust him again, and that would take work and time.

**

The spectacular fall colors of vibrant amber and crisp gold created a seasonal masterpiece of scenery along the east coast of Prince Edward Island. Each helicopter flight became a memorable, enjoyable experience. Adding to the seasonal effect of my wonderful job, the light, gentle touch of the Jet Ranger with its sleek lines and spacious fuselage made that October in PEI a pilot's dream. Even the time I spent on the rig waiting for my next flight became tolerable after the intense encounter with Stan, which seemed to alter his attitude toward me.

Too soon, fall became winter, and two large tugboats arrived and pulled the rig off the location. They would tow it across the world to the Far East for its next drilling assignment. No one would tell me if they had found oil near PEI or not, but I suspected they hadn't because I had overheard the term "dry hole" whispered around the office.

From my company's point of view, the assignment ended well, and we had finished with a good relationship with our customer. After saying goodbye to all the Hudson's Bay people, the local staff at Georgetown and the drilling crew, I took Paul Williams to the airport in Charlottetown. He was truly a good guy to work with and had helped me with the old Bell 47 and our beautiful Jet Ranger.

"Thanks for all your help," I said, standing behind my car as Paul unloaded his big suitcase out of the trunk.

"Lord Jesus, b'y. Don't worry 'bout it," he said, extending his hand and smiling.

"Hope we work together again somewhere, Paul."

"I'm sure we will," he said, lifting his bag and giving me that broad Paul Williams smile. "And if we do, boy, I'll keep working on you and convince you that folk music and country is crap. I'll teach you about real music."

"What's that?" I asked, as if I didn't know.

"Hard rock, me son, hard rock: The Who, Led Zeppelin, good stuff, good stuff." At that, he smiled and walked into the terminal.

That afternoon I called Jack Murphy and found out that my next assignment would be working a winter project in Northern Quebec. He told me to find a house in PEI for the family to winter. Barbara and the kids loved our summer cottage, but the colder days made it obvious that we couldn't stay in the cottage all winter. Mr. MacLean had built the cottages for summer visitors, not frigid Atlantic winters. We needed to move into the city.

***

In the late '60s, due to the overcrowded conditions at the Oklahoma State Prison in McAlester, paroles for nonviolent prisoners were obtainable if the inmate kept his record clean. After being shot by a Tulsa cop, Marve had served one year of his two-year sentence and hoped to be paroled soon. He worked hard on detail, kept the straw bosses and guards happy, and had managed to stay out of serious trouble. Other prisoners were getting "early outs," and he looked forward to his parole hearing in two weeks.

Late one afternoon when the sun set behind the hills west of the barn, Marve sat on the ground and leaned against the whitewashed walls of a cattle stall. He had scored the best work detail of them all, cleaning the barns and taking care of the animals.

Marve, working on his own, was responsible for a couple of dozen cattle and four horses in the west section of the barn. He had finished his chores and sat down to enjoy the peaceful moment. To celebrate, he pulled up his pants leg up enough to expose a small cloth bag tied around his calf. He carefully removed a joint, then took a match from the opposite sock and lit the marijuana. As he inhaled the sweet-smelling cannabis, the pot soothed his senses and relaxed his mind and body. It had a warm, calming effect.

Soon he felt high, surprised that the cannabis could affect him so quickly. He figured it was because he wasn't using other drugs. He thought of it as a self-administered afternoon parole. The tension in his aching body slowly evaporated. Now, free to think his own thoughts and dream his own dreams without interruption. Several times during the next few minutes, he took deep gulps, indulging his selfish inner needs, allowing his thoughts to shift inward.

After a while, his imagination became unfiltered, and his hearing more sensitive. In the far distance, he heard a guard yell at someone, and the familiar sound of picks and shovels striking the ground. In his mind he saw his ill-tempered father driving down a highway, steering the family car with his left hand, then turning around to reach far into the backseat with his right hand. While the family begged him to stop, his father grabbed Marve by his neck, screaming at him, barely able to keep the weaving car on the road.

As Marve sat on the hay with a mixture of delusion and fear, it took him a few seconds to notice a shadow that had fallen across his hand. The shadow wasn't there a moment before, but now it inched slowly across his arm. Quickly Marve dropped the joint onto the floor and turned toward the barn door. His heart beat faster as he saw the outline of a bulky frame in the doorway. Marve knew he was about to get busted, but as he adjusted his eyes, he could make out the long, wide frame of a wandering milk cow.

Marve jumped up, removed the smoldering joint, and kicked at the hay to extinguish the now smoking pile. As the inmate led the chestnut animal back to its stall, he grinned and took a deep breath, glad that he had avoided detection by one of the only honest guards in the prison. Bill had a reputation for appearing at any time without making a sound. If that had happened, there would be no talking him out of the righteous punishment. But not this time, Marve thought, grinning. Not this time.

***

In late fall we left our cottage and moved to a house in Charlottetown. But before we drove away, we said goodbye to our friend, the kindhearted Mr. MacLean. We let him know how much we appreciated him. His charming personality, his patience and love for Leslie, and the special, unselfish manner he had cared for an alien family made it difficult to say goodbye.

A few days after we got settled into our warm house in Charlottetown, I got the call from Jack Murphy letting me know more about my new assignment.

"As I said, we have a job for you up in Quebec," Jack said. "You'll be living in a rough camp with forty or fifty men, and you will be hauling them to and from their work site every day. Be ready for some cold weather."

"Yes, sir," I said. "How long will I be there?" Jack hesitated, then said, "It's hard to say, but plan on three or four weeks. Get Barbara set up where you are, and, like I said, it's going to be cold in Quebec, so take lots of gear."

I knew this wasn't going to be good news for Barbara, but at least I had her in a nice, comfortable home.

That morning I broke the news to Barbara, and, as I expected, it upset her to learn that I would be away for three or four weeks and she would be left alone again. New location, two kids, and no family. She talked about going back to Oklahoma, but we found a pleasant neighborhood with nice, friendly people.

"I'll be back in three weeks," I said. "And remember what the guy across the street said. It doesn't snow much in PEI, so I'll be back before it does."

"I'll help Mommy while you go away," Leslie said. I took her into my arms and hugged her and Barbara at the same time. "I know you will, Pumpkin. I know you will." Barbara hugged me and tried to keep from crying. While we lived in the cottage, she had enjoyed the nights together as a family, and now we were saying goodbye again. She didn't want to face the prospect of being alone, once again.

***

As usual, Jack was right! Quebec is a cold, cold place. The assignment took place in Eastern Quebec, around eighty miles north of a city called Seven Islands. Our company would be providing helicopter support to a famous construction project in the early seventies which transferred electricity from Churchill Falls, Labrador, to Quebec. At that time, Churchill Falls was the largest construction program in North America, producing over five million kilowatts of electricity. To connect the Churchill Falls electricity to its client, Hydro-Quebec, hundreds of V-shaped transmission towers were being erected along a five-hundred-mile stretch of rugged, isolated land. The helicopter would work at a construction base camp on mile 84 of the Quebec North Shore and Labrador Railroad, QNS&L. A large camp, strategically located near the rail line so that people, equipment, and steel could be moved efficiently by railroad. The helicopter would be used daily to move construction workers and supervisors to and from their job site, deep in the interior.

Large, crowded, and smelly are the best words to describe the Mile 84 camp. Fifty men slept on cots in one enormous room with few toilets and even fewer showers. At times, during the twenty- or thirty-below-zero winter nights, toilets froze, only to be replaced by large metal cans. A few of the toilets remained frozen until the spring thaw. And adding to the depressing, overcrowded situation, French-Canadian workers smoked the powerful, foul-smelling French cigarettes named *Gitanes*. It made the immense room almost unbearable.

Although I despised the dreadful living conditions, I respected the vigorous men working there. They were tough, hardworking French Canadians, descendants of lumberjacks, trappers, and railroad men. They were accustomed to extremely cold conditions. Each winter morning, after a meager meal, I flew them to their work sites, ten, twenty, and sometimes thirty miles from the camp. They climbed the giant, unfinished towers and worked eight to ten hours at temperatures as low as thirty-five below zero, and in winds as high as twenty miles an hour. In the late afternoon, I flew them back to the camp, where they ate supper and slept. There were no TVs, radios, telephones, or any other form of entertainment or communication except books and card games, and yes, of course, more *Gitanes* cigarettes.

It was a dry camp, which meant that they allowed no alcohol. However, on one occasion, booze played a key role in a major incident. Each evening the workers returned from their job site for supper after spending the day freezing on top of a steel towers. They had one thing on their mind: a hot meal. And believe me, they devoured it.

One night I brought the men back from the field, and after unloading the helicopter, I followed several of them into the dining room. Inside, I heard a horrible commotion in the kitchen. Several men were screaming and cussing in French, as pans and dishes crashed onto the floor. Since they swore in French, I couldn't understand what the quarrel was all about. Then, two or three of the workers I had flown in pulled several terrified cooks out of the kitchen and into the dining room.

"Here," one of the irate construction workers yelled. "You eat this shit." He grabbed a cold sandwich from a large stack of sandwiches and shoved it into the sobbing cook's mouth. The cook put his hand up to defend himself, but to no avail. The workers were furious. Within minutes three cooks lay on the floor with cuts and bruises ranging from a broken arm to a black eye and an assortment of lacerations. As it turned out, the cooks had spent the afternoon getting drunk and failed to prepare a hot meal. The construction workers had to eat cold sandwiches, and they were furious.

Two of the cooks required serious medical attention, but I couldn't fly to Seven Islands until the next morning at daylight. As I watched the ruckus die down and the construction workers pick up their cold sandwiches, I learned a serious lesson: don't screw with tough, hardworking men. Feed them, respect them, and leave them alone.

Despite the crowded, primitive condition of the camp, and extreme weather conditions I learned a lot that first winter in Canada. The Jet Ranger is a good utility aircraft, capable and reliable in arctic weather. If, that is, the aircraft is well maintained and preheated.

Another thing I learned: it takes a good man to keep a helicopter running in tough environments, and I had one: Brian Baker, the engineer I worked with, proved to be an expert Bell Helicopter mechanic, *and* a master scrounger. Most of the time, Brian could come up with anything we needed, right in the camp. He could get along with anyone and knew how to trade, bribe, or borrow. Unlike other helicopter crews in Eastern Quebec that might miss a few days of work while waiting for a certain piece of equipment or tool to be shipped in, Brian could *procure* what we needed and keep us flying. Brian Baker, what an asset.

Since there were no phones available in the camp, every week or two, after I flew passengers or cargo to

Seven Islands, I called home. Each time I called, Barbara cried and asked when I would be coming home. As the weeks and months went by, she became more and more depressed. But I could never tell her when I planned to come home since I didn't know. Then, after one month turned into two, then into three, I finally got to go home. In early March of 1971, I left Quebec and flew home to my family.

***

In the taxi, I rode along the outskirts of Charlottetown, PEI, amazed at the incredible snow accumulation and wondered if somehow the flight had been diverted to Russia by mistake. It was unbelievable. I thought of that day in November when we moved into our home and one of our friendly new neighbors had said, "Don't worry, PEI gets very little snow." But the snow was piled eight or ten feet high along the road. And on some side streets, instead of two-lane roads to drive on, there were only walking paths carved out of the snow, six and eight feet deep. Streets where it would be impossible to get out of the driveway, let alone drive to the store.

Near our house, the taxi driver slid through dicey snow-covered streets as I tried to determine which house my family lived in. We were lucky, it seems; the snowplow had been able to get down our street. But even still, the snow had accumulated to the point that most of the addresses were covered with it. Snow had amassed in great wavy layers in yards, on housetops, and atop idle, frozen cars. Sidewalks were nowhere to be found. My best bet, since the house numbers were covered, was to try and spot our little green Pontiac in the driveway. Only a few cars were visible, but then I saw it, our little car, stranded in a snow-filled driveway with only the faintest section of its green roof showing through a soft white blanket of snow. On the top of the car, the ferocious wind whipping around the house and driveway had created a mountainous snow peak. It looked like a parking lot at the North Pole.

I walked up the driveway in knee-high snow, across the unseen lawn, and carefully up the steps to the porch. With my suitcase in hand, I stood shivering on the front porch and waited for Barbara to open the door. I had looked forward to this moment for so long. So many cold, lonesome nights in Quebec I had dreamed of the day I would return to her, and now it was about to happen. Like a Norman Rockwell painting, or a John Denver song, my dream of coming home would finally come true. I smiled broadly as Barbara opened the door, but my childlike smile evaporated in an instant. It wasn't my beautiful wife that welcomed me home, but someone else. Someone that barely resembled my wife.

Barbara stared at me with a dazed, empty look on her face as she held little David on her hip. She looked exhausted, miserable, as though she were about to scream. The baby cried, and by the disgusting smell that greeted me, probably needed a clean diaper. Standing beside her mother, Leslie, wearing filthy pajamas and one house shoe, clutched her mother's leg and looked up at me as if she didn't recognize her own father. I smiled at Leslie, then my gaze went back up to Barbara. Barefoot, wearing a worn-out gray housecoat, grungy jeans, no makeup, and wispy, tangled blond hair which looked like it hadn't been washed in a month.

"Well," she said, drawing out the word, taking a deep breath. "It's been a long four weeks, hasn't it?"

"Can I come in?" I asked, not sure if I wanted to.

"I don't care," she said, stepping back, shrugging her shoulders. "I just don't care."

Inside the unfamiliar house, I was overcome by the disheveled condition of the stuffy living room. Toys were scattered everywhere and dirty clothes lay in several piles. The TV played loudly, while an overfilled diaper pail sat next to it, contents strewn across the carpet. Several empty coffee cups and plastic juice glasses sat on the coffee table. Looking at the mess, I thought back to her letters during the winter. They depicted a mixture of anger and despair, but in no way had they prepared me for the downward slide she had taken.

Barbara had spent her first winter in Canada housebound due to a record snowfall, forced to survive inside an overheated house with two small children. The isolation and pressure had taken a physical and emotional toll on her. She suffered from the strain of being cooped up with her small children for over three months. I looked at her carefully, perhaps too carefully. She noticed me staring, then snapped indignantly, "What are you looking at?" "Nothing," I lied. "I'm glad to be home."

I wanted to change the subject, so I spoke to Leslie. "Hey, Pumpkin," I said, holding out my hands. "Come and give Daddy a hug." Leslie let go of her mother and ran to me. I swung her high above my head while Barbara stood with that same brooding look on her face.

"Don't you want to hug me?" she asked, in her gloomy tone. Her face showed the deep-seated hurt inside her frazzled, exhausted body.

I put Leslie down and held out my arms to Barbara. Leslie stood by, watching carefully, a faint smile on her little face, but Barbara didn't move. She stepped back as a tear fell down her cheek.

"You told me three weeks!" she said, now getting louder. "*Three weeks!* Now it's been *thirteen weeks!* Do you know how hard it has been to live in such a cold place with two children, no family, and no transportation? Do you even care?" Her voice was resentful, hurt, and when she spoke, tears ran down her pale, despairing face. Wet, bitter tears, as numerous and sorrowful as the lonely days she had endured. Now she cried, head bent, body sagging as she released a tiny portion of the hopeless pain she had held in for so long. I took the baby from Barbara as she leaned against the wall, looking toward the floor, staring at nothing.

"I thought we had nice neighbors," I said. "Wouldn't they help you dig the car out of the driveway? Wouldn't they offer to help with the kids once in a while?"

She looked up at me, shaking her head. "They did," she said, her voice monotone, a faraway stare on her wet face. "They came over here four or five times. Dug our car out after several storms, and three times they had to connect those long wire things to the battery. Several times they took me to the store. I can't tell you how many times people brought food over. So many times that I was embarrassed to ask them again."

"I didn't know about all this," I said, feeling ashamed.

"I'll bet you didn't," she said, accusingly. "Want to know something else? The woman who lives across the street won't let her husband come over here anymore. She didn't say anything, but I think she worried that I might seduce him."

"I'm sorry," I said.

As Barbara caught her breath and tried to stop crying, the thick, repugnant odor from David's diaper rose from his little body and into my face.

"David has been sick—a lot," Barbara said. "Leslie was sick a few times, and I was sick of this house. I couldn't go anywhere or do anything. That's the wonderful life you gave me when you flew off to Québec. I hate my life, and I hate you and your damn helicopters. I just want to go home. Do you hear me? I want to go home," she yelled.

After a moment or two, her voice went back to a more normal volume, but her pale, upturned face remained serious, mournful. "Sometimes I don't love you. I hate you. I hate you so much I wish you would have drowned when you put that helicopter in the lake. Then I could go home and never have to worry about when you will be coming home." She cried again, but stood with a look of defiance and resolve, as her tears of hurt betrayed her, running uncontrollably down her cheeks.

I put the baby in his crib, then wrapped my arms around Barbara and held her for a long time. She cried and cried, sobbed, and took a deep breath. Pulling her close to me, I felt her warm tears on my neck, and welcomed them. When she finally relaxed, she looked up at me and let me kiss her softly. Near us, Leslie leaned over the top of the crib and spoke baby talk to her little brother. He giggled and crawled closer to her.

I looked into Barbara's sorrowful blue eyes, red from crying. My words were useless at that moment, so I stood there, silently holding her, and tried to caress some of the infinite hurt from her tired, wounded soul.

Chapter Twenty

Marve proved quite convincing on the day of his parole hearing. Perhaps to the parole board he resembled a model prisoner, or maybe they were under tremendous pressure to free up space in the massive Oklahoma prison. Whatever their motive, it didn't matter to prisoner number 76964, because the board granted him a parole and he would soon walk out of Big Mac a free man.

The day Marve left OSP, Bill stopped in to say goodbye. The crusty old guard acted as if he had just noticed Marve packing. He only liked a few of the inmates, and Marve was one of them. But even though everyone knew Marve had been granted a parole, Bill acted surprised to see the tall inmate folding up his bedding.

"What the hell is this?" Bill said. "You moving to Death Row?"

Marve looked at the old guard and smiled. "Come on, Bill. Not much goes on around here that you don't know about. You come by to give me a speech?"

"Hell, no," Bill shot back. "You didn't listen to it last time, so why waste good words like that."

"Did ya come in to give me some traveling money?" Marve quipped.

"No," Bill said in a more serious tone. "I figure you made more money while you were in here than I did. No, this ain't about money."

Marve stood still for a moment and looked at the old guard. This time, his face showed more consideration. Though Bill was the enemy, Marve respected him. He extended his hand and spoke politely, "You've been square with me, sir, and I appreciate it."

Bill shook his hand with a strong, solid grip that surprised the young inmate. He looked deep into Marve's dark, brown eyes. "You got along pretty good this trip," he said. "You didn't give me any trouble, and whatever you did on the side, I never found out. Otherwise we wouldn't be having this conversation."

"Thanks, Bill."

"Don't thank me, that ain't no compliment. You got along good in here. Too damn good. So good that the thought of coming back to prison doesn't scare you anymore. And when prison doesn't scare a man, he'll probably keep bein' an outlaw."

Before Marve could respond, Bill put his hand up and continued, "There's something about you, Marve. Something that people like. Even me, I like your sorry ass. You got more friends in here than any ten prisoners put together. But whatever you got that makes people like you—charm or personality—you been using it for the wrong reasons. When you get back out on the street, you can use those qualities to have a good life or you can use them to get deeper into the hard life. And if you keep at it, you'll wind up back here or wind up in a wooden box with fancy lining."

Marve studied the wiry old guard, unsure how to respond. "Thank you, Bill," Marve said sincerely. "I'll remember what you said."

Before Bill could answer, a couple of other prisoners arrived and stood outside, waiting to talk to Marve.

Bill left them there, and when he got back into the hallway in front of the cell, he glanced through the bars at Marve. From his heart, he had wanted to say more, but his head and his years of experience told him he had said enough.

He walked carefully along the massive east cell house and turned off the part of his mind that cared. Prisoners yelled at each other from cell to cell, guards shouted orders, and steel doors slammed shut. Continuous noise ran along the corridor of the cell house like the yellow lines painted on the floor. They were familiar sounds; men laughing, yelling, and sometimes sobbing. Noise unfiltered by the hot, humid air, unyielding but somewhat lonesome.

Unconsciously, the old, prison-weary guard switched on the part of his mind that kept him alive. He put the young, tall inmate out of his mind, and once again, he went into full readiness mode.

***

During the next few weeks, I helped Barbara get the house back to normal. That seemed easy compared with slowly bringing her out of the protective shell she lived in. And just as she finally settled down, our chief pilot called once again.

"You're going back to Newfoundland," Jack said.

"But Jack, remember our talk yesterday?" I reminded him. "I told you I can't do another bush job right now because my wife is still trying to get over the three months I did in Quebec."

"It's gonna' be fine," he said. "You will be the base pilot on the Newfoundland government contract and live near Corner Brook. You'll be home every night."

"Home every night?" I asked, suspiciously. "Are you sure, Jack?"

"Well, almost every night," he said, less convincingly. "You will only be away from home when you get forced to stay in another town or village due to weather."

"That does sound pretty good. When do we need to be there?" I asked.

"Next week," he said, then explained the situation. Universal Helicopters had one Bell Jet Ranger based in Western Newfoundland to support one of several regional government contracts. The helicopter worked with three divisions of the provincial government: Forestry, Wildlife, and Medical Services. And, from time to time, provided VIP flights for provincial and federal government officials. One of the hallmarks of the contract was medical emergencies. Given the vast remote areas of the province, the pilot would be required, at a moment's notice, to drop any other projects he flew on and proceed to various villages, outports, and camps to pick up sick or injured patients and fly them to the nearest hospital or nurses' station.

"It will be a demanding job," Jack said, "With a variety of missions, difficult weather and terrain, and a lot of flight time."

"What do you call a lot of flight time?" I asked, because all pilots love as much flight time as they can get. Jack paused, giggled, and said, "Last year we did seven hundred and fifty hours. Does that sound like a lot to you?"

"Yes, sir," I said. "I can't wait to get started."

The current pilot on that job, James Jones, would be moving to St. John's, Newfoundland, to start his training on the big Sikorsky S-61 offshore helicopter. Universal Helicopters and Okanagan Helicopters were working together on a large offshore oil project and James would be one of their first pilots. I had heard a lot about J. C. Jones and had met him briefly while in Gander. Another Vietnam vet, James was an experienced helicopter pilot with California good looks and a mind for detail. His leaving gave me an opportunity for my first long-term contract, and I couldn't say no to such an exciting prospect.

It took me a few days to talk Barbara into going, but she liked the idea of my being "home *almost* every night." A few days later, we took our second ferry ride from Sydney, Nova Scotia, to the coastal city of Port aux Basques, Newfoundland.

The next morning, we drove across Western Newfoundland to the little community of Pasadena,

Newfoundland. Located on the shores of Deer Lake in the beautiful Humber Valley, Pasadena got its name, not its population, from Pasadena, California. In 1971, there were less than nine hundred people living in the tiny, rural community. There were a few farms and apple orchards, and one general store. We saw beautiful little cabins beside the lake and got our first peek at our house in the woods. Barbara loved the little house from the moment she saw it, and I knew then that this would be a new, exciting chapter in our life.

***

On a cold, February morning, after two months being out on parole, Marve wandered what the day would bring. In a small, rented house in North Tulsa, the tall ex-con sat in bed and looked at the sunshine coming through the frost-covered bedroom window. His house was one of several hundred tract houses built near the Tulsa Airport during World War II. Now an older, less-maintained sub-division, originally constructed to accommodate aviation laborers and their families during the peak years of the war. Companies like Spartan and McDonnell Douglas needed workers and were desperately trying to keep up with the war's demand for aircraft. Marve, however, was desperately trying to keep up with his personal demand for cash.

That morning he felt a slight hangover, but it wasn't as bad as the day before. As he reached for his first cigarette, he briefly thought about looking for a job. He inhaled and felt the familiar sensation as he contemplated the challenges of working for a living. He knew that finding a job and making money were two different things. He needed a job to keep his parole officer off his back, but he could make more money several other ways.

He stood up, stretched, and walked barefooted to the tiny bathroom. After relieving himself for what seemed like several minutes, he felt behind the medicine cabinet for his little green book. He returned to the bed and continued to smoke while he sat and looked up the phone number of an old prison pal.

Several years ago, Ben had suggested creating a "little black book." And once Marve started, it didn't take long to accumulate over fifty names and phone numbers along with a few addresses. Most of the names were listed using a simple code he alone understood. The little book was dark green, small enough to fit in the back pocket, and easy to hide. Marve quickly located the number he needed, then walked into the kitchen and used the yellow wall phone located near the fridge. Surprisingly, his friend picked it up on the first ring.

"Hello," a deep, familiar voice said.

"Damn, Phil," Marve said. "You walkin' around with the phone tied to you? Maybe you were expecting a call from an old cell mate."

"Don't worry about it," Phil said. "How's the wife?" he asked, bandit code for "How's business?" Marve assumed that Phil's phone might be tapped.

"She's pissed at me right now," Marve replied jokingly, meaning that there wasn't much going on. Then Phil said, "Need to get the oil changed on my car today. Let's talk about our marriage problems." The two ex-cons finished talking and planned to meet later in the day.

Marve had called his mother the day before and learned that his father would be out of town on business. A perfect time to pay his mother a visit. While in prison, she alone, visited him on a regular basis, and she had somehow managed to pay most of his legal fees. He could at least stop in and pay her a visit.

His parents lived in a small, older home across the street from Will Rogers High School, and as he drove along their street, he watched a number of neatly dressed students walking along the sidewalk.

A few minutes later, in his parents' living room, Marve sat nervously drinking coffee, while he chatted with his mother. She asked all the usual questions: how are you, where do you live, why don't you come over more often.

"When is Dad coming home?" Marve asked as he stood. He walked to the front window and looked out to see if anyone had pulled into the drive.

His mother removed a hardback book from the bookshelf and opened it, exposing an envelope she had hidden from Marve's father. The envelope contained a detailed invoice from Marve's attorney with an outstanding balance of fifteen hundred dollars, more than two month's pay for the aging telephone operator.

She had waited to talk to Marve in person, hoping a face-to-face conversation might persuade him to take it off her hands. But as she opened the invoice and started to speak, Marve interrupted her.

"Shit," he said, shaking his head in disgust.

"What's wrong?" she asked, taking her glasses off.

"Dad's here," Marve grumbled.

"Oh, my," she said, quickly inserting the invoice back in the envelope.

"Now, son," she said, in a pleading, almost begging tone. "Don't start anything, please."

"*Me* start something?" he asked, offended. A few seconds later, his father walked in the front door with a familiar scowl on his rugged face. "Who's got their damn car in the driveway?" he asked. When he looked across the room and saw his tall, ex-con son, his face transformed from grumpy to insolent.

"Un-huh," he uttered. "Finally came around to visit your mother?" Then, in an even more disgusting tone, "Bet you're here to borrow money."

"Not at all," he said. "How ya doin', Dad? How's business?"

Marve's father sat his brown, beat-up suitcase on the floor and closed the front door behind him. He took off his overcoat and walked into the bedroom, glancing suspiciously at his wife, wondering why she was holding a book. When his dad disappeared into the bedroom, Marve saw his opportunity to escape. At the front door, he stopped and looked back at his mother and shrugged his shoulders. Then, he called out to his dad, "Dad, I have to go," Marve said, trying again to sound friendly and avoid a fight. "I have a job interview, and I need to go change clothes first."

"Honey!" Mom shouted toward the closed bedroom door. "Come and say goodbye. Marvin Allen has to leave now."

There was no answer from the bedroom. Marve whispered to his mother, "Call me, Mom. Just call me sometime."

"Please, son," she whispered, gripping the book tightly in her hands. "We need to talk soon." Marve smiled at her, glanced quickly toward the bedroom, then slipped out the front door, as quick and silent as a cat burglar. His worried mother stood looking through the large picture window as he backed out of the driveway and onto the street. Marve glanced back at her and smiled broadly. She held the book for another moment, watching Marv's car speed away. Worrying again about the unpaid bills hidden in the book, she knew down deep she would get little or no help from her wayward son. Then she thought how strange and beautiful it had felt when he smiled at her. After all the trips to court, the visits with him in prison, and the frightening times at his side in the hospital, she still had this wonderful, yet fearful love for her troubled son.

For a moment she blocked out her endless worries and focused on his deep, endearing grin. As she looked out the window, students hurried by her house, chilled by the winter wind. A few cars with frost-covered windows passed along the street. Beyond the cars stood Turner Park with its silent oak trees, bare-limbed, cold and lonely. Just like her. And, like her, the windswept trees clutched their memories of warmer days, and the gentle, more forgiving seasons of their lives.

Chapter Twenty-One

Our small house in Pasadena was located between the Trans-Canada Highway and Deer Lake, only a half mile from a farmer's field where the helicopter was based. Since I could walk to work, Barbara would always have the car and loved that idea. We lived in a small, peaceful community, but the helicopter would be my passport to a wider range of people and problems.

Our first afternoon, while unpacking and getting settled in, a few of the neighbors came over to welcome us. It would be the first of many occasions we were to enjoy the famous Newfoundland hospitality. One couple brought a bottle of homemade bakeapple wine, and another neighbor brought a warm loaf of homemade bread, which filled our house with its heavenly aroma.

Later that evening, Paul Williams, the stocky, long-haired engineer who had worked with me in PEI, surprised us by showing up at our door with his wife, Kay. They lived less than a mile away and told us the good news: we would be working together again. They stopped in with a bottle of wine to welcome us back to Newfoundland.

Paul was his usual jovial self and kept us laughing while we drank wine, ate the fresh bread, and discussed the various ins and outs of living in Western Newfoundland. His pretty wife, Kay, a short, petite brunette, seemed quiet and more laid-back in contrast to Paul's rough, outspoken personality. While Paul enjoyed telling a good story or freely offering advice to a "mainlander," Kay was more introverted, preferring to listen and study people, considering everything around her. They seemed to fit the rule that opposites attract.

The next morning, after our special evening with Paul and Kay, I expected to fly anywhere, since my territory covered eighty percent of Newfoundland and Labrador. I would be taking orders from a government manager who lived near Pasadena and who had the authority to approve flights.

That first morning, I flew my newly assigned Jet Ranger, registration GAM, to the forestry office on the Northern Peninsula, a little over one hundred miles away. I landed near a small village called Roddickton, located on the north end of Canada Bay. With only a few dozen houses and a fewer dirt roads scattered around Roddickton, I easily located the forestry office. When I landed, I was met by the regional wildlife officer, Earl Pilgrim.

A large, muscular man in his late 20s, Earl carried a parka and wore khaki slacks, a beige Newfoundland Forestry jacket, and dark green rubber boots. By tracing his forefinger across his throat, he motioned for me to shut the helicopter down. I had met Earl once before and had heard stories about his exploits. Stories about the brazen poachers burning down the government cabins he and other wildlife officers had built. How they might do anything to discourage Wildlife Enforcement. But the officers rebuilt those cabins and continued the fight against illegal hunting and the senseless extermination of moose and caribou.

A tall, strapping, good-natured man, Earl Pilgrim had a reputation of being a serious big game regulations enforcer, and everyone knew he would go to any lengths to capture a poacher and protect wildlife. In his younger days he had been a successful boxer and gained notoriety as the light heavyweight Canadian champion.

That morning, he led me into his office and introduced me to his partner Norm Muse, and together, they briefed me on their plans for the day. Norm was an easygoing, friendly guy who tended to let Earl do most of the talking. Both men were fit and enthusiastic, and somehow their passion for justice was infectious. They explained that they were following up on reports of several cagey moose poachers hunting on snowmobiles around the upper Cloud River. "Let's catch them red handed," Norm said.

"This time of year," Earl said, "when a poacher kills a cow moose, she is probably carrying a baby inside her. That means they have actually killed two moose at once."

I had never given much thought to wildlife preservation, but his statement got my attention. "Dave, that's not only illegal, but it's barbaric, senseless killing. A helpless little baby moose murdered inside the mother, before it's born."

At that point, I felt ready to help. "How do we do this?" I asked, looking closer at his map. "The area you're talking about is nearly all forest and hills, so where do we land?"

"That's the point," Norm said. "They hunt in the forest because they think we can't or won't land. We find ways to fool them, and then we catch them." I still wasn't sure how it would work, but I wanted to be part of it.

Thirty minutes later, we were flying along the eastern edge of the snow-covered Long Range Mountains. Earl sat in the front of the helicopter beside me, and Norm sat in the back. Their technique was simple: watch for snowmobile tracks in the snow, mostly around large, wide-open fields where the poachers cross on their way to their hunting cabin. Then, follow the tracks and find the culprits.

Earl pointed at the sky and said, "This weather is perfect—cold and overcast with a nice north wind. It's cold enough to cause them to pull their thick hoods over their head. That will decrease their chances of hearing the helicopter."

After only twenty-five minutes of searching the area, Earl pointed to the ground and shouted in his headset. "Right there, look right there!"

"I got it," I said, then turned. Our view was perfect. The snowmobile tracks crossed a small open field and were easy to see, so I followed them into the woods, flying slower now and watching carefully below me as the tracks wound around from one trail to another. For a second, I lost the tracks, but then I picked them up again. We crossed another open area and down into a valley. On an adjacent ridge we saw smoke along the trees, perhaps from a cabin. "That way," Earl said. "Follow the smoke."

"Got it," I said. A few minutes later I spotted a small log cabin with three snowmobiles parked nearby. We circled the cabin, and Earl pointed to a patch of bright red blood scattered in the snow nearby. I found a narrow open area to land, and after we landed, I followed the two wildlife officers to the cabin.

Three rough-looking, sullen-faced men stood at the door outside the cabin, not at all pleased to have company. Smoke rose from the cabin's chimney, up through the birch trees and into the sky. Ahead of me, the two wildlife officers walked toward the suspects without a word spoken. Earl and Norm walked up together and faced their hunters. Earl's composure was calm and friendly, as if they were his old friends. "Morning, boys," Earl said. "Some cold today."

"Hi, Earl. So, what do ya need?" the older of the three asked.

Earl continued as friendly as can be, asking them the normal questions about the weather and Newfoundland politics. One might think you were listening to neighbors talking across the backyard fence. But then he played his hand.

"Jake," Earl said to the leader of the group. "Have a report there's been moose killed up this way, and I saw blood behind your cabin. I need to look around to make sure it isn't you doin' the killing."

"Like hell you will!" Jake said, as he took a large axe from the man standing beside him and held it with both hands. It was an obvious threat and challenge to Earl's authority.

Earl, without a gun, knife, or weapon of any kind, kept the same friendly look on his determined face and stuck out his massive right hand, now tightened into a fist. "Boys," Earl said in the same neighborly tone, "you know you really don't want to fight me, do you? Now give us the axe and get out of the way so we can do our job."

The angry older man knew Earl wasn't bluffing. His bearded face showed the disgust he felt for Earl, and reluctantly, he turned over his axe to Earl and moved out of the way. Earl and Norm walked past the three men and entered the cabin. I followed them, feeling the hateful stares from the outraged hunters.

Inside, the two officers searched the cluttered cabin for rifles or any evidence of poaching. They looked under the bunk beds, the mattresses, and under a stack of dirty clothing. Norm went outside and searched behind the cabin but found nothing.

I stood out of the way and noticed the smug look on the two younger hunters. Earl finished his search and was about to leave when I thought of something. I tapped on Earl's shoulder, and he followed me to where the two younger hunters were standing. "Excuse me," I said. The two men moved slightly. I kneeled and tapped the floor with my knuckle. A hollow sound.

Earl, using his pocket knife, pried the muddy board loose and removed it, revealing a long, thin cavity below the floor. As he placed the board beside the bed, the cavity beneath the floor revealed several rifles, all of which were considered illegal to have in a cabin out of season. All the wildlife officers needed to prove the three men were indeed poachers.

The livid hunters looked at me as if for the first time. Jake, the rugged spokesman for the group, walked over to me, his eyes narrowed, face black with rage.

"Where's your badge?" he asked.

"Don't have one," I said.

"Yank, you better pray we never meet up somewhere, because I'll even the score."

Earl quickly stepped between Jake and me before the situation escalated. He inventoried the rifles and wrote down the serial numbers. Norm carried the confiscated weapons to the helicopter, and when he returned, he informed Earl that he had found the remains of the slaughtered moose not far into the woods.

"What happens now," I asked.

While Earl herded the poachers out of the cabin, Norm came over and explained, "We take their guns and they go back home. Then we bring our case against them as soon as it comes before the magistrate."

Five minutes later, with the three miserable poachers on their snowmobiles, Earl stood in front of the cabin and gave them a warning.

"We took your guns, and we will turn them in with the charges against you. We'll see you at the magistrate in a few weeks. Take your ski-doos and go home, and as you leave here, look at the blood of the animal you killed. What you're doing isn't right. Boys, if you're having thoughts about trying this again, keep this in mind: if we catch you, we'll confiscate your snowmobiles and anything else you have, and you might even go to jail. I have legal right to do it now, but I'll give you one more chance before I do that."

The three men started the engines on their snowmobiles, and Jake, the obvious ring-leader, looked at me, his eyes demonic, direct, as he fumed. When the three poachers were far away into the thick forest, the three of us walked back to the helicopter, stopping to see the bloody moose carcass Norm had uncovered. It was a terrible mess where the moose were quartered, gutted, and the remaining thick skin and bone lay scattered about for the scavengers. Tree limbs and shrubs had been cut and placed over the mess but failed to hide the obvious from Norm.

I would later learn that the wildlife officers had the right to confiscate weapons, and in some cases take vehicles, including cars, trucks, or snowmobiles. And Earl Pilgrim, the most highly respected and often most hated wildlife officer in Newfoundland, had a reputation for vigorously prosecuting hunters who defied government authority.

What an interesting first day on the on the Pasadena job-watching the fearless, self-driven wildlife officers. It had been sad looking at the bloody moose carcass partially hidden in the snow, but as I flew back to Pasadena toward sundown, what bothered me most was the haunting, somewhat eerie feeling of being threatened by a vengeful poacher.

***

Marve sat alone in his house and thought about the brief encounter that morning with his father. It had bothered him more than it should have. It wasn't so much that he worried about being told off by his dad, but there had been something else. He had experienced a strange sensation the moment his father walked in the front door. A brief fragment of hope or love or something he couldn't name. Then, immediately, listening to his father's rude remarks, it changed back to that old familiar feeling of rejection. Somewhere, down deep in his mind, he had often fantasized about someday having his father look at him and smile, maybe shake hands, like men do, in a show of respect. Or maybe, maybe even a hug.

He decided those useless thoughts had no place in his mind. And he knew the best way to get rid of them was to get high. But getting high isn't easy when you're broke. Then he remembered his meeting with Phil.

An hour later, Marve met Phil at a hamburger joint called Brownie's. They chose the place because it offered a small, noisy place to talk, and the hamburgers and pie were the best in town.

Marve knew Phil from his first stretch in McAlister. The ex-con had a reputation for being connected. A tall, balding man in his mid-forties, Phil had a square face, dark eyes, and he dressed well, giving him the appearance of a businessman. But even though Marve knew Phil could help him make money, he also knew Phil had a passion for revenge. He had once "iced a rat in Chicago" and had tied the lifeless body to the bottom of a freight car, where it remained undiscovered until the train reached the West Coast. Without a doubt, Phil's reputation preceded him, and Marve had no intention of crossing the man.

The two ex-cons sat facing each other, eating their hamburgers and fries. They talked about old times and old friends. For the moment, they avoided business until it they were satisfied no one around them were listening. When their waitress busied herself choosing a piece of pie for a man sitting at the counter, Phil opened the discussion.

"How long ya been out of the stir?" he asked, as he poured more ketchup on his French fries. "Two months," Marve replied, as he looked at Phil, but watched people near them. "You picked up any swag?" Phil asked, wanting to know if Marve had any stolen goods.

"No," Marve said, shaking his head. "Tried to find regular work just to keep my parole officer off my back. They don't like my looks or my record."

Phil looked at the few remaining French fries on his plate and whispered, "Guess you need some bread?" "Damn right," Marve snapped, a little too loud.

"Easy, Ace," Phil said, a gentle smile crossing his face.

"Sorry, Phil," Marve said, relaxing a bit and grinning nervously. "Anything going on that I can help you with?"

Phil motioned to Marve, with a slight movement of his head. A few minutes later the two men stood outside while they smoked and talked about mutual friends, as well as some road trips that Phil needed. Trips to Kansas and back.

"Got good wheels?" Phil asked.

"Over there," Marve said, pointing to his Ford sedan.

"Yep, that looks good. Looks like she's got a big trunk."

"Sure does," Marve said. Phil threw his cigarette to the ground and rubbed his hand across the top of his head. "First, I need you to bring in a load of hard stuff," he said, referring to liquor. "I'll give you the information tomorrow."

"Yes, sir," Marve said, excitedly.

"When can you leave?"

"I'm ready when you are, stud."

Phil grinned and looked up at Marve, who stood at least four inches above him and had the wavy black hair he had always longed for. He reached into his pocket and removed several folded bills, then handed them to Marve.

Marve took the advance and listened carefully as the more mature ex-con explained the job. Five minutes later, with one hundred and forty dollars in his pocket and a job to look forward to, Marve drove north on Harvard to visit his dealer. In the back office of a car parts store, he purchased a small amount of grass, then drove back to his rented house. It felt good to have some work to do and a bit of spending money in his pocket.

That night as he sat on his bed smoking weed and drinking beer, he thought about the irony of it all. He remembered the years as a kid when the bootleggers came to the house and brought their precious bottles to his father. He had looked up to them and couldn't remember a time he didn't think about being one. Now his dream had come true. He would drive to Kansas City, fill his Ford with twenty cases of liquor, and bring it all back to Oklahoma, where it would be sold for triple the purchase price paid in Kansas.

As he relaxed, his memory brought back the image of that tall stocky bootlegger who had stood up to his father. He could still see the man standing in the front door, afraid of nothing. He glanced Marve and smiled. A slight nod that took less than a second, perhaps without thought or reason. But it meant something to Marve, and he never forgot the benevolent gesture.

***

During the next several months I flew a variety of missions in Western Newfoundland. Each day seemed more like an event than a job, and most of the time it was more fun than I could have ever imagined. One day I would be flying the Jet Ranger on a wildlife project, perhaps with a couple of wildlife officers on board counting the number of caribou in a square-mile grid, searching for poachers or even hauling equipment for the officers. And sometimes, when things were getting a bit boring, a call would come in on the radio that I should drop everything and go to the south coast for a medical evacuation. These were urgent medical flights that would typically entail pickup of an injured person, or a premature baby, or sometimes a man who'd had his arm chopped off in a sawmill accident. Because the helicopter was equipped with a small fold-out stretcher, I could transport patients to hospitals or medical clinics either sitting up or prone. But the threat of bad weather constantly hung over us.

One day, weather made it nearly impossible to transport a dying, premature infant. I picked up the child and a delightful midwife at Burgeo and flew as fast as I could to Corner Brook, dodging low clouds and evening fog all along the way. Often, the low cloud and fog forced me to fly right above the highway. So low, in fact, that at times I had to pull up to avoid hitting trucks on the road.

After an intense 40-minute flight in which I broke every aviation rule in the book in order to get the baby the medical care she needed, I could finally see the hospital ahead. As I reduced my airspeed and set up to land near the hospital, I felt the nurse pat me on the shoulder. I looked back at her as she frowned and shook her head, letting me know that it was too late. The little preemie had passed away. I can still remember the horrible feeling as we landed and they took the poor lifeless body into the hospital. Though I had done everything possible to rush her to safety, it hurt to know the little girl hadn't survived the flight.

Luckily for me, I made it through the fog on those flights. Young and inexperienced, I had allowed my emotions to get the best of me. I should have said no to the flight request since the weather made the flight far too dangerous.

As the months in Western Newfoundland went by, I learned that the most important word in a pilot's vocabulary is no. It's a word you don't use much, but when you're asked to fly in unflyable weather, you must learn to say no or pay the price as so many dead pilots have done. In the months to come, I found that lesson a hard one to learn.

Chapter Twenty-Two

In a run-down Tulsa bar, Marve sat with a voluptuous young girl he had met a few hours earlier. They drank beer, smoked several cigarettes, and listened to the Troggs sing "Wild Thing." She was small-waisted, with dark eyes, long, jet-black hair, and substantial breasts. Breasts that were partially visible due to the top two buttons of her blouse being undone.

During the late '60s, *free love* characterized an important part of the counterculture in the United States. And that night Marve fully supported the term free love. He felt proud that during the past eight months his work for Phil had gained Phil's respect. Using his Ford, Marve moved more liquor and color TV sets than he could count. Phil was pleased, and Marve was pleased, and if Marve could talk this long-legged girl into going back to his house, he would see to it that she was pleased.

They left the bar giggling, holding onto each other, and enjoying the buzz from the night's drinking and flirting. He became so worked up while driving that he thought about pulling into a motel, but remembered he had some good weed at his house. She kissed his neck, put her hand into his shirt, and stroked the hair on his chest, knowing full well it drove him crazy. Everything about her turned him on.

As they pulled into his driveway, he wasted no time getting her out of the car, then hurried her across the front yard and up to the porch. Facing the door, he keyed the lock as she stood behind him, pressing her body against his. She sang softly, but slightly off-key, "You're a wild thing." She grabbed the back of his jeans with both hands, feeling his hips. "Your butt is groooovy."

He pushed the door open, pulled her into the house with him, and they stood facing each other, holding off their growing passion. He grinned, then kicked the door shut with his foot and locked it. Marve pulled her closer to him and slowly unbuttoned the few remaining buttons on her white cotton blouse. She wore a black, lacy bra, which revealed an abundance of well-developed breasts. He had planned to get high before they made love, but now he was way past that. "You really are a wild thing," he said. "Want to see the rest of my house?" he asked.

She nodded and winked, but before they turned toward the hallway, they heard a loud knock at the front door. "What the hell?" Marve said.

"Are you expecting someone?" she asked, teasingly. "Maybe you got another girlfriend?" She giggled.

"Shit, no," he said, his face showing worry now. "Hurry and button up, just in case."

"What is it?" she asked, noticing the worried look on his face. And now showing her own concern, she said, "Really, what is it?" She quickly buttoned her blouse.

"Button up, button up!" Marve urged her insistently.

"OK, OK!" she said, now becoming frightened.

They heard another loud knock on the door. "Police!" someone yelled. "Open the door. Now!"

"Oh, shit," Marve said. She put her hands on her face, "Oh my God."

When Marve opened the door, three Tulsa cops barged into the living room. Two officers grabbed him, and the other policeman grabbed the frightened girl and led her out of the house. "Marve, what's going on," she screamed as she went out the front door.

Marve watched them take the beautiful girl out of the house and felt a wave of hate and fear swell over him. In a moment they had him cuffed and were busy searching the house. Going from room to room, they worked quickly and efficiently.

"What are you looking for?" Marve asked. One of the larger cops stopped, then looked at Marve. "Shut up, asshole!" While Marve stood helplessly, they continued to wreak havoc on the house.

"Right here!" someone shouted from the bedroom. At that moment Marve slumped onto the divan. The police removed two stolen television sets hidden under a sheet in the bedroom closet and a stash of marijuana in plain sight on top of the chest of drawers.

The same barrel-chested cop returned to the living room and spoke to Marve. "I'm not going to ask you where those TVs came from," he said. "But I will ask you something else. How old is that girl you were about to nail?"

"Nineteen or twenty, I believe."

"She's sixteen, dummy," the cop said. "You should have stayed home and watched *Bonanza* on one of those stolen TVs."

Marve hated cops and wasn't about to show his concern. He squinted and gave the surly cop his best James Dean stare, "I don't watch *Bonanza*. I'm more of a *Perry Mason* guy myself." The cop spun him around and led him out the door without another word.

That night the Police booked Marve into the city jail, and when he was able to call, he phoned Phil. Hearing the news, Phil swore at Marve, "You dumb shit, how could anyone be stupid enough to hide two TVs in their own bedroom?"

"I don't know, man," Marve said.

After cussing at Marve, Phil said he would make a few calls. "Keep your mouth shut and sit tight, and I'll work on this."

"Don't worry," Marve replied, trying to sound convincing.

"Are you shitting me?" Phil said. "How could I not worry when you've caused this shit storm?"

"I'm sorry, Phil. I know what to do," Marve said.

During the next few days Phil called a few of his cop buddies who did him a favor once in a while and appreciated a favor in return. They were the ones who got a case of liquor from time to time and sometimes tried out the talent at one of Phil's girly houses.

Luckily, Phil managed to help Marve. He got the marijuana charges and the statutory rape charges removed. The latter of which had no chance of standing up in court, because the cops broke in before anything serious happened to the girl. But the charges for possession of stolen property stuck since the TV sets had serial numbers which matched a police report in Missouri.

Marve was freed on bail but would be standing trial in a federal court. Phil arranged for a lawyer, partly to help Marve, but mainly to keep his own name out of the mess Marve had created. Four months later, after a two-day trial, which his mother attended, Marve was found not guilty on the charge of transporting stolen goods across a state line. And guilty on the charge for possession of stolen goods. The smooth-talking attorney convinced the jury that Marve had nothing to do with bringing the TVs across the state line. The strict, impartial judge sentenced him to eighteen months in the Springfield, Missouri, federal prison.

After standing up to hear his sentence read, Marve looked behind him in the courtroom and spotted his mother. She tried desperately to smile at him, but couldn't, barely able to hold back her tears. After the bailiff escorted Marve out of the courtroom in handcuffs, she walked three blocks to the bus stop, rode the city bus home, and then cooked dinner for her cranky husband. She ate sparingly, and after the meal, washed the dishes while her husband smoked one cigarette after another and watched TV in the living room.

Without saying a word, she went to their bedroom and quietly closed the door. Alone in the dark, with the image of her tall, misguided son in her mind, she ignored the constant noise from the television and the black acrid smoke streaming in beneath the bedroom door. She sat on the unmade bed, took a long deep breath and released her warm, fleeing tears.

**

The summer of 1971, seemed short, like most summers in Newfoundland, but our family enjoyed each sunny day. Often people joke by saying "Newfoundland summers are so short that if you happen to sleep late, you're liable to miss summer altogether." During those warm months, Barbara made lasting friends with our neighbors, while Leslie played with the other children. David Jr. walked now and kept Barbara busy looking after him. Often, I would bring home fresh fish I had either caught or had been given. I was a novice hunter, but even a novice in Newfoundland had no shortage of tasty, nourishing food in his freezer. Barbara learned several new recipes from the ladies who lived near us, and out of necessity, baked her own bread. Stores in that part of Newfoundland did not sell bread in those days.

But too soon the weather changed: the days became cooler and the leaves on trees turned yellow and orange, signaling the advent of autumn. Conversations were filled with the excitement of the upcoming hunting season. And that fall, there was something else going on. Something unusual that had nothing to do with migratory birds, fish, or even big game. It wasn't hunting season but election season. Time for the election of the premier of Newfoundland.

Almost on a daily basis, the news media featured stories of a young schoolteacher named Frank Moores who had switched parties in order to challenge the current premier and political icon, Joey Smallwood. Smallwood, a political giant, having been elected as Newfoundland's first premier, had somehow managed to hold that office for the past twenty-three years. Self-educated and well-traveled, Joey Smallwood had established himself as a populist candidate in the political ring. He was known as the Father of Confederation due to his courageous, successful efforts to bring Newfoundland into the Confederation of Canada, making it Canada's tenth province. Some people considered Mr. Smallwood Newfoundland's founding father and favorite son all in one. His reputation and power were legendary, and anyone who seriously challenged him was met with skepticism. [2]

Stories of the upcoming election dominated the news, but I was more interested in flying or hunting than the boring political events going on. But somehow, that fall, politics got my full attention.

In early August 1971, I flew north to St. Anthony to carry out a series of VIP flights for the famous premier, Joey Smallwood. Even though I wasn't interested in politics, it came as exciting news. Having flown to the Northern Peninsula and St. Anthony several times that year, I was familiar with the unique weather patterns and challenging geography of the region. But it would be my first time to fly with such a famous person.

Located at the northeast edge of the Northern Peninsula, St. Anthony is famous for the Grenfell Mission Hospital, and for some of the most severe and hostile weather conditions in the world.

Premier Smallwood arrived on time on a cold, wet afternoon at the St. Anthony Airport. He had flown in on a small twin-engine turboprop airplane chartered from St. John's. When his plane landed, people were relieved that he had made it in such horrible weather.

A short, balding man in his seventies, I instantly recognized Joey Smallwood by his size and his famous black, horn-rimmed glasses. He came toward the helicopter, walking quickly and purposefully through the mud, accompanied by three other men. Mr. Smallwood shook my hand and let me know that he was ready to go.

"Sir, which of these men will be going with you?" I asked.

The premier smiled and shook his head. "No, lad," he said, "It's just you and I."

"Yes, sir," I answered, a bit surprised, since every minister, mayor, and government official I had ever met in Newfoundland had at least one aide that traveled with them. Now the famous Joey Smallwood would be going it alone. When the other men walked away, I stowed Mr. Smallwood's suitcase and helped him into his seat in the front of the helicopter. I gave him a short briefing, checked his seatbelt and closed his door. In few minutes we took off and flew slowly into a nasty afternoon sky.

Jack Murphy had called the night before and briefed me on the trip. I would be flying the premier from St. Anthony to Labrador, stopping along the Labrador coast to land anywhere the premier wished. He would be conducting various meetings and giving political speeches.

After we departed St. Anthony that cold afternoon, I climbed to 300 feet and quickly hit light rain and fog, reducing our visibility tremendously. During the next forty-five minutes I was to cross the final sections of land on the Northern Peninsula, then fly across the frigid, ice-filled waters where the North Atlantic meets the Labrador Sea. Once across the water, I would land at a small outport called Mary's Harbour, on the eastern edge of Labrador. It would take at least thirty minutes to cross the treacherous water where I had often spotted icebergs and transport ships. Since there were no navigation aids, it was to be dead reckoning all the way. I had made the crossing several times before, but always during good weather, and always with the Labrador land mass in sight. Not today.

As we crossed the last point of land along the island of Newfoundland, I flew lower toward the water, and within minutes, the fog and rain forced me to fly about fifty feet above the choppy ocean waters. Worried, and ready to turn back, I said, "Sir, this isn't looking good."

"Do your best," he said. "I'd like to make it across today if we can."

"Yes, sir," I replied, looking at the pathetic weather and sea in front of us.

"So, I hear you're a Vietnam pilot," the premier said. "I've read a lot about Vietnam. What did you think of the war?"

"That's right, sir," I replied, worried about our flight but intrigued that he wanted to talk about Vietnam. He didn't seem at all worried about the weather and continued to carry on a most interesting conversation on subjects ranging from Vietnam to President Richard Nixon. An intelligent, articulate man, Mr. Smallwood seemed to enjoy talking about anything and had the ability to make you at ease chatting with him. And even more surprising, he wasn't at all nervous about flying in dense fog just above the spotty patches of ice below us.

After twenty-five minutes of overwater flight, we hit the worst layer of fog I have ever flown into. It became difficult to see the water's surface, and impossible to see more than fifty yards ahead. At that point it was far too late to turn back, since the weather would be as bad behind us as it might be ahead. I flew slower now and brought the aircraft as low as possible above the water. And with all that going on, the laid-back premier kept talking, so I kept flying and pretended to know what I was doing. With only a magnetic compass to guide us and no landmarks to correct our course, I was now flying by the seat of my pants, unable to see and unable to judge our distance or direction.

My first concern centered on keeping the aircraft out of the water, and after that, of course, reaching our destination, Mary's Harbour. Making it safely to Labrador but missing our destination wouldn't be too bad, but far worse, and more dangerous, would be to fly too far northeast and miss Labrador altogether. Since the winds had changed direction several times during our flight, it would be possible to misjudge our course and break out at Belle Isle, twenty-five miles to the east. And it would be possible to break out of the fog too far west, around Red Bay, Labrador. But the worst scenario of all would be to steer too far northeast, missing Labrador completely, sending us on a never-ending path across the vast Labrador Sea. If that happened, the helicopter would run out of fuel and crash, creating one of the worst tragedies in Newfoundland history.

I noticed my palms were getting sweaty and I wanted to turn down the cabin heater, but I wanted to make sure the premier remained comfortable. After a moment, I realized I wasn't hot, but nervous. In fact, I was scared as hell. I had to find Battle Harbour, the rocky point of land right before you get to Mary's Harbour.

Glancing at the clock, I noted we were ten minutes past my estimated arrival time at Mary's Harbour. I touched the microphone switch on the cyclic to let the premier know I would be changing directions. But then I saw it.

At first, I saw five or six seagulls, which is often a good sign that you're approaching land, but then I saw a faint, dark object in the fog. I wasn't sure if it was a boat or another iceberg, but I knew the hidden form before us wasn't far away. I slowed my airspeed and carefully approached the vague, mysterious object in front of us.

"Yes, boy," the premier said. "I think you found it."

"Well, yes, sir," I replied, not sure where we were, but glad to see something. Finally, I could see the rocky formation of the land on both sides of Battle Harbour and knew we had hit our target right smack in the middle. Mary's Harbour would only be a few miles farther west. I don't know how we made it, but we *had* made it.

"Yes, boy, I think you found it," he said, looking over at me with a fatherly smile. I returned his smile, relieved beyond belief.

A few minutes later we circled the small outport of Mary's Harbour to announce the premier's arrival. After landing, the wiry politician walked toward the docks like a maritime pied piper, gathering a long line of onlookers as he went. Without fanfare or a proper introduction, the premier, standing on the soaking wet wooden dock, ignored a gentle rain and held a small meeting with a few dozen surprised and introverted residents. His audience was mostly Labrador fishermen and their families, and it seemed an amazing thing for them to have the father of Newfoundland among them on that cold, foggy morning.

I had visited Mary's Harbour a few months before, since the Mary's Harbour Nursing Station is part of the famous Grenfell Mission and is supported by the Newfoundland government. The friendly people who work at the nursing station are accustomed to helicopter pilots dropping in to pick up or drop off medical patients. So that afternoon, while the premier gave his political talks and held his various meetings, I enjoyed tea and biscuits in the small, orderly building that served as an outport nursing station.

Walking into the building, I thought of the other nursing stations I had visited in Labrador and their impact on the isolated communities throughout Labrador.

The International Grenfell Association, named for its British founder, Sir Wilfred Grenfell, has provided health and social services to the remote areas of Northern Newfoundland and the Labrador Straits since the late 19th century. The backbone of the Mission is the hospital in St.

Anthony, staffed by British doctors and nurses in addition to a vast number of skilled, hardworking Newfoundland doctors, nurses, and medical specialists. Sir Wilfred Grenfell worked with aboriginal people, establishing schools and orphanages and often traveling by dog sled. On one dogsled trip, Doctor Grenfell, traveling alone to a medical emergency, became stuck on the ice and drifted in open water for several days. Without food or fresh water, he was forced to kill some of his dogs to make a warm coat and shelter. He managed to stay alive until he was rescued by local villagers.

Since transportation in the harsh region has always been a major problem, the mission established a network of cottage hospitals, now called nursing stations, along the Labrador coast, connected to Saint Anthony Hospital by dogsled, boat, airplane, and now helicopter.

During my temporary assignments at St. Anthony, I transported a variety of patients to and from the hospital, including expectant mothers, heart attack and stroke patients, and of course, premature babies. On one trip, during a time when the harbors and rivers were still iced over, I flew a young British doctor to small outports where he held medical clinics. In a few of those villages, when we were pressed for time due to deteriorating weather conditions, I parked the helicopter on the thick ice of a frozen harbor. As I sat in the front seat, keeping my eyes focused straight ahead, the busy young doctor examined one patient at a time in the back seat of the helicopter. While he worked with that person, several other villagers, cold and anxious, dressed in hooded parkas, their breath steaming upwards, stood in line ten feet away. They stomped their feet to keep warm and awaited their turn to see the much-needed doctor.

Those trips caused me to appreciate the work the Grenfell Mission is doing along the Labrador coast and the vital role they play in providing healthcare to such a scattered, lightly populated country.

That afternoon, in the clean, simple kitchen of the Mary's Harbour Nursing Station, I drank my hot tea and talked to the pleasant British midwife, Margaret Harris. After chatting awhile she asked me, "Have you signed our guestbook, Dave?" She pointed to a small table near the front door which held a well-worn blue book. "We don't get many visitors."

"No, I haven't signed it, but I will be happy to sign it right now."

I wrote my name and the date in the guest book. Then I became curious and turned the pages backwards to see who may have visited Mary's Harbour recently. There were few visitors that year or the year before. Becoming even more curious, I looked closer, continuing to turn the pages backwards through the many years recorded in the visitor's book. There were several years with only a few signatures, and even more years with no visitors at all. Then as I looked closer, I it amazed me to see that only ten or fifteen pages back the name and signature of the famous American explorer, Robert Peary. He and Newfoundland ice captain Bob Bartlett had visited the nurse's station during one of their North Pole expeditions some sixty years before.

"Wow," I said, as I realized the historical value of that name. "Robert Peary came here?"

Looking across the room, she smiled. "Yes," she said. "This clinic was over to Battle Harbour first," she said. "Then, around 1930 they moved to our location here in Mary's Harbour. You're looking at the same guest book we had in Battle Harbour, and yes, that's the famous Robert Peary."

"Wow," I repeated, then looked one last time before carefully replacing the book. I thanked the nurse for her hospitality, then went for a walk to see if I could find Premier Smallwood.

His first meeting that day was one of several informal sessions Premier Smallwood held during the next few days in a handful of small, isolated fishing villages along the rugged Labrador coast. The sessions seemed to follow the same general pattern. Sometimes he gave a speech in a home or school, and a few times people gathered outside by the post office. For me, this afforded a rare opportunity to observe firsthand a man who managed to hold his position as Premiere for more than twenty years and fully understood the need for each vote. It had been widely reported that the opposition party was pressing hard for a change, and his rival, Frank Moores, a younger man full of promise and personality, seemed to be gaining momentum.

Since Mary's Harbour is such a small outport, it wasn't hard to find the lively Mr. Smallwood. When I saw him, he stood on a muddy walkway not far from the wharf, talking to a group of fifteen or twenty people.

The rain stopped, and hungry seagulls flew overhead in the hopeless gray sky, then congregated in clumps along the empty dock.

At the meeting, shy men in thick turtleneck sweaters, heavy wool slacks, and black rubber boots stared at the ground, glancing up occasionally to peek at the premier. Freckle-faced children giggled nervously and held their mother's hands, while elderly folks, fully realizing the rich history behind the speaker, stood a bit farther away, but never missed a word. That day the people of Mary's Harbour watched and listened as the celebrity politician walked among them.

Mr. Smallwood spoke of their history, their problems, and their village. And while he was at it, he threw in a few offhand statements about more roads in Labrador and the protection of valuable fishing waters.

When he finished, people seemed pleased with his little speech. Of course, they had heard promises of help before and didn't put much faith in political talk, but they were impressed that the famous Joey Smallwood had dropped right out of the sky to see them. It was a day they would talk about for years to come and an exciting experience they would tell and retell during cold winter nights in the beautiful, isolated village called Mary's Harbour.

Chapter Twenty-Three

We departed the coastal town of Blanc-Sablon on a stunningly beautiful morning, and began our trip across the choppy waters of the Gulf of St. Lawrence. We were on our way back to the island of Newfoundland. After several days of political speeches along the Labrador coast, it was time for Mr. Smallwood to head back to his imperative duties in St. John's. With a slight tailwind, we flew at five hundred feet above sea level and were doing around one hundred and ten miles per hour ground speed. The brilliant blue-green water below us and the clear blue sky above stood in stark contrast to the dense fog and light rain we had encountered during our crossing a few days before. Like a giant curtain being lifted on a Broadway stage, the clear sky revealed a new and stunning world, and the two of us were the only members of the audience.

Thoughts of fog and missed destinations were far from my mind as we soared high above the miles of open water toward the Northern Peninsula. While enjoying the vast, crest-filled water and blissful blue sky, the rugged hills waited for us on the other side of the gulf. It was as if the island of Newfoundland waited patiently to welcome its founding father back home.

"It's a lovely day," the premier said cheerfully. "I don't have to be in St. Anthony till noon." Then in a more serious tone, "We need to land right at noon, if you know what I mean. There will be several reporters on hand doing stories about my visit to Labrador, and I want to time it right. Time it just right."

"Yes, sir, I understand," I said, checking the time. "Sir, what would you like to do for an hour or so? We are a bit early."

"You decide," he said, surprising me. The premier was in a wonderful mood that morning and seemed to be enjoying the scenery. He wore a dark gray suit, white shirt, and black tie. More formal than he had dressed during his visit to Labrador. I thought for a moment, then gave him a few options.

"Sir, I have a fishing rod. I can land near a lake or river and we can catch a few trout. Or, I have some plastic containers if you'd like to land in the hills and pick bakeapple."

He thought for a moment, glanced at me and grinned. "Bakeapple."

"Yes, sir," I said, trying to decide the best place to land along our route. We still had a few minutes before we would reach land, and it gave me time to think. We were about to pass a medium-size iceberg floating south. Brilliant white, virtually blue-white in places, and around it, the water lay dotted with small fragments of ice. Mr. Smallwood leaned forward, looking carefully at the tubular-shaped berg. "Can we get a better look?" he said. "Yes, sir," I replied, as I lowered the collective and flew closer.

This was a rare opportunity to get a close-up view of a floating boulder of ice. As we approached the berg, I decreased our airspeed and flew to the right, putting it on the premier's side, allowing him the best view. Now we could see two large pools of clear, opaque water standing on the iceberg, as well as several dark brown stones or boulders embedded in the ice, the size of a small car. With nothing around it, it was difficult to determine the actual size of the iceberg, but it seemed as large as a two-story building, perhaps a large church.

"Bet you never saw one of those in Vietnam," Mr. Smallwood said.

I chuckled, then replied, "No, sir, I did not." He grinned as we passed the beautiful sight and I climbed back into the sky. Then, as we completed our gulf crossing, I steered southeast toward a captivating range of wooded, low hills a few miles past Castors River. It was off our route, but worth the effort on such a gorgeous day. The hilltop I headed for wasn't as striking or majestic as the mountains around Gros Morne National Park, eighty miles further south. But the high, wooded hillside offered a large open space near the top. I picked a flat, treeless spot that seemed to be a perfect place to land.

I hovered into the wind, then sat the aircraft down softly, in a large level area of wet, blanket bog which overlooked the Gulf of St. Lawrence. When we were out of the helicopter, the morning sun felt surprisingly warm. The premier took off his suit coat, removed his shoes and socks, and rolled up his trousers. He stood in the bog ankle-deep in water and fauna, a pleasant smile on his smooth, clean-shaven face. Barefoot, sleeves rolled up to his elbows, he looked as content as any man I had ever seen.

Mr. Smallwood took one of the plastic containers and walked away in search of the popular wild plant called bakeapple. A golden-yellow fruit, bakeapple grows wild in the high country, along bogs and marshes, and is harvested in late summer and fall. The fruit has a tart taste, and it is used to make jam or liqueurs. Bakeapple is a popular fruit with my family and a well-known Newfoundland favorite.

While the premier commenced his search, I sat on a large rock thirty feet away, in a wonderful position to watch him and the beautiful scene beyond. Our green-and-white helicopter shined in the sun while parked on a lush emerald bog. The oval-shaped area was partially surrounded by a dense hazel thicket, with the majestic waters of the gulf behind it. Halfway across the gulf, a white, motionless object appeared as a tiny dot on the horizon. Yet another iceberg floating silently, gradually melting as it traveled at a snail's pace toward its final resting place. And on this rare day, with unlimited visibility, and clear, perfect air, you could see beyond the gulf waters and icebergs to the vast, mysterious black and barren shoreline of Quebec, forty miles away.

In that stunningly picturesque setting, the most famous man in Newfoundland stood barefoot with his gray suit pants and white shirtsleeves rolled up, enjoying the simple pleasures of a warm fall day in a boggy marsh.

Joey Smallwood wasn't a politician at that moment, but just a kind, simple man, enjoying a special, quiet moment in the morning sun and forgetting, for a time, the extreme pressures of reelection. I sat quietly enjoying the breathtaking scenery, wishing I could capture the moment with a photo.

I glanced again at the azure, indescribable waters of the gulf, then turned toward the premier. Suddenly, fifty feet away, a small, innocent black bear cub walked toward the premier. Bent forward, preoccupied with filling his container, the premier was unaware of the furry visitor.

"Sir, watch out," I said, standing slowly, careful not to frighten the animal.

"OK, I see it," Mr. Smallwood said, as calm and composed as an old country preacher. He pushed his thick black glasses up on his nose and stood still for a moment, watching carefully as the playful little animal continued to walk toward him, curious, unafraid.

Maybe Mr. Smallwood wasn't worried, but I was *very* worried. Scared as hell. The furry, inquisitive animal had appeared out of nowhere. The cuddly cub strolled past the premier, beside the helicopter, and made its way down the hill. For a brief time, I watched it, mesmerized by its cute little body. And then I smelled something strange in the air: a foul-fetid odor.

I quickly turned in the opposite direction and saw it. The massive mother bear, at the crest of the hill, following her cub's path, walking directly toward the premier. Mr. Smallwood had innocently broken the golden rule of the outdoors: never stand between a mother bear and her cub. "Get into the helicopter, sir!" I yelled. "Go now!"

The premier smiled, stood for a moment, and walked slowly toward the aircraft. I yelled again, this time with more authority. "Sir, run like hell! She might look tame, but that bear is ready to kill."

"OK," he said, now hurrying toward the aircraft. Once we were inside, I quickly started the helicopter. I worried that the huge bear, now unseen behind the aircraft, might run into the spinning tail rotor, but there was no time to consider the possibilities. We had to get out of there.

As I pulled the collective and rose into the air, I saw the surprised mother bear on the ground and watched the massive animal reel backwards from the violent winds of our rotor wash. Quickly, I took off, then circled around the hill. Below us the mother ran toward her cub. The premier smiled and pointed toward the happy reunion.

"Sorry, sir," I said. "But I couldn't take a chance on you getting attacked."

"I understand," he said. "I understand."

On our flight to St. Anthony, Premier Smallwood seemed quiet, reflective, and I assumed he was thinking about the bears, or bakeapple, or perhaps his political battles. Whatever they were, I decided it would be best if I left him alone. We landed at St. Anthony at exactly twelve noon, and when we touched down, my prestigious passenger thanked me for an interesting trip. With the helicopter as a dramatic backdrop for his arrival, the premier walked toward a small group assembled nearby. Local businessmen, politicians, along with a handful of eager reporters were there to greet him. Joey Smallwood was back in his own pressure-filled environment.

After refueling, I flew back to Pasadena, enjoying more of the lovely weather. Paul Williams was there when I arrived but seemed unusually quiet. I assumed he might be arguing with his wife, so after we put the helicopter to bed and I finished filling out the logbook, I walked home. Barbara met me on the front porch, excited about something, and before I could get into the house, one of our neighbors shouted from across the street. I couldn't understand what he wanted, so I glanced at Barbara, who had a strange look on her face. I shook my head.

"Don't tell me," I said. "Problems with the water pump again?"

"No, not that," she said, smiling. "It was all over the news."

"What are you talking about?" I asked. Barbara grinned again, and I repeated, "What are you talking about?"

"About you saving Joey Smallwood from the black bear." She grinned like a child who had just stolen a cookie.

"What? I didn't save him. We saw a bear and got out of its way."

"That's not what they reported on the radio. They said a Vietnam helicopter pilot named Dave Eagleston saved the premier from a black bear attack."

"Oh, good grief, it wasn't a big deal at all," I said.

As Barbara led me into the house and our two playful children ran up excited to have Daddy home, I remembered the thoughtful look on the premier's face as we were flying toward St. Anthony. I had tried to guess what he might be thinking about. Of course, he must been thinking about the bears. But not like I imagined. With his lifelong experience as a politician and former newspaper reporter, he saw a story in our bear encounter. A story too good to pass up.

During the next few weeks, Paul and the other Universal Helicopter people enjoyed teasing me about the *Joey and the bear* story. But soon, that was old news, and in a few months the real bear story in the news centered around Frank Moores, Joey Smallwood's political rival.

The young, wealthy businessman and leader of the Progressive Conservative Party won the election and became the second premier of Newfoundland and Labrador.

Chapter Twenty-Four

At the federal prison in Springfield, Missouri, Marve arrived in early 1970 to serve a two-year sentence. The huge, massive facility, which provides medical care and training to federal prisoners, was part of a deal negotiated by Marve's lawyer. That's the good news. But even though the facility was kind of a "garden spot," he still had to survive in a cell block filled with dangerous men who had spent their lives learning how to steal, cheat, and lie. And all too often, they learned how to inflict pain. At first, the new inmate drew the tough work details like laundry, cell block cleaning, and kitchen duty. But that didn't bother Marve. He knew how the game was played, and he was ready to defend himself when the time came.

Not surprisingly, the time came all too soon. After beating two men so badly they were sent to the infirmary, Marve became known as a guy you didn't mess with. Springfield wasn't the madhouse he had lived in back at McAlester, but the prisoners still had a code, and the key to that code was respect. After the news of his fighting traveled throughout the cell block, and Marve kept his mouth shut around the guards, he slowly earned the respect of the gang bosses.

Like other inmates in Springfield, Marve looked forward to visitors. He knew that every three or four weeks his mother would make the four-hour drive from Tulsa to be with him. She arranged her work schedule around her trips and always wrote to let him know when she was coming. After he'd been there four months his mother came for another visit. But this time she wouldn't be alone.

***

A few months earlier, his mother had written him about Brenda, one of the ladies she worked with at Southwestern

Bell in Tulsa. Like his mother, Brenda was an experienced telephone operator. Described as a slim, pretty girl about Marve's age, divorced and raising her young daughter, Katy.

It all started when Marve's mother, Zelda, asked Brenda to send Marve "one letter." Brenda agreed, but it didn't end there. She was intrigued by the interesting reply she received from Marve, and soon they wrote to each other regularly.

It wasn't long before their letters revealed intimate details about their lives, and Brenda was overwhelmed by the attention he afforded her. Unlike her ex-husband, Marve freely gave her the admiration she relished. Marve wanted to learn everything about her, and their letters grew more frequent and more personal.

At first, Brenda told herself not to become attached to this man. After all, she had never known a criminal, and had it not been for her coworker's encouragement, Brenda would have never written the first letter. But now she rode in the car with Zelda, on her way to Springfield, Missouri, and Marve sat in his cell, counting the hours until Brenda's arrival.

At the end of their long drive, the stone fortress-like prison came into sight. Brenda started to feel frightened, but also strangely excited. She had deep, conflicting feelings, but kept her feelings to herself while she parked her car, then walked quietly to the visitor's entrance with Marve's mother.

After being informed of a visitor's arrival, Marve was searched and allowed to walk along the shiny well-mopped hallway toward the most cherished place in the prison—the visiting area. As he walked in the noisy room, other inmates chatted with their families, girlfriends, or lawyers. Several inmates, knowing it was Marve's first time to meet his pen pal, giggled and made muted catcalls which got the guard's attention.

Standing a head taller than anyone in the room, dressed in clean prison-issued khaki shirt and slacks, Marve ignored his buddies and searched the room for his two visitors. He tried to look calm and casual, but when he spotted the two women and got his first look at Brenda, he grinned like a kid at a circus. He had expected someone nice, but not pretty. Certainly not this pretty.

Brenda was an adorable, dark-eyed beauty with a slim waistline and long auburn hair. Though she wore a modest, long-sleeved blouse, he could tell she had a somewhat generous bustline. He would dream about that for the next two weeks.

After he hugged his mother, she introduced Brenda, "This is my friend, Brenda, and this is my son, Marvin." Then giggling, she said, "We call him Marve."

Now Brenda had her first close-up look at the man she been writing to. He wasn't at all what she expected. Taller, ruggedly handsome, with thick, jet-black hair, and deep-set dark eyes. She was overwhelmed by his robust good looks and broad, eager smile.

As she gazed into Marve's eyes, Brenda got over the nervousness she had felt walking into a dark joyless prison for the first time. She got over her deep concerns about his problematic past and her constant worries about dating an inmate. She even forgot they were in a room filled with other, somewhat hopeless inmates and visitors. She focused on Marve and blocked everything else out.

At first Marve's mother led the conversation while the two younger people stared at each other. Slowly, they followed her lead, talking about anything and everything except prison life. When Marve relaxed and asked Brenda questions about her daughter, his beautiful visitor grew talkative and more animated, relating a few sweet stories about her Katy. It had been a successful first visit, and when the time came for his visitors to leave, Marve hugged his mother and politely shook hands with Brenda. From the moment he saw her, he had wanted to hold her close to him, but knew he had to make a good impression, otherwise he might scare her off.

Later, on the drive back to Tulsa, Brenda thought of the handsome, charming man she had just met. She had also felt a touch of depression while leaving the prison, looking at the sad, often cheerless faces of wives and families as they said their goodbyes and headed back to their lives without husbands and fathers.

She decided she would never be like them. As soon she got to know Marve better, she would help him start a new life. It wasn't clear to her how to make this work, but she had sensed something warm and extraordinary about this man and she was willing to make the effort.

Marve's mother seemed quiet, introspective as she stared out the car window and watched the farms and trees as they passed. She thought about their visit and knew Brenda well enough to know that she had been impressed with Marve. As they passed a large field of wheat, Zelda watched a hawk dive down and snatch a field mouse, then land on a barbed-wire fence. She thought of how critical timing is to nature, and how important it is to love. Brenda's timing was perfect. Right now, more than anything Marve needed a strong, loving woman, a woman just like Brenda.

***

During the next few months, letters between Marve and Brenda were exchanged at a frantic pace. They were both lonely and in love. Soon, instead of the chitchat and daily description of their activities, each of them went into minute detail describing what they wanted to happen the first opportunity they had to be alone.

If anyone would have told Brenda a year before that she would fall in love with an incarcerated man, she would have laughed out loud. But that's exactly what was happening. When she looked into the mirror, she saw a woman fed up with the ordinary, tired of the horrible struggle it took to be a working, single mom. Tired of going to work every day with nothing to look forward to at the end of it all. Brenda had started this as a simple favor to her friend. She had started with a thousand reservations, but now she stood neck-deep in quicksand and didn't want to be saved.

As the weeks went by and the relationship grew stronger, Brenda kept Zelda informed. Zelda daydreamed about the couple being married and having children, but she couldn't share her dreams with her drunken, short-tempered husband. She had tried to talk with him before, but he had crushed each remnant of hope she possessed. She decided she wouldn't go through that again. She would simply keep quiet about the romance between her friend and her son.

During that year Brenda devoted as much time and resources as she could manage to helping Marve, and her efforts included an arduous campaign aimed at securing his parole. To a discouraged, overworked parole officer, Brenda came across as the wholesome girl-next-door type. A pleasant change compared with the hard, damaged women he normally met with. Women who were often used by their convict boyfriends to score drugs or work as prostitutes.

Brenda also convinced Marve to take part in the prison outreach program, and soon he joined the "Outreach of Springfield." She wrote, encouraged, visited often, and even took the major step of bringing her daughter Katy with her on those visits. Katy was a cute, well-mannered four-year-old with long brown hair and a ready smile. Un-inhibited, Katy talked freely with anyone and became a popular visitor, often entertaining inmates in the visitor's lounge while Brenda and Marve sat nearby.

Brenda, now with Katy's help, worked miracles in Marve's life, and for the first time, he began to be less selfish, putting someone else's interests above his own.

After more than a year of medical training and having reached a higher trustee status, Marve moved into a work status where he performed regular duties in the prison hospital: taking blood, dispensing medicine, and even giving shots to inmate patients. Although he worked hard, he felt the prison hospital conditions were horrendous, and during one of Brenda's visits, Marve described the treatment of sick patients as morbid and cruel.

"Sometimes I go to the psych ward," he said, looking down at Brenda's beautiful hands, wanting so badly to touch them. "They have guys in there handcuffed to their beds, crapping all over the place and staring at the ceiling all day. All I can do is give them a tranquilizer, talk to them a little, then move along to the next bed."

Marve lit another cigarette, blew the blue smoke into the air, and continued, "Some of those guys are there because they got in a fight or broke a guard's nose. But many of them don't know why they're in there. I guess it doesn't matter; they all get the same treatment."

"What can you do?" Brenda asked. She glanced across the room to see if the guards in the visitor's room were watching them. The couple had learned how to sneak a little touching in here and there, but they knew full well where the lines were drawn and knew which guards were more lenient. Brenda had seen other couples reprimanded for hugging and kissing, and she wanted to keep Marve as clean as possible for his parole hearing when it came up.

"There's nothing I can do," he said, his eyes sad and thoughtful.

"What about that guy you met at outreach?" she asked.

"Mr. Johnson. Oh, he's a great guy," Marve said, smiling. "We really get along, and hell, I can talk to him about lots of stuff. I even told him about you. He talks to us about business and how to interview for a job."

"OK," she said. "Then think about this: in your letter last week you mentioned that Mr. Johnson is respected in the community. Were you serious?"

"Sure, he's a businessman in Springfield and has lots of connections."

Brenda looked at Marve and narrowed her eyes. Marve understood. In his more serious voice, with a shade of inflection, Marve said, "The answer was right in front of me and I didn't see it. But you did. I'll talk to Mr. Johnson, and maybe he can help."

Marve looked at Brenda, his head cocked to one side, a slight grin on his face. It wasn't the first time she had come up with a good suggestion or an answer to a problem. And it certainly wasn't the first time he realized that Brenda wasn't just a beautiful woman: she was thoughtful, intelligent, and caring, and she continued to make a tremendous difference in his troubled life.

Chapter Twenty-Five

January is a cold, windy month in Newfoundland, and most people stay out of the woods. But poachers are not like most people, and there were far too many of them on the Northern Peninsula that January. One cold day I took Earl Pilgrim for another airborne search for the persistent out-of-season hunters. This time, it wasn't an ordinary search, and the results were anything *but* ordinary.

With Earl on board, we flew southward in the Jet Ranger, along the Long Range Mountains, past Soufflets River, searching the woods and open areas for snowmobile tracks. We were hindered by a brisk wind and cloudy sky, making it difficult to see tracks of any kind. As we flew across snow-covered bogs and forest areas, I watched the ground beneath us while remaining mindful of our gusty flight conditions. In the downdrafts, I could easily get caught unawares and lose control of the aircraft.

About forty-five minutes into our search, Earl spotted two snowmobiles in the thick forest below us. He pointed to his right, and I turned the aircraft around carefully to see them. Sure enough, the hunters were right below us in the thick forest, trying desperately to hide. After we circled a few times, it was obvious to them that they were spotted. But equally obvious that were unable to find a suitable place to land. It was a stalemate of sorts. The two men, with what looked like a sledge, or trailer, filled with moose meat, lay curled up near a tree. They didn't want to be recognized.

I searched desperately for a place to land in order to drop Earl off, but there was nothing but thick forest for over a half mile, and the wind blew so strong and gusty, I couldn't take any chances. The poachers knew they were spotted, but they also knew that helicopters need a clear landing area. Earl, as passionate as ever about catching poachers, cussed and swore he would catch them. But after ten minutes of burning jet fuel and hovering in the horrible wind, we were forced to move on.

I climbed upward, circling overhead and surveyed the area. Earl said he thought the men looked familiar and were from Eddies Cove or Hawke's Bay. He figured they would be heading back that way after we left, thinking it was safe. That's when I got an idea of how we might catch them. Earl liked it.

I climbed into the sky, high above the mountains, and headed southwest, as if we were flying back to Pasadena to refuel. That round trip would take us a few hours, and the poachers knew it. I made it obvious which direction we were headed, and when I was 20 miles from them, flying lower, I cut back to the east along a series of ponds south of the Blue Mountains. At that point I turned north while the vast mountain range kept the poachers from hearing or seeing us. I had flown in a large, thirty-mile circle, ending up a few miles behind and downwind from the poachers.

With the wind directly on my nose, I landed on a hill a little more than a mile northeast of the poachers. We were now in an excellent location to watch two large open fields between their current hiding spot and their village. Because of the strong wind and the distance between us, I felt certain they would not be able to hear our helicopter. We would sit and wait for them to make their run.

I shut the helicopter down, and we waited with our eyes fixed on the open fields in front of us. Earl and I talked to pass the time. After two hours, cold and disheartened, we were about ready to call it quits. That's when I saw two black dots moving across a snow-covered bog on the horizon.

"There they go!" I shouted.

"Hurry, Dave!" Earl said. "Got to catch them before they go into the woods again."

I started the helicopter, took off into the gusty wind, and flew down the mountain toward our escaping targets. In less than two minutes I was able to catch up with them from behind. The two snowmobiles cut across the snow-covered terrain, bouncing and bumping as they went. With the wind and snow blowing across their face and their winter hats pulled tight over their head, the poachers couldn't hear the helicopter coming up behind them.

As I flew low-level, five feet above the snow, the fleeing snowmobiles scurried across the open field in tandem. I maneuvered the helicopter slowly and silently forward just enough to come into view of the second snowmobile. Glancing to his left, the driver jumped as if he had been electrocuted.

I flew past him to the first snowmobile, whose driver showed no sign of being surprised when he saw us. He raised his fist in defiance, making it clear he planned to keep running to the thick patch of forest only a half mile away. If he made it to those trees, they would be gone.

"Stop, you idiots!" Earl shouted, holding his fist up. I had to stop them. I had to do something drastic.

With little thought of the danger involved, I flew toward the lead snowmobile, adjusting my airspeed to match his groundspeed. I carefully maneuvered the aircraft into a position beside the fleeing poacher. Closer and closer, but he wouldn't stop. With time running out and the thick forest looming, I carefully placed the helicopter's right float on top of the snowmobile, pushing it down slightly and forcing the shocked driver to lean completely forward in order to dodge the massive black rubber float. Seconds before we reached the trees, the frightened hunter gave up and stopped. I had only touched his vehicle for a split second, but it made a believer out of the tough, hardened poacher.

After we landed, Earl stood in the blowing snow arguing with the furious poachers. The man on the lead snow vehicle yelled at Earl while he removed his frost-and snow-covered balaclava cap. It was Jake, the stubborn, defiant leader of the group we had caught the year before.

"You almost killed me," Jake yelled, as he started toward me. Before he took his second step, Earl grabbed him by the arm and pulled him back. "Damn shame he didn't kill you," Earl said. "You stand right here and cool off. I'll have a look at what you're transporting. Don't think you boys would be hauling firewood this far into the woods."

I helped Earl as the two men followed Earl's orders and stood out of the way. The second poacher, young and embarrassed, seemed reticent and respectful of Earl's authority. A search of the sledge trailer produced two moose, quartered and stiff, along with two .303 Enfield rifles, a box of shells, several ropes, saws, and some blood-soaked skinning knives.

"Well, what a surprise," Earl said sarcastically. "And you can be sure I'm confiscating everything this time."

"You can't do that," Jake yelled. "You can't, by God, you can't."

"Yes, boy, I can, and I will. You don't like what I'm doing, then you tell Judge Jenkins."

The man's face grew even darker at the mention of the famous "Wildlife Jenkins," known for supporting the efforts of Newfoundland Fish and Wildlife Enforcement.

Earl took me off to the side and explained that we would be taking everything, including the snowmobiles, rifles, and moose meat. Then he told me how he planned to do it.

"Dave, you'll need to make three flights out," Earl said. "The first flight I need you to take both these men and one snowmobile. The second flight will be with me and the second snowmobile. I'll gather the meat and equipment and tie it up on the sled for the third flight. You come back and get that one on your own."

"OK," I said, "but I don't have my sling gear."

"Can you use some of the rope in their snowmobile?"

"I guess so," I said, sounding a bit worried. Earl pulled me farther away from the two poachers and said, "What's wrong. Are the snowmobiles too heavy?"

"No, Earl," I said, "but listen, it isn't legal to fly with passengers in the helicopter while you're hauling sling loads. Second, look at Jake. He's pretty pissed off, and he's liable to try anything. I'm not sure what he might do once he's away from you."

"You'll be all right," Earl said. "They won't try anything, and as for the helicopter, no one cares. It's a kind of emergency work you're doing."

"OK," I said. "Let's get it done." But the plan still bothered me. Somehow in the cold wind, looking at Jake's miserable face, I wasn't sure this was such a good idea.

We used one of the confiscated ropes and rigged the first snowmobile with one end of the rope. I made a double loop on the other end and snapped that into the aircraft's cargo hook. With the two poachers on board and a snowmobile dangling from a fifteen-foot rope below us, I took off to the west, toward Eddies Cove. Glancing down, I saw Earl below us, already preparing the second load. Once we were airborne, Jake, the smelly, unshaven poacher in the front seat, started cussing. Furious because of being caught and arrested. He knew full well that this time he stood a good chance of losing his precious snowmobile. Listening to him holler, I could barely concentrate on controlling the helicopter. After I told him to shut up several times, it started to wear on me.

Before the flight, Earl had suggested we put the quiet poacher in the back seat and the loudmouth in the front so I could watch him. Even though his buddy tried to calm him down, Jake wouldn't shut up.

"Yank!" Jake shouted, from three feet away. "You're a son of a bitch, and I'm gonna find you."

"Shut up," I said.

"I know you live in Pasadena," he said. "If you're not there when I get there, then I'll speak to your wife."

"Shut. Up!" I shouted, now ready to slug him. He saw my reaction and slammed his fist against the plexiglass window, cracking it.

"I know how to even things, Yank. Yes, b'y, I do."

At that moment, with both hands busy flying the aircraft, I wanted to hurt the man, but I couldn't let go of the controls to slug him. Then I thought of something better. Something he would never forget.

"Shit!" I yelled, "Something's wrong with the cargo hook." At that instant I touched the tiny cargo release switch on the cyclic and immediately the hook below the helicopter opened, releasing the rope connected to the snowmobile. The helicopter shifted, as it adjusted to the change in balance.

I grinned, then banked the helicopter hard left, putting the aircraft over on its side, Jake's side, and watched as the bulky snowmobile glided through the air like a giant boulder. Time stood still as Jake screamed, "Noooooooooooooo," and his treasured vehicle free-fell toward the ground. Then to my delight and to the horror of my two un-law-abiding passengers, the ski-doo smashed into a large, rock-covered hill, breaking into hundreds of pieces. The debris bounced into the air, then blew across the hill like a shattered wine glass. Jake for once was silent, his ugly face limp, unbelieving.

"Sorry," I said. "Technical problems."

I brought the nose of the aircraft to the right and leveled out, then flew toward our destination. Beside me, Jake sat with his mouth open, as if frozen in midsentence, his face a seasick greenish color. He appeared lost, dazed, and totally unsure of what was happening to him.

He had pushed me over the limit, and I fought back the only way I could. The cabin remained silent as I made my approach to Eddies Cove. I don't know if it was shock or resignation, but luckily, Jake kept quiet the rest of the flight. When we landed, I told the young poacher in the back seat to get out and walk toward the front of the helicopter and wait there for Jake. I grabbed the second headset off the hook and handed it to Jake, then motioned for him to put it on. When he had it on, I calmly asked, "Can you hear me?"

Jake's face flushed angrily, and he said, "Ain't right, Yank. You did that on purpose, you dropped it on purpose, and you know it."

I looked at him and thought of the things he had said. The threats to my family. "Maybe I did and maybe I didn't," I said. "But if you even come close to my family or threaten them again, you better be careful on your hunting trips. Sometimes hunters get shot by other hunters." Jake started to answer, but I put my hand up and said, "Think of how ironic that would be: a moose poacher being mistaken for a moose."

Jake threw the headset at me, then got out of the helicopter and joined his friend. They walked away, knowing that Earl would be filing the paperwork later in the day. I flew back and finished hauling Earl and the equipment out of the woods. Of course, I had to tell Earl about the "equipment malfunction." He was surprised, but thoughtful. Then he smiled and said, "It wasn't your fault, Dave."

"Really, then what was it?"

"Gravity," Earl said. "No one, I mean no one, can defy gravity."

"Wow," I said, in a jovial tone of respect. "Earl Pilgrim, champion Canadian boxer, wildlife officer, and now, Newfoundland philosopher."

***

Around 9:30 one evening right after Barbara had put the kids to bed, I received yet another surprise call from Jack Murphy, who never called past 8 p.m. I knew he had something important on his mind, but I would have never guessed just how important.

"How's the guitar coming along?" Jack asked. Barbara shot me a dirty look from across the room. She had finally managed to get the kids asleep, and based on her body language, it hadn't been easy. I had worked behind the house most of the evening, trying my best to repair the sorry excuse for a water pump that our landlord refused to change.

"I'm learning a few basic guitar chords and some songs," I said. "Only some simple stuff, really."

"Well, that's good, son," he said. "We'll be watching you on CBC before you know it." He chuckled.

"What's going on, Jack?" I asked in a quieter tone than normal, knowing little David was a light sleeper.

Jack got to the point and explained that the next day I would be flying to Stephenville. Nothing unusual about that, I thought. But then he proceeded to tell me that I would be flying Newfoundland politicians to Stephenville to meet with the prime minister of Canada, Pierre Trudeau. As I tried to grasp this surprising news, I glanced at Barbara, who had tiptoed down the hall to check on the kids and had returned to the front room. I smiled at her and in an overdramatic tone repeated my instructions.

"So tomorrow," I said, seriously. "I will pick up passengers in Deer Lake, then fly them to Stephenville where they will meet with Prime Minister Trudeau, and I suppose, Margaret."

Barbara stopped in midstride and shook her head. "Really?" she asked, loudly.

"Really," Jack replied, having heard Barbara. "Make sure you're looking good. There will be more photographers at that airport than sand on the beach."

I hung up the phone as Barbara sat next to me, as excited as a schoolgirl. I sighed and pretended everything was normal. Putting my arm around her, I asked, "How are the kids doing? Did little David get to sleep yet?" Playing the part of the dutiful father, I stood up and started to walk toward the bedroom. "I'll go and check on him. You stay here and relax."

"You sit down right here and tell me what's going on tomorrow," she said.

"No, I better go check on our kids. I thought I heard one of them crying."

Barbara grabbed my hand, pulled me back to the couch, and we both giggled. When she stopped giggling, I told her what little I knew.

"I'm not going to fly the first couple," I said. "I'm only going to take a few VIPs from Deer Lake over to see them."

"It's still going to be fun," she said. "A lot more fun than I'll have watching our kids."

We turned off the TV and talked for a while, amazed at how quickly things could change in our crazy life. Then she made me promise to tell her everything about Margaret Trudeau: What dress was she wearing? What shoes? Did she wear a hat?

"Sure," I said, grinning. "I'll tell you everything. But for now, tell *me* something. What are you wearing to bed tonight? What dress, what shoes, and will you be wearing a hat?"

"You'll find out soon enough," she said, her lovely eyes narrowing seductively.

***

The next morning three well-dressed passengers, local politicians, sat in the Jet Ranger chatting with one another as I flew across the hills on my final approach to the Stephenville Airport. As we landed, I could see that in front of the terminal a group of Liberal Party faithful and excited citizens waited to greet the first couple. My passengers quickly joined that group as the prime minister's Canadian Forces aircraft taxied up to park.

A few hundred excited, curious Newfoundlanders stood anxiously on both sides of a red-carpet walkway, hoping to catch a glimpse of their 51-year-old prime minister and his 22-year-old bride.

Along the decorated walkway a thin yellow tape hung as a barrier, and inside that barrier stood a handful of tall Canadian Mounted Police. Dressed in their scarlet tunics, midnight blue breeches, brown riding boots, and light brown flat-brimmed Stetson hats, the Mounties were the symbol of everything good and safe about Canada, and on that momentous day they seemed even more than that. They were a tangible symbol of law and order.

During the past year, peace-loving Canadians in all ten provinces had suffered through one of the most disgusting and shocking national crises in Canada's modern history. Two cells of the infamous revolutionary group, Front de Libération du Québec, FLQ, had kidnapped British Trade Commissioner James Cross and Quebec Labor Minister Pierre Laporte in Montreal.

Prime Minister Trudeau, who had a reputation for standing up to violence, went into action by sending federal troops to Quebec and invoking the War Measures Act. All of this was still fresh on the nation's mind since it had played out on national television in the fall of 1970, while Barbara and I were on Prince Edward Island. The dramatic situation had become known as the October Crisis.

When the "crisis" finally ended, Labor Minister Pierre Laporte had been killed and left in the trunk of a car. James Cross was released after having spent over eight terrifying weeks as a hostage. There was no real victory for either side, and the aftermath seemed to create a country even more divided by cultural and geographical differences.[3]

But today, the famous, flamboyant Pierre Elliott Trudeau and his young, lovely wife Margaret, were about to make an appearance in the small community of Stephenville, Newfoundland. People wanted to forget the October Crisis and think about this unique, attractive couple.

The prime minister was an intellectual with a broad smile, a rose in his lapel, and a friendly, open manner. He seemed to have a face for every audience: smiling, quizzical, mocking, serene, and very handsome blue eyes. He was always in the news in what was called "Trudeaumania." [3]

Part of his image came out of the October Crisis, but there were other surprises. Being a well-known fiery debater, Trudeau outdid himself during an argument with John Lundrigan, a member of Parliament. It sounded like the prime minister used a well-known four-letter cuss word, but later he later told everyone that he had only said "Fuddle Duddle."

The term "Fuddle Duddle" became an overnight household phrase and the title to a popular song. And then, as if the charismatic politician wasn't satisfied with just being the most popular and widely known prime minister Canada had ever elected, he shocked the world by marrying a rich young girl from Western Canada named Margaret Sinclair. A youthful, fun-loving woman who enjoyed rock and roll and was rumored to indulge in drugs, Margaret Sinclair Trudeau was known as a flower child and she fascinated Canadians with her pleasure-seeking attitude and rock-star lifestyle. They were more than celebrities, and the world couldn't get enough of them.[3]

And today, as the first couple descended from the four-engine Canadian Armed Forces plane, a polite round of applause rose from the onlookers, who strained their necks to get the first, eagerly awaited glimpse of these famous newlyweds. At the bottom step of the stairway, Premier Joey Smallwood, wearing a black suit, white dress shirt, and black tie, shook hands with his friend, the prime minister, and welcomed the beautiful Margaret Trudeau. After exchanging pleasantries and being introduced to a few local politicians, the first couple followed their host along the walkway toward the terminal building.

As the dignitaries strolled through the crowd of well-wishers, the prime minister shook hands with a few people and Margaret accepted a small bouquet of flowers. People responded politely, respectfully, and one of the ladies curtseyed as the youthful Margaret walked past.

Then, as several people gathered closer to the dignitaries, someone handed Margaret a second bouquet, and the woman standing nearby reached across the tape barrier to touch Margaret's shoulder. From my vantage point, it looked harmless, but Margaret recoiled and stopped moving forward.

Before anyone could grasp the situation, Margaret pulled away from the group and scurried back toward their airplane. People watched in amazement and tried to make sense of it. The prime minister hurried back to his wife to comfort her, and soon a small conference convened near the aircraft. The diminutive Margaret stood a few feet from the group as her husband whispered to her, attempting, I suppose, to calm her.

A few Newfoundland politicians took part in the conference, and after several minutes the prime minister and Joey Smallwood, along with other dignitaries, walked briskly back toward the terminal. Behind them, Margaret stood with a man who appeared to be a plainclothes policeman. Then, to my amazement, the man in the suit, along with Margaret Trudeau, walked directly toward me. She seemed frightened, and the man with her appeared protective but avoided touching her. I stood nervously beside my helicopter as they walked right up to me. I was stunned.

The man in the blue suit turned out to be a federal officer and said, "Will you take us up for a slow, local flight and let her relax a few moments? I'll go along and help with this." "Yes, sir," I said. "Yes, sir."

***

High above the tree-covered hills northeast of the Stephenville Airport, Margaret Trudeau sat quietly in the back seat of the helicopter, looking down at the forest and creeks that passed below us like a beautiful, borderless park. The muscular bodyguard explained that Mrs. Trudeau was feeling nervous about the crowd back at the terminal.

"I need you to fly around the countryside for a few moments and let her get away from it all. If you see a safe place to land with no people, put us down there so she can get out and walk around."

"Yes, sir," I replied.

I turned toward the back seat and said, "Let me know if you need anything, Ma'am." She looked at me for a brief second but didn't reply. Perhaps the "Ma'am" thing was her first indication I might be an American, but she said nothing. I suppose a hundred other things crossed her mind.

Beside me, the muscular bodyguard's stoic manner led me to believe that it wasn't a good time to chat. He was highly professional, never taking his eyes off Margaret Trudeau for more than a few seconds.

With his approval, I landed in a small open area, roughly half the size of a football field. During the next thirty minutes, Mrs. Trudeau sat in the helicopter, then walked around a small, open area bordered on two sides by tall trees and thick shrubs. The unfettered grass, sometimes knee deep, was adorned with several varieties of wildflower. The setting reminded me of Premier Smallwood and the bear cub that surprised us. But fortunately, no animals made an appearance that day, and soon the quiet, reserved Mrs. Trudeau so near in age to my own wife, walked back to the helicopter and climbed into the back seat. She seemed more relaxed as I carefully buckled her seatbelt. More gentle than usual because I knew this beautiful lady would be having their first child in a few months. She looked toward the forest, and her charming face seemed peaceful now. Perhaps she understood that even in a small, out-of-the-way place like Western Newfoundland, she would always be around people, and they would always want more of her than she was willing to give.

With the Prime Minister's wife on board, I flew back to the Stephenville Airport. When I let the reluctant Mrs. Trudeau and her bodyguard off at the terminal, I didn't feel as starstruck as I had expected. My feelings were more personal at that moment. This complicated lady struggled to find her way in a dark, crowded tunnel. The prime minister's young, somewhat introverted wife walked away from the helicopter with a slight smile on her lovely face. I waited, hoping she would turn and say goodbye, but she didn't.

She walked purposely toward the terminal, her arms swinging at her sides, bravely stepping back into her life of meeting and being met. An arduous and demanding life fraught with unwelcome intrusions. She was warily becoming the focus of all attention while embracing each distinctive Canadian culture and acting pleasantly impressed while doing so.

I can't recall what designer clothing she wore, but I do remember her youthful, mesmerizing face. A gentle woman, almost soulful in her yearning, who somehow, during her time alone, walking on that quiet, distant hill, found the calm, quiet strength she needed to accept her bittersweet fate.

(1)Marve *left* and unidentified inmate to his right at Prison Rodeo 1969.

1

(2) Bell 47 with fixed floats near iceberg
credit: archive P. Füllemann
https://www.heli-archive.ch/

(3) Dave Eagleston with headset.

(4) Bell Jet Ranger with Fixed Floats.

(5) Barbara Eagleston

(6) Sikorsky S61N

(7) Dave Eagleston in Alaska with Erickson Aviation before his retirement in 2016. Credit Micah Ness, Silverline Films

Chapter Twenty-Six

After more than a year of letters, cards, and visits with and without her daughter, Brenda finally got her wish, driving her tall, handsome fiancé from Springfield, Missouri, to Tulsa, Oklahoma. Because of his good behavior while incarcerated and the fact that Brenda's determination had impressed the authorities, Marve received another parole.

The tall Oklahoman walked out of Springfield Prison as a free man, determined to do exactly what he had promised Brenda he would do—become an honest person. It was the opportunity of a lifetime because she was a strong, beautiful, God-fearing woman, capable of taming the wild animal in his heart.

On the drive to Tulsa, they stopped in Miami, Oklahoma, and were married by the county clerk. On the outskirts of the small town, they were delayed by a flat tire on Brenda's car, which Marve quickly changed. When he got back into the car he smiled and said, "Is that my wedding gift?" Brenda smiled and said, "No, your gift won't take near as much work and will be a lot more fun."

The newlyweds quickly drove the remaining hundred miles to Tulsa and parked near the courthouse. They were about to start their new life together, but part of Marve's parole condition included a mandatory meeting with his parole officer on his first day out of prison. Brenda made sure they didn't stop at a cheap motel on the way, or most likely they would have missed the meeting.

The young parole officer, who had recently met with Brenda, looked across his cluttered desk at the newly married couple. Brenda's ambitious dreams were becoming a reality, and he envied her. Her lovely face reflected all the hope and love she had for her husband. He listened as Marve, the nervous parolee, explained that he planned to start a new chapter in his life and now, thanks to Brenda, he had a home and a family, and would be getting a job as soon as possible.

They talked for a little while, and after the PO laid out the rules, the couple walked out of his office and down the steps of the courthouse. Now, free to have their much-anticipated honeymoon, they drove straight to Brenda's house.

Inside her modest, cozy living room, Marve set his small bag on the hardwood floor and slowly surveyed Brenda's comfortable home. Brenda had enjoyed spending time during the past week preparing her house for his arrival. She had placed cut flowers, artfully arranged, on the coffee table, and two place settings of silverware and dishes on the glossy white laminate dining room table. There was a new white coffee mug on the table with the message "Not till I have my coffee" in bold letters. As Marve took it all in, a huge smile crossed his calm, handsome face. Brenda walked into the bedroom and lit several candles she had purchased the night before. She turned on the radio, and the intoxicating, lyrical sounds of the Carpenters played low and gentle, like the candles. Glancing back at her husband, Brenda motioned for him to follow her as the Carpenters sang their popular love song, *We've Only Just Begun.*

As she lit the last candle, she turned toward Marve, who leaned against the doorway, overwhelmed by his newfound freedom and love. His eyes were focused on Brenda as if she were the first woman he had ever seen. Now she felt the same freedom and sensed his vulnerable sexuality. In that moment, she knew that he adored her, and she had never felt anything so personal and intimate in her life.

Marve walked slowly across the candlelit room, took off the brown leather jacket Brenda had given him, and put his strong arms around her. He held her there, close enough to feel her heartbeat, close enough to take in the hypnotic fragrance of her perfume, and just long enough to let his new wife know she was loved.

"I don't think I can wait that long," he said.

She looked up at him. "What do you mean," she whispered, unbuttoning his shirt, running her finger across his chest. "Wait how long?"

"Like it says in there," he whispered.

"What do you mean?"

"Like it says in there, 'Not till I have my coffee.'"

She giggled as she grabbed his shirt tightly and pulled him toward the bed.

"You will never have to wait again."

***

The late spring of 1972 brought wonderful news to our little family in Pasadena, Newfoundland. First, I found out that I might be transferred to the Sikorsky S-61 offshore contract in St. John's, and if so, I would be trained on the huge, twin-engine, twenty-one-passenger Sikorsky helicopter. Second, we received a wonderful letter from Mom letting us know that Marve had been paroled, married, and now lived in Tulsa with his new wife and her daughter. I couldn't wait to talk to him.

And, if that wasn't enough, we found out that Barbara was going to have our third child. Not the best news since Barbara seemed overwhelmed with our other two children. Unlike Leslie, little David had been a sickly child who needed more attention and never seemed content as his sister had been. Leslie often sat on the floor, to play while her mother worked in the kitchen. But not little David, who always needed more from his mother. We considered it a blessing to have a third child, but the timing wasn't such a blessing.

While we waited for news about the St. John's job and Barbara started her familiar morning sickness, I had work to do. In late May the ice along the Labrador coast had started to thaw, so I flew north to St. Anthony to work for the Grenfell Mission for a few weeks. It was to be my last trip to Northern Newfoundland, and I expected it would be somewhat boring since I often spent most of the day waiting for patients and doctors. But I could be wrong.

The morning I left the house, Barbara stayed in bed feeling sick. Luckily, our neighbor across the street took our kids for a few hours. I kissed Barbara goodbye and rode to the hangar with Paul Williams. As we drove away, Barbara came to the window and waved at me, trying her best to smile.

Due to the length of time I would be away, Paul Williams went to St. Anthony with me to look after the aircraft and keep up with maintenance. I would be filling in for the airplane which provided air ambulance services at the International Grenfell Mission. The airplane, a de Havilland Otter, was equipped with skis in the winter and floats in the summer. Between seasons, it couldn't fly because the lakes and harbors were part ice and part clear water, which meant the airplane would crash into the thin ice if it attempted to land. As a result of those conditions, the hospital needed a helicopter to transport patients between the hospital and the outlying communities along the Labrador coast.

When we arrived at the coastal community of St. Anthony, I flew past the hills, up the harbor, over choppy water and ice. On both sides of the inlet we passed fishing boats, storage sheds, and wooden houses, and I landed on a long wooden dock down the hill from the busy hospital. Jet fuel was stored on the dock for airplanes and helicopters, and Paul, knowing the routine, jumped out and moved the fuel hose, then filled our aircraft.

With Paul back on board, I lifted the helicopter into a hover, then took off into the wind, flying across the open water of the harbor, headed toward the airport. We were in the air less than 30 seconds when the familiar drone of the helicopter's engine went dead silent. A horrible, nasty silence that instantly shattered the calm within the cockpit and bled each precious ounce of engine power along with it. As the instruments retreated from full power to zero power, I shoved the collective down and pulled back slightly on the cyclic control to cushion our landing. Out of the corner of my eye, I saw Paul's huge hands fly right up to the ceiling as he yelled, "Shit, we're going in!"

***

While Paul's hands were still in the air, the helicopter splashed into the St. Anthony Harbor, and the large black rubber floats kissed the shallow waves perfectly with minimal impact. Within a few seconds we were bobbing up and down in the water with no power, controlled only by the wind and the receding tide. It was a safe landing, which had little to do with my talent but everything to do with the few hundred auto-rotations I had practiced. I quickly made two calls on the HF radio to alert the hospital and Universal Helicopters of our situation. I let them know we were all right but needed help quickly.

As Paul and I watched in silence, the strong westerly wind blew us in an easterly direction, away from the tiny coastal community. Soon we would be leaving the protection of the harbor and heading out to sea with no help in sight!

Ten minutes later, as we watched helplessly, our little helicopter rode the higher waves in the frigid waters of the adjoining bay. We were entering French Bay, only a few miles from the Atlantic Ocean. The few seconds of pride and relief I had felt after the successful landing were now replaced by the fear of floating helplessly in the frigid, ten-foot waves of the Atlantic Ocean.

"Lord Jesus," Paul said, his worried eyes showing the fear we shared. "Newfoundland all my life, b'y, and I never seen anything like this."

"Hang in there, Paul," I said. "The hospital's sending out a long-liner as soon as they can."

"Can't be too soon," he said.

Ten minutes later, a short time that felt more like an hour, we saw a boat headed our way, but it seemed a bit small.

"Paul, is that a long-liner?"

"No b'y," he said, breathing in as he said it. "That's a skiff. But it should do. She's a beautiful sight right at this moment."

Paul opened his door and stepped carefully onto the top of the floats. Wind and water slapped at him, soaking his pants and boots, a wet reminder of our precarious situation. I got out the other side and we greeted the two men in the skiff.

When the small, open boat pulled closer to us, one of the two rescuers, local fishermen, cut the engine and they coasted beside us. One man threw a rope at the helicopter, and Paul quickly rigged the rope under our aircraft by tying it tightly around the front cross tube. As soon as the rope was secure, Paul motioned for the boat to head back to the docks.

"Thank you, b'ys!" Paul yelled in his thick Newfie accent, "You're a couple of heroes, sure!"

The two fishermen grinned and checked the rope on their end to make sure it was secured. The man in the rear of the boat stepped back into the tiny, semi-enclosed cabin, which looked no larger than a phone booth cut in half. We listened, but there were no engine sounds coming from our rescue vessel. After ten minutes the fisherman shook his head and cussed out loud.

"Damn it, Harold!" he shouted. "The shitten' thing won't turn over," he said. Then to us, he said, "B'ys, you better get on your radio and call for another boat."

As he gave us the bad news, I glanced back to the west again and noticed the sun sneaking behind the hills like a bandit. As if the helicopter's engine failure wasn't enough, we now had to put up with a skiff that wouldn't start and the sun going down. It was like mother nature giving us the finger. Quickly, I made my second call to the hospital, this time feeling more worried. We were now five miles from the safe confines of the harbor as the helicopter rocked up down with the waves, and the unsecured main rotor blades thumped against the mast.

On the radio I said, "We're east of French Bay, and the boat you sent out to tow us is here with us, but it is disabled and tied to the helicopter."

"That's good, b'y," Terry, the dispatcher said.

"I don't think you heard me, Terry," I said. "The skiff can't get its engine started, and the wind is blowing us farther away from shore. We need another boat, and we need it fast."

After a few seconds of silence, the dispatcher finally grasped the situation and said, "Yes, b'y, I'll send her as fast as I can."

"Thank you," I said.

It took another half hour for the second boat to arrive. While that may not seem like a long time, in the cold, choppy waters off the Newfoundland coast, it was a lifetime. We had spotted one small iceberg three or four miles north of our position and, according to Paul, we would have seen a few more bergs and a couple of whales had it been daylight. But now help was on the way.

When I finally spotted the boat, I pointed to it and said to Paul, "How 'bout that one, is that a long-liner?"

"Yes, b'y," Paul said, pointing to the second boat. "She's a proper long-liner this time. We'll be fine."

Paul was right. The large wooden vessel had a small, enclosed cabin, a three-man crew, and a ready supply of ropes and cables. Paul and I shivered in the cold, but were thrilled as the vessel drew near to us.

"Are you okay?" One man yelled. "Is anyone hurt?" "No," Paul yelled, "but I'm freezing my arse off out here." The three men in the long-liner laughed and invited any of us to join them on their boat. Paul lowered his voice and said to me, "Don't leave this aircraft. I'll tell you why later." We declined and thanked them, and when we were all tied on, we headed back to St. Anthony, slowly moving through the choppy water. At first the helicopter had a tendency to roll over in the water, so the long-liner took it slow and easy.

Paul and I took turns climbing onto the upper deck of the helicopter to hold the main rotor down. Otherwise, it would slam against the tail boom or impact the mast. Holding it down safely wasn't easy, and Paul did most of the work.

Once again, the crew of the rescue ship invited us to come aboard for a cup of tea, but Paul thanked them and we stayed aboard the helicopter all the way back to St. Anthony. From time to time during a calm section of water, Paul and I talked about how hungry we were getting and how much ice was building up on the floats. Then, as Paul stood on the side of the aircraft with his foot near the baggage compartment, looking down from the helicopter's upper deck, he jokingly said, "What kind of a write-up should we put in the logbook for this? This one will be worse than that float-eating dog down on the south coast."

I slipped on the step on my way down the other side of the helicopter, then regained my balance before falling in the freezing water. "Yes, it will," I said, eager to talk about something other than the mess we were in. "That one was a world-class logbook entry. I swear, that dog could have chased away a polar bear."

Paul chuckled and the men in the small boat looked back at us, wondering what we were up to. I grinned again and said, "I'll never forget that one, Paul. I needed to land in that little outport on the south coast and a giant, moose-hunting Labrador dog jumped up and bit the helicopter floats. A group of people came out to see the helicopter and watched as I struggled to hover over a small school yard. The people from the outport kept a safe distance, but each time I got within five feet of the ground, that damn dog jumped up and put a fist-sized hole in the left float. Then, when he ran around to the front, I could see him through the chin bubble as he bit a hole through the right front float. He was large and mean and he looked up at me as he violated the thick rubber floats. I'm glad he couldn't jump any higher or he would have jumped into the cockpit with me."

Paul laughed uncontrollably, and this time, he almost fell in. I continued, "By the time the dog got tired and ran off, the left side of the helicopter sat so low on the ground, I was afraid to shut down the engine."

Paul chucked, and I guess he was trying to picture in his mind the sight of a crazed dog ravishing a helicopter. Paul looked out into the choppy water and said in his official, mock voice, "Yes, boy. That night I wrote the proper Department of Transport entry in the aircraft journey logbook:

"Aircraft unserviceable due to excessive float damage and multiple bite-shaped lacerations in left rear float caused by wild-ass Newfoundland dog."

At that point, there wasn't enough light to see Paul's face, but I knew he was smiling. Ahead of us, two boats moved slowly through the dark, frigid water, pulling us back to the same dock where we had refueled only a few unforgettable hours before.

"So," I said. "You should start working on a good logbook entry for this little voyage, because we're almost there." In the dark night air we could smile because we were close enough to the harbor and dock to relax. It was wonderfully safe and familiar. I had flown across the little harbor several times, but I had never seen it as I did that night—with the frosty, distant stars twinkling overhead, deep, fluffy snow along the trees and hills, and wood-framed houses with light gray smoke rising into the frigid sky from their numerous chimneys. St. Anthony at night, as peaceful and inviting as anywhere I had ever been.

Chapter Twenty-Seven

It may be hard to believe, but after all the drama associated with the helicopter floating into the Atlantic Ocean, the next day they had my Bell Jet Ranger up and running again. And it's a good thing, because our role was about to be reversed. We would be the ones searching for a downed helicopter.

Luckily for us, the hospital had a construction project going on in St. Anthony, and their large crane crawled down to the dock and pulled the helicopter out of the water. Slowly and carefully, the driver placed it gently onto the dock. As Paul had suspected, the cause of the engine failure turned out to be the fuel control unit, and a newly overhauled FCU was transported by truck from Gander. One of the engineers from Gander, Larry Gibbons, brought the part and stayed to help Paul.

A careful search of the engine, airframe, and floats revealed no damage, so the FCU was the only thing that needed repair. Of course, Paul had to write up the engine failure in the logbook, and Jack Murphy submitted a report to the Department of Transport. Otherwise, we were back in business. While Paul and Larry worked on the helicopter, I helped as best I could by handing them tools or bringing coffee, and by being there to support them in the cold weather. Paul, his usual jovial self, told and retold the *engine failure and out to sea* story and Larry listened politely, letting Paul talk away.

In the late afternoon I handed Paul another cup of coffee and he said, "Remember when I told you not to go aboard the long-liner?" "Yes," I said. "Why not? I could have warmed up and come back to help."

"I'll tell you why," he said. "It's the international Law of the Sea. If the captain and crew abandon a vessel at sea, any other vessel can claim salvage rights. In this case, the helicopter belongs to the long-liner captain if we leave the helicopter and he pulls it in."

"He's right, b'y," Larry said. "Good thing you stayed on the helicopter."

"I never knew that, Paul." Then I said, "I don't make a habit of taking advice from hippies, but this time I made an exception."

Larry looked at Paul, but Paul grinned and said nothing.

During the next three weeks I flew five to six hours a day, back and forth across the straits to Labrador. Things went well, considering the changeable, Arctic-like conditions in that area. With only two days left before the fixed-wing operation was to begin, we woke up to a horrible snowstorm. The wind howled, and the wet snow came down so thick that visibility decreased to less than a half mile—far below our operational limits.

Late that afternoon, Paul and I sat in the hospital's radio room and drank coffee with the hospital dispatcher, Terry Simms. We were in the radio room because a determined helicopter pilot had decided to brave the blizzard and fly from Blanc-Sablon, Quebec, to St. Anthony. He was on his way to St. Anthony with a baby and a nurse on board, and planned to drop off the baby and return to Blanc-Sablon with the nurse.

When the helicopter arrived, we couldn't see across the harbor due to the heavy, blowing snow. I went down to chat with the pilot and stood with him on the dock while Paul put fuel in his helicopter. I tried desperately to talk him out of returning to Blanc-Sablon, emphasizing that he and the nurse would be safe and warm if he stayed the night in St. Anthony.

"Paul and I will help you secure your aircraft," I said.

"No way," he said, in his French-Canadian accent. "I got to get back soon, but t'ank you."

I stood on the dock as a lovely young nurse, dressed in a hospital uniform, parka, and stocking cap, got into the front seat of the helicopter. She smiled and waved at us through the window. As the helicopter lifted off and turned to fly above the harbor, it disappeared into the blowing snow within a few seconds.

"Lord Jesus," Paul said. "Buddy is tryin' to get 'em all killed."

"You got that right," I said, standing with Paul as the wet snow blew against my face.

***

In his new role as stepfather, Marve sat with his family of three in the kitchen of their little house near Riverside Drive. As he listened attentively, his energetic stepdaughter chatted away about the *Muppets* special they had all watched on TV the night before. Katy was eager to tell Marve, who she called Papa, all about the pretty lady on with the Muppets.

"Papa, remember?" Katy asked. "That lady was real pretty, and she could sing good. Just like a *moo-vie* star," Katy said.

"Sure, I remember," Marve said, grinning at Brenda. "That's 'cause she *is* a movie star. Her name is Julie Andrews."

"Who?" Katy asked, frowning.

"You know," Marve said. "Mary Poppins."

"That's right," Katy said. "Mary Poppins was on the *Muppets*."

Brenda giggled as she stood to clear the table. She seemed more at ease lately, aware of the relationship Marve was developing with her daughter. Marv's first two months with them had gone so smoothly that Brenda began to relax, knowing that Marve loved her and adored Katy. He had gone out each day bright and early to look for work, and finally found a job at a sheet metal shop. From then on, he came straight home at night, and if he drank at all, he only drank at home, with Brenda.

After supper, Marve walked up behind Brenda while she faced the sink, finishing the dishes. She glanced over her shoulder as she felt his muscular arms wrapped around her waist.

"Who wants to go for a walk?" Marve asked.

"I do, I do!" Katy screamed. "Mommy does too, don't you, Mommy?"

Brenda wiped her hands on the dishtowel and hesitated. She still felt the impact of a rough day at work, and she only wanted to sit on the front porch and relax, but she gave in.

"I do, I do!" Brenda said, in mock eagerness.

"Yeah!" Katy yelled. "Everybody's going for a walk!"

"Yeah," Brenda echoed with much less enthusiasm than Katy. When Marve went for "a walk," he went for "a run." Brenda and Katy rode bikes while Marve jogged along the beautiful sidewalks. It had become their nightly ritual, and she didn't enjoy it nearly as much as Marve or Katy, but it felt good once they were out of the house pedaling along.

Even though it provided good exercise, the main reason Brenda enjoyed their "walks" was the proud, excited feeling she experienced as they passed other people walking on the sidewalk. She saw the admiring looks women gave Marve when he wore his gym shorts and tee shirt. At first it had bothered her. But then, as she gained confidence, she felt like telling each one of them, *Go right ahead and look, because he's all mine.*

***

An hour after the helicopter left St. Anthony in the blowing snowstorm, Paul and I sat in the Grenfell Mission's radio room awaiting word from the Blanc-Sablon dispatcher. We were anxious to see if the pilot had successfully made the 60-mile flight. But now, fifteen minutes past his ETA, their dispatcher confirmed what we feared: they had not arrived and had not been heard from for the past forty-five minutes.

I wanted to jump into my helicopter and search for them, but the treacherous weather and impending nightfall prevented any hope of flying. I immediately contacted the aviation authorities and made a Missing Aircraft Report. During the next hour, as the sun disappeared and the heavy snow continued to fall, I contacted other aviation authorities in Quebec and Newfoundland and discussed the missing helicopter, giving them all available information. Before nightfall the hospital received several calls from news sources, but according to protocol, we gave out carefully worded responses. With a horrible guilty feeling I sat there and did nothing. Then I thought of one thing that might help: I called Barbara to let her know I was okay and needed to warn her not to worry when she heard the radio reports about the missing aircraft near St. Anthony.

"When are you coming home?" she asked, as I heard the children crying in the background. "Hopefully in three or four days," I said. "I just wanted you to know I'm okay." I had called her so that she wouldn't be worried about me, but after that call I became more worried about her. I knew I couldn't keep beating the odds in this business much longer. I had to find another type of flying. Between the accidents, the time away from home, and the horrible weather, Barbara's depression grew worse. I had to somehow get that job on the big helicopters in St. John's.

The next day brought more horrible weather and prevented a search. But on the second day the storm abated, and we welcomed beautiful, sunny skies, which gave us perfect flying conditions. The Canadian Armed Forces and various provincial and federal authorities launched a full-fledged search.

Of course, the worst part of the missing aircraft's sixty-mile course was the untraceable 20-mile stretch of open water between Flower's Cove and Blanc-Sablon. The 20 miles of treacherous water across the Strait of Belle Isle which I had flown over several times. On each crossing, I had tried to remain as high as possible above the water. But on the day the helicopter went missing, the pilot had less than two hundred feet between his aircraft and the water below. If he had crashed into that massive body of water, chances were the aircraft would never be found.

The morning of the search I flew two emergency flights for the hospital, then joined the search. I tried my best to follow the route he would have taken in the storm. Searching for any sign of a crash—perhaps a piece of clothing, foot tracks in the snow, or maybe a signal or smoke—I flew south along the harbor, made a quick right turn at Goose Cove, and hugged the shoreline until I was over Hare Bay. I flew west across Hare Bay around ten miles or so and went onshore, thinking he might have crossed over the peninsula in that area.

After crossing back and forth along a fifteen-mile area, I found the crashed helicopter, nestled perfectly in the tall trees. To my disappointment, no one could be seen around the crash site. With my adrenaline pumping full speed, I circled the lifeless helicopter and called the rescue team leader. About that same time, Tom Green, flying a small airplane, spotted two people on the ground five miles from the crash site. The survivors, walking along a rocky beach, were picked up and taken to the St. Anthony Hospital. The pilot and nurse had spent a horribly cold night out in the open, huddled together, trying desperately to survive the howling wind and unbearably cold temperatures. The helicopter pilot had tried in vain to lead his passenger to shelter, but had given up in the blowing snow and was forced to huddle with the nurse when they could walk no longer.

The pilot survived but suffered severe frostbite and would possibly lose one foot as a result of spending two nights in the open. The nurse also suffered from frostbite, as well as blunt trauma. She would remain in the hospital for quite some time while they worked on her foot and she recovered from emotional stress.

After refueling, I returned to the crash site with Paul Williams and Terry Simms, the hospital dispatcher. I parked as close as possible, and we walked through the woods to the crash site. Perched in the tall fir trees, the helicopter, a Bell Jet Ranger 206 A, sat four feet off the ground, suspended in place by tree limbs which had miraculously cushioned its crash landing. From all indications it appeared the pilot had lost engine power, most likely as a result of wet, blowing snow which caused a flameout.

Surprisingly, the fuselage was completely intact. There were a few broken windows and slight damage to the main body of the aircraft, owing in part to the cushioning of the trees. The only visible damage was to the main rotor and tail rotor blades, which had obviously hit a few trees on their way down. Inside the aircraft I found the collective control lever in the upward position; higher, in fact, than I thought possible. Because I wasn't a trained accident investigator, I could only speculate on the cause of the accident. I called Jack Murphy later that evening.

"Jack, it looks like the wet snow had caused a flameout," I said. "So, the engine failed while they were flying low-level over the forest with zero visibility. The pilot, unable to find an open place to land, did a pretty good autorotation and somehow managed to stop the aircraft's forward and vertical movement a few seconds before it fell through the trees."

"You mean there was no damage to the aircraft?" Jack asked.

"No, not really," I said. "Only the main rotor and tail rotor, and of course, I can't tell if there's any damage to the tail boom or transmission."

"Why didn't the pilot stay with the ship?" Jack asked.

"I don't know," I said. "I checked out the battery, and it still has juice. So he might have been able to use his radio if he would have stayed there. I checked the fuel and found he still had the better part of a full tank of jet fuel. And another thing, the woods around the crash site are thick with undergrowth that is brittle and plentiful, perfect for making a fire. Hell, he could have set up a nice little camp, built a fire with all that undergrowth, and waited for help to arrive."

"Too bad he tried to walk out," Jack said. "We all make mistakes, but the trick is when you make your first one, stop there. Looks like this guy kept on making them, just like dominoes falling. Guess it was one bad decision after the other."

"Yes, sir," I said. After a moment, Jack said, "Learn everything you can from this, because any of us could be in his shoes one day."

After I finished talking with Jack, I went back to the hospital and found the injured pilot resting in his hospital bed. I felt upset about the whole unnecessary ordeal, and when I entered his room, I planned to tell him off. But the guilt on his battered, swollen face, and the sight of his bandaged hands and arms changed my thinking. He didn't need me to shame him. He seemed to be doing a good job on his own. He spoke openly about the events and his crucial, regrettable decisions. He went over each dismal detail of the flight, and for once, I listened carefully, appreciating the unique opportunity it provided. When we finished talking, I told him I would come and see him again the next day.

"Get some rest," I said. "Probably a good idea to write down everything you can remember while it's still fresh in your mind."

After leaving the pilot's hospital room, I walked along the hospital corridor searching for the nurse who had survived the ordeal. For some strange reason *I* started to feel guilty about the crash. But I wanted badly to talk to the nurse and listen to her story. I might be able to glean some bit of survival information to benefit pilots and passengers in the future.

It wasn't hard to find her room, and when I did, I stood in her doorway. She lay in her bed, covered with several warm blankets, while being carefully attended to by two Newfoundland nurses. This lovely nurse, now an injured survivor, looked across the room at me with a shy, pitiful expression. As I caught the patient's eye, one of the attending nurses crossed the room, looked at me expressionlessly, and, without saying a word, closed the door in my face. I felt a mixture of surprise and guilt. They knew that I wasn't the pilot who had flown into the snowstorm. But perhaps they thought I didn't try hard enough to keep the pilot from going into the horrible weather.

Who knows, maybe she wasn't thinking about me at all. Perhaps it was only my imagination. I guess I'll never know. But I know that the rest of my life I will regret not trying harder to convince that pilot to stay on the ground.

I walked along the quiet hospital corridor toward the radio office, passing several hospital rooms along the way. Some were empty and a few held patients and their visitors. The pleasant, fresh scent of clean laundry mixed with a trace of antiseptic in the narrow hallway. I walked and watched and listened, but I was not alone. Two injured, mournful people walked with me in that dark, second-floor passageway. And as the floor creaked with each step, those silent souls whispered their prophetic warnings.

Chapter Twenty-Eight

In so many wonderful ways, life had improved for Marve and Brenda. After years of confinement and forced structure, Marve's job at the sheet metal shop was a challenge, but he kept at it. He went to work day after day and put up with a skinny, arrogant boss who wouldn't last an hour in McAlester Prison. It wasn't that Marve couldn't take orders from a short, annoying clod of a man. But Brian, his boss, made it a point to speak loud enough for everyone to hear each time he criticized Marve's work.

"Look at this," Brian said, as he stood beside a large hand brake machine and kicked a pile of metal across the floor. He spoke loudly, causing the men at the other end of the shop to look his way.

"You're making a mess on this floor," Brian said. "You got a job working on the break because you're a big guy and the owner likes to give ex-cons a chance. But you better clean this place up if you want to work here." Now it went through Marve's mind how much fun it would be to pick his boss up and hold him in the air for a few minutes. But he let that pass and said, "Yes, sir, I'll get it cleaned up." Walking away, the disagreeable little man turned and said, "See that you do."

After work Marve drove along Harvard Avenue, passed the familiar bars on Harvard, then turned right and drove straight home. He enjoyed the family meals and loved every moment with his stepdaughter. He often told Brenda that he wanted to adopt her little girl.

Of course, Brenda's life had changed drastically. She was proud of her job as a telephone operator and maintained a stellar work record. But, because she had married an ex-convict, there were several coworkers who didn't approve. They never said anything to her, but their pious, upturned faces gave away their unbelief. Most days at work went well, and once or twice a week she managed to spend a few minutes with Zelda, her mother-in-law. Brenda wanted to tell Zelda the latest news about Marve and how well he had adapted to married life. Zelda felt encouraged at how well things were going and how Marve, for once, managed to hold on to a job and a relationship. She gave Brenda most of the credit and gave God the rest.

At home, Brenda enjoyed cooking more than ever before. Now she had a man who bragged about her cooking. That was a reward in itself, but she also loved the way he came into the kitchen, breathing in deeply, then smiling as he savored the aroma of her corn bread or chicken casserole. Sometimes, before dinner, she leaned against the sink and watched as Marve and Katy sat at the table talking about their day. Or times when Katy sang one of her favorite songs and Marve listened carefully, encouraged her, then looked up at Brenda and winked.

In the evening, after they had gone for a walk or watched TV, Marve carried Katy into the bedroom and put her to bed. This became the routine. But some nights in the living room when "Popa" was tired and pretended to be too sleepy to move, little four-year-old Katy stood by his chair pulling and pulling, trying desperately to get him on his feet.

"Come on, Papa," she said, straining to pull him. "You promised to tell me a story tonight."

"I'm sleepy," Marve said, his eyes closed, his head bobbing back and forth. "If I get up, I'll have to walk in my sleep like a monster." Katy giggled, then tugged at his arm again. "Come on, Papa."

Sitting next to Marve, Brenda smiled and pushed her sluggish husband toward Katy. Slowly, Marve rose from the divan, then stood tall. He stepped forward in slow motion, sleepy-eyed, hands stretched out in front of him in classic sleepwalking form. Behind him, Katy giggled as she pushed him out of the living room, into the hallway toward her bedroom. A few steps from her bedroom door, her sleepwalking stepdad ran into the door, pretending to bang his head against the wooden frame. "Ouch," he said, holding his forehead in mock pain. Quickly, he turned around, wide awake, looking down at Katy as if seeing her for the first time.

"Grrrr," he said. "I am Count Dracula. Who is this little girl?" Katy screamed and tried to run the other way, but Marve quickly grabbed her and lifted her up off the floor. With his best Transylvanian accent, he said, "Youuu Kant Runnn from Count Dra-cu-la, little girl. I must put you to bed-da."

Katy shrieked as Marve carried her into the bedroom tickling her. He kissed her on the neck and said, "Count Dracula wants your blood." Katy screamed again. "Yuk, you can't have it. Put me down, Papa."

Marve carefully lay little Katy in bed and pulled the covers up to her chest, tucking her in snugly. Still smiling, Katy looked at him and said, "Will Dracula read me a story?" Marve squinted mysteriously, then said, "About vampires?"

"No, Papa, no." For a second Marve rubbed his chin thoughtfully. "About Transylvania?" Katy giggled, "No, Papa, no."

"Okay," he said, giving in. "How about the duck that couldn't find her mommy?"

"Yeah," Katy said, clapping her hands.

Marve leaned toward the small bookshelf near Katy's bed and removed a yellow children's book with a cracked, well-worn cover. It was one of her favorites, and Marve had read it to her so many times he could practically quote it by memory.

In the familiar comfort of her little bed, Katy clutched the soft pink fur of her stuffed Easter rabbit, and felt warm and cozy. As her stepfather started reading, Katy listened carefully, telling herself that she wouldn't fall asleep this time, like she had so many times before. *I'm going to listen carefully this time to make sure I hear the end of the story.* But then something happened to her eyes; she blinked. Marve noticed, then rubbed her cheek softly. *He better stop that, it makes me blink even more.* Now, they came to her, those soft, steady blinks. *Stop that, Papa. It feels wonderful, but stop, Papa, I want to hear ...*

At the bedroom door, Brenda stood quietly watching. From the living room, the low sounds of a commercial on TV were heard floating along the hallway and spilling into the room. The clean, fresh scent of baby shampoo lingered in the cozy bedroom as Marve switched off the Mickey Mouse lamp next to Katy's bed.

Brenda watched as Katy drifted off to sleep, Marve next to her holding a book in one hand and tenderly stroking Kathy's cheek with the other. For the past eight months, Brenda had watched the relationship grow between Katy and Marve, and how he began to anticipate the little girl's habits and win her boundless trust.

As Marve stopped reading, Katy's eyes remained shut and the warm, family-based theme of *The Waltons* came from the living room. Marve placed the yellow children's book back on the bookshelf and stood up slowly, careful not to wake his little Katy. He turned toward the door and, seeing Brenda there, smiled. He walked the few steps to her and put his arms around her. She said, "Can you put me to bed like that?"

"I guess I can," he said. "But what would John Boy say?" She giggled as she led him down the hall and into the bedroom. He stopped and turned toward the living room. "I better turn off the TV," he said. "Later," she whispered, pulling him closer. "Later. I want you all to myself right now."

***

After two and a half years of flying in the Newfoundland bush, years of seeing far too many exciting and dangerous situations, I finally had an opportunity to move into a more sophisticated, "safer" helicopter program. At least that's what they called it.

In late 1972, offshore oil exploration off the east coast of Newfoundland was in its infancy. Mobil Oil, one of the most active players, carried out drilling operations in the Atlantic Ocean on wells located between 150 to 200 miles east of St. John's.

The drilling rigs, with names like Sedco I and Sedco J, were manned by a hearty, well-paid group of rig hands that needed helicopter transport on a daily basis. In order to keep the best workers on board, the oil company needed at least three things: good food; a safe, reliable helicopter; and excellent helicopter crews. That's where Okanagan Helicopters came in.

A joint venture was formed between Universal Helicopters, a Newfoundland company that operated smaller, bush-style aircraft, and Okanagan Helicopters, a British Columbia company that operated smaller bush-style aircraft as well as a fleet of larger Sikorsky S-58T and S-61 helicopters. Okanagan sounds more like a Japanese name, but it isn't. The company was named after the beautiful fruit-rich Okanagan Valley in British Columbia. For offshore work at long distances and the extensive challenges of the Atlantic Ocean, the Universal-Okanagan partnership was born.

Based in a large WWII hangar at the Torbay Airport in St. John's, Newfoundland, the huge Sikorsky helicopters were capable of transporting up to eighteen passengers two hundred miles out and two hundred miles back in good or bad weather. If *bad* weather is a bit of a nebulous term, think of months and months of fog, separated by months of snow or freezing rain. If fact, if anyone wished to create a list of locations in the world with the worst possible flying weather, St. John's, Newfoundland, would be at or near the top of their list.

To make matters worse, not only do you have the horrible weather conditions to contend with, but sharks and whales were commonly seen around the oil rigs in the Grand Banks, along with icebergs. Floating like nature's silent battleships, bergs range in size and shape up to the length of a football field and weigh over 500,000 tons. They start their journey near Greenland, float past Labrador, then drift south and east along Iceberg Alley. Some of them drift directly toward a working oil rig, endangering and possibly destroying the drilling platform and the men on board.

It was into this "safer" environment that I was now headed. But first, I had a major technical hurdle to cross: transitioning to visual flight rules, VFR, to instrument flight rules, IFR. Basically, instrument flying is the method by which airplanes and helicopters navigate in bad weather. As the helicopter goes through clouds or fog, or flies at night with no horizon, instruments in the cockpit guide the pilot to his or her destination and keep them on track, at the right altitude, and prevent them from turning upside down. Airlines have used instruments for over forty years, but IFR was a relatively new thing in the commercial helicopter world in 1972. So new, in fact, that in Canada helicopter instrument training had to be completed on an airplane first, because there was no official rating for instruments on helicopters. The pilots who wished to fly offshore in a helicopter had to take their airplane (fixed-wing) check ride first, then do an IFR check ride in the giant Sikorsky helicopter. I spent five weeks in Montreal, Quebec, training on an airplane while leaving Barbara to look after our growing family back in Pasadena. While I worked in Montreal, Barbara had a difficult time with our two small children and one on the way, and to say the least, she was not happy. And after my training, we quickly moved to St. John's.

One day, after we had moved in, we were in the back yard with the kids. As we watched the children play, I tried to explain the whole IFR/VFR thing. Barbara listened carefully.

"It's all pretty complicated," I said. "Complicated and worrisome, and compared to the Bell 47 and Bell Jet Ranger, this will be a major leap in technology. To be honest, and less technical, the whole thing scares the crap out of me."

"What are you worried about?" Barbara asked, as we sat together on the back porch of our basement apartment. It was late fall, and we were enjoying a warm afternoon in the backyard. Little David played with a small dump truck in the mud, and Leslie had her Barbie doll on top of a pink blanket right at Barbara's feet. Barbara, now in her second trimester, sat with me while we watched the kids.

"See if I have this right," Barbara said. "You went to Montreal and got your fixed-wing instrument training, we moved here and you got your S-61 training, and now you're about to start flying to oil rigs." Before I could answer, Barbara turned toward little David, who was getting hungry again.

"Cake cup, Mommy," he said. "Cake cup."

"We don't have cupcakes today," she said. "Let's stay outside a while longer and play, then Mommy will make supper. OK?"

David, disappointed with his mother's response, stared at his truck. "Cake cup," he grumbled, ignoring his mother and directing his request to his dump truck. "Cake cup."

Barbara and I giggled, and it was wonderful to see her smile.

I leaned closer to Barbara and said, "I guess I'm worried about instrument flying in general. Bush flying wasn't as complicated, and sometimes I flew with no passengers. In this aircraft we could be hauling seventy or eighty people a day, and I'm younger than most of the pilots. Some of them have flown IFR for years."

Barbara acted like she wanted to stand, so I helped her up and held her a moment while she got her balance. She turned to me and her beautiful smile faded, quickly replaced by a scowl. In a cold, hateful tone she said, "We left Texas and came to Newfoundland because you wanted to. We moved to Prince Edward Island for the same reason. Then, back to Newfoundland, settled in at Pasadena where we had a nice little house and made a life for ourselves. I guess that wasn't good enough, so we moved here. We now live in a basement apartment again where we hear people walking on top of us all day. Oh, and then you went off to Montreal for five weeks, leaving me alone with the kids and the house while you lived in a motel room and got your meals in a restaurant. So, tell me again, why have we done all this?"

I started to answer, and Barbara cut me off. "Because of you and your damn helicopters, that's why. I'm sick and tired of helicopters."

I stood quietly for a moment. Then, thinking Barbara was finished, I stepped toward her to try and calm her down. But I was wrong, she still wasn't finished.

"I have three things to say to you: I don't ever want to move again, that's number one. And number two, I don't want to hear you whine about being worried you might not be good at flying this aircraft or that aircraft, or V … FR or I … FR, or any other damn FR!"

I remained silent as my very pregnant and very upset wife turned and stomped away. Little David ran over a rock with his dump truck, and our daughter Leslie, who had listened carefully to our conversation, looked at her brother and whispered, "Daddy's in trouble again."

Chapter Twenty-Nine

The airport at St. John's, Newfoundland, has a rich aviation history, but now it had a new and exciting chapter to write, as the large, powerful Sikorsky helicopters became part of the thrilling pioneering days of offshore petroleum in Newfoundland.

Steeped in its early contributions to WWII and built near the coastal community of Torbay in 1941, the St. John's International Airport services Newfoundland's largest city and capital. It was first used to support the war efforts of the RCAF (Royal Canadian Air Force), RAF (Royal Air Force) and the United States Army Air Corps. And in 1972 a few aircraft hangars and other structures left over from the war were still in operation. But it had developed into a busy commercial airline destination with excellent weather and navigation facilities, including a Category 2 (Cat II) IFR approach system.

Standing in one of the massive hangars, once used to house B-17 Flying Fortresses and B-24 Liberators, I looked up at the giant Sikorsky S-61 helicopter. It was an amazing sight at 18 feet tall and 60 feet long. Configured to hold up to 21 passengers in a comfortable cabin six feet high, you could almost store my old Jet Ranger inside. Fully loaded, the Sikorsky weighed slightly over 19,000 pounds and was purpose-built for offshore work.

Familiar to Americans, because of the special military version painted dark green with a classic white roof, which flew the president of the United States. And who could forget the naval version, called the Sea King, seen often on TV as it recovered astronauts during the exciting missions of the Apollo Program. In Canada, the Sea King was widely used by the Canadian Armed Forces, the Royal Canadian Navy, and the Royal Canadian Air Force.

In commercial aviation, there are two versions of the aircraft: S-61L (L for land) used for overland projects, and the S-61N (amphibious) used for over-water flights. The bottom of the *N* model's fuselage is made like a ship's hull and has two large Sponson stabilization floats, enabling the aircraft to land in the water in an emergency.

The S-61 is a twin-engine, two-pilot aircraft, and the pilot's seats are well built, comfortable, and totally adjustable—a feature practically unheard of in smaller helicopters. Often called a pilot's helicopter, the S-61 has a large, spacious cockpit with weather radar, AFCS (autopilot), and an incredible cluster of instruments and gauges which were quite intimidating to a young pilot fresh off a bush flying assignment. I loved the aircraft, and even though my flight training was a challenge, I felt relieved that it was finally over.

The chief pilot of Okanagan Helicopters was an older man named Don Jacques. A tall thin Canadian, Don was all business. He wore his hair short in a flattop style, and ate and slept helicopters. Well known for being a company man to the point of washing his clothes in a sink when staying in a hotel to avoid excess expenses. He was old school all the way, expecting his pilots to memorize aircraft systems and become experts on emergency procedures.

Don seemed skeptical of a Vietnam vet flying this larger, more sophisticated helicopter and warned me during our training that I needed to transition to a more professional way of thinking. He also let me know I would never become a captain until I convinced him I could handle it. At that moment, I was proud to get the training over with so I could start flying the line and get into some semblance of a normal work routine.

On the day of my endorsement, I walked through the long hangar, then into the office where Don Jacques was waiting, along with an older Canadian pilot named Roy Webster. A twenty-year employee of Okanagan, Roy was getting his rating at the same time. Roy was a short, husky-built guy, jovial and spirited, taking nothing seriously and preferring a good laugh over a solid conversation. But Roy had a reputation as an excellent helicopter pilot, having flown for years in the Canadian Arctic and throughout Western Canada. His transition into instrument flying wasn't much of a challenge to him because he had flown the C-47 during his military days in the RAF. Since we had finished our training, Don Jacques was about to give us the written endorsement on the S-61.

Don was standing in the office when I walked in. Not much for small talk, Don said, "Dave, give me your pilot's license and radio permit."

With a sense of accomplishment, I removed my Canadian Commercial Pilot License and Radio License from my wallet and handed them to Don. In those days, the chief pilot wrote out the endorsement and signed your license, a practice later discontinued. Don held my documents and stood there for a moment, looking closely at them. I did not like the look on his face. I glanced at Roy, who had a naughty twinkle in his eyes. Something was wrong.

"Dave," Don said, with an icy stare that would freeze the bravest pilot. "Did you take a pair of scissors to your pilot's license?"

I thought for a second. "Yes, sir," I said. "I had to trim the edge a tiny bit to be able to keep it in my wallet. Aren't we supposed to carry it on us at all times?"

Don shook his head, and I felt the shame. He wasn't joking. "Son," he said. "That's like taking scissors and cutting pages of the Bible." I glanced at Roy, who had a slight grin, enjoying my embarrassment.

For once in my life, I was at a loss for words. What could I say to the man who many in Canada considered the "father of helicopters"? Don Jacques had flown almost every type of helicopter throughout all of Canada and most of the United States, and had been sent to Russia by the Canadian government to evaluate Russian helicopters for commercial use. He was a legend, and I was a young American pilot with barely enough experience to be considered for this job.

"Yes, sir, I understand," I said respectfully. "I will never do it again."

Don endorsed my somewhat shorter, disfigured license, and handed it back to me. I thanked him and quietly walked out of the office and into the hangar, where several engineers were working on the S-61. I felt a mixture of pride and humility as I stood there looking at the huge aircraft. It felt like going from a small sailboat to an aircraft carrier, but I was ready. I might be the youngest pilot on the S-61, but I was going to show Don Jacques that I could do this. I was going to show him that he would *never* regret endorsing me.

***

During the winter of 1972–1973, the drilling off Newfoundland went into high gear, and our company had two aircraft and a large group of pilots and engineers to cover the increased workload. Each pilot flew between four and eight hours a day but was able to get a few days off each week. This was something I had never experienced during my bush flying days.

Now I could spend more time with my family, and Barbara seemed more relaxed since I was home on a regular basis. There were a few nights when I came home late due to a night crew-change flight, but overall, it was a normal lifestyle.

Because I had taken Jack Murphy's advice, another opportunity opened for me in St. John's—music. A few years back, I started carrying my guitar in the back of the helicopter and learned to play. In St. John's I auditioned for a CBC Radio program, and it led to a chance to sing on the air. I didn't play the guitar that first time but chose instead to sing with a piano accompaniment provided by the studio. After a few radio programs, one of the CBC folks suggested I try out for a well-known Newfoundland television show, televised coast to coast in Canada, called *All around the Circle*. I contacted the host of the show, Doug Laite, who let me audition, then gave me a solo spot on a program. During the next few months I was singing on the radio and television regularly and did an occasional bar gig. All this was going on about the time Barbara was close to having our third child. She wasn't sure about the whole music scene, but she faithfully encouraged me to keep trying. Looking back, I don't know if I could have been as generous if the tables were turned. But I kept at it, and soon our passengers, the tough, energetic rig workers, recognized me from TV and enjoyed cracking jokes as they boarded the helicopter, or if they saw me grabbing a meal on the offshore rig.

But the weather was no joke. The horrible, disagreeable, offshore Newfoundland weather. We encountered numerous snowstorms, sleet, rain, and endless amounts of fog. As a copilot, I had to learn the necessary skills of offshore flying, and my teachers were some of the best pilots in the business. Pioneers of long-distance, offshore aviation in North Atlantic conditions. Energetic pilots like Doug Hogan and Dave Whyte, experienced, self-driven aviators that expected a lot out of a copilot and forced you to think through difficult situations. Some were more laid-back in their personality, like Al Winter and Mike McDonagh, but they all had one thing in common:

they insisted on professional standards and strict use of company procedures.

Since our flights were between 150 and 200 miles offshore, the weather forecast offshore was seldom accurate. As we flew further away from land, it could be sunny one moment and fifteen minutes later low or no visibility due to dense fog or blowing snow. There were times when we picked up ice on the blades and fuselage so thick and heavy that after we landed, the ice fell off in chunks.

In between those flights, I often spent time talking with the engineers who worked on the Sikorsky, and they were a huge help in teaching me more about the various aircraft systems and functions. But not all the engineers were experienced, since a few were new to the job, just like me.

One of the young engineers was a hardworking guy that could be a bit distracted at times. His name was Jim Johnson. Jim was a sharp, energetic helicopter engineer, but always seemed to be watching the pilots and listening to us talk about the weather or how the aircraft handled.

One evening Jim stood on a ten-foot rolling ladder outside the parked helicopter, cleaning the windows as I sat in the cockpit. With me in the cockpit was James Jones, the captain and base manager, who everyone called J.C. Jim listened carefully as J.C. and I discussed the weather. We were about to do a night crew-change flight and were worried about the possibility of icing.

Jim leaned into the window and said, "I'm going to fly this helicopter one day." J.C. glanced at him, but said nothing, and Jim continued cleaning the outside window on my side of the aircraft. Our helicopter was parked near the hangar in St. John's, fueled and ready to go. The passengers, dressed in orange flotation suits and lifejackets, walked from the hangar toward the helicopter. I sat in the right-hand pilot's seat and J.C. sat in the left seat. Like the

passengers, we wore our immersion suits and life jackets.
Jim Johnson continued to clean the windows while
watching us carefully. Once again, he stuck his head in. "I
will," he said.

"OK, Jim," I said, rolling my eyes.

"Watch me," he persisted. "I'm gonna get my
pilot's license and work my way up to be a S-61 driver."

I pointed to the window in front of me and said,
"You missed a spot." Jim frowned, but rubbed the window
again, grumbling as he worked.

"Hey, Jim," J.C. giggled. "Don't worry, you can't
be any worse than Eagleston here." But the young
mechanic didn't catch on that J.C. was taking his side. The
moody engineer climbed back down the ladder and rolled it
away from the helicopter. A moment later we got the signal
that all the passengers were loaded. When the area was
clear, we started the engines and taxied out for takeoff. Jim
stood near the hangar watching us as we headed out for
another four-hour flight across the stormy Atlantic Ocean.

***

After taking off, J.C. and I went through the post-takeoff
checklist and I made my radio calls. The busy part was
over, so I sat back. After several months of flying as copilot, I would be taking my captain's check ride in another
month or two. Most likely, J.C. would let me fly most of
the time on this flight. But it was not going to be an easy
night since blowing snow, fog, and occasional freezing rain
were forecast.

The distance from the airport to the rig was 186
miles across open Atlantic Ocean water, and we were using
a Decca Navigation System with a rolling map. We also
had the NDB (radio beacon) as one of our navigation aids.
These were far from accurate, and with all the changes in
our course due to strong winds, it was impossible to fly in a

straight line, so we made certain we carried as much fuel as possible.

One hour into the flight, J.C. turned the flight controls over to me. However, before doing so, he briefed me on the routine.

"Tonight, I'll turn the control over to you. For all practical purposes, you will be the captain. I want you to make all decisions, and I want you to tell me what you're doing and give me my instructions as if I am the copilot. This is your flight."

"Roger that," I said.

"You have control." he said, as I gently put my feet on the pedals and both hands on the flight controls.

The sky was as dark as a tomb, and I flew along depending solely on our instruments. There was a warm glow from the cockpit lights which lit J.C.'s silhouette. He had his small flashlight out, leaning forward, peering through the front window at the metal base of the windshield wipers. He was searching for any trace of freezing rain or an ice buildup. Normally, rime ice can be detected on metal surfaces like the outside air temperature gauge, or the edge of a window, or the base of the wiper assembly. It was crucial that we see it early.

Heavy snow obscured our forward visibility, but the aircraft cabin heater worked well, keeping us comfortable. Most of the passengers were sleeping, and had it not been for the possibility of ice, it would have been an enjoyable evening. Some nights we flew in clear weather with a full moon. And on those tranquil flights, the moon's brilliant reflection on the ocean's waves created a splendid, serene image.

But not tonight.

The aircraft was as smooth as silk, and the controls felt wonderful in my hands. The Sikorsky is easy to control due to its three-axis stabilization. A far cry from the less complicated, but far less stable Jet Ranger that requires both hands and both feet to stay on course. Our only concern was ice. Rime ice or freezing rain can form on the fuselage and weigh the aircraft down. And since the helicopter's main rotor blades were not heated, ice accumulation on the leading edge could render them useless, causing the blades to lose lift and the helicopter to fall out of the sky.

During the past four months too many flights came with dangerous threats of blade icing, and I wanted to avoid it altogether. Fortunately, J.C. found no ice at that moment. But after fifteen minutes I noticed the outside air temperature increasing.

"J.C., look at the OAT," I said.

"Oh, shit!" he said, grabbing his flashlight. "You know what to do."

"I'll keep my speed up and hold my altitude. You look for ice."

As J.C. grabbed his flashlight, I scanned the instrument panel, watching for signs of power changes. Within seconds, I knew we were into the bad stuff. There are two rows of engine instruments on the large panel in the S-61; they display the engine power parameters. There are several flight instruments like the artificial horizon and vertical speed indicator which give you the navigation and horizontal positioning of the aircraft. As I watched these instruments, I saw something that made my skin crawl.

In a split second, the airspeed dropped from 115 knots to only 80 knots, while the engine torque spun upward to 100%. We were falling out of the sky, and it was all because we had hit the dreaded icing conditions. We couldn't see it, but we knew the surface on the main rotor blades, as well as the outside of the helicopter, was beginning to ice over, becoming less aerodynamic. There was no time to discuss the situation. I had to act fast or crash into the water one hundred miles from the oil rig.

Sometimes in this situation it would be expedient to gain altitude and fly above the clouds, thereby eliminating the moisture and the icing. And sometimes (in an inversion) climbing to a higher altitude can put you into warmer air, thus eliminating the threat of ice. However, since we were over eighty miles from St. John's, in a snowstorm with no accurate weather reporting station, we didn't know the conditions above us and couldn't take the chance of climbing higher only to discover the same or even worse conditions.

"Call St. John's," I said. "Give them our position, the time, and let them know we have encountered icing conditions."

J.C. did exactly as I said, and as he made his first radio call, I quickly lowered the collective, turned on the searchlight, and put the helicopter into a dive. We were headed straight for the frigid waters of the Atlantic Ocean, but we could only see the thick white, blowing snow in front of us.

Diving toward the water at over 130 knots, I felt the aircraft strain from the g-forces. I expected right then that J.C. would take the controls, but he didn't. All of a sudden, I heard one of the passengers yell behind me in the cabin, most likely awakened to the frightening flight conditions. I'm sure they were scared out of their wits, thinking we were crashing into the water. But that didn't matter. I had to regain control of the helicopter and there was only one way to do it. As I watched the precious flight instruments, I waited until we were 100 feet off the water before I started to level out.

A few seconds later, with our searchlight showing the first signs of the furious whitecaps below us, I leveled off the aircraft, nudging closer to the water, slowing our speed to 90 knots . . . 80 knots. I let the helicopter slip down to 50 feet—a mere 30 feet above the violent surface of the Atlantic Ocean.

Now I watched anxiously as the stiff wind blew the saltwater spray up from the mighty ocean waves, and over the helicopter across the frozen rotor blades. As I held the cyclic and collective controls, I felt a rousing vibration as the saltwater tore off strips of ice and the blades returned to their normal smooth surface. We were now close enough to the churning waves to see bits of sea spray as it blew onto the windshield.

The yells from the cabin subsided as I increased our speed to 120 knots while remaining 40 to 50 feet off the water. The sudden dive had frightened our passengers, but it had worked. Now we were back at normal power settings and J.C. could see no sign of ice on the outside of the cockpit.

"If you had waited thirty more seconds," J.C. said. "We would have lost all lift from those blades, and your wife would be collecting your life insurance check."

"Roger that," I said. "I'm kind of surprised, though."

"About what?" J.C. asked.

"You didn't take the controls back."

"I was ready to, but you did fine. Like I told you during my briefing, when I turn the aircraft over to you, continue on as if you're the captain, and you give me my instructions as things happen. If I need to take back control, I'll tell you."

"Thanks," I said.

We flew on into the night and stayed low over the churning ocean, occasionally seeing the ominous black fins of sharks cutting through the water. Mile after mile the foamy waves passed below us as I watched our instruments, and truly appreciated my instrument training. As the never-ending waves churned and ripped, churned and ripped, I listened to the beautiful drone of the two General Electric engines. That sound, that safe, secure sound, was heavenly music to my ears.

An hour later we were ten miles from the oil rig, and J.C. called our distance as he watched the rig on our weather radar. The radar was able to show the rig clearly as well as any icebergs that were nearby. On a few occasions, pilots had reported icebergs sighted in clear, calm weather that didn't show up on radar. It seems they don't always show up on radar if they are dry and the sea is calm. But that night, there were no icebergs. As we got closer and closer to the rig, J.C. called out the distance and other important information according to our company IFR offshore approach procedures.

"Five miles, five hundred feet, airspeed 100 knots." I maintained altitude, heading and airspeed throughout the approach. J.C., performing the duties of a copilot, confirmed all necessary information in his highly professional radio procedures. As we passed over the rig, J.C. called in our position to our base in St. John's and I started our figure-8 IFR approach. Five minutes later, through a series of turns and step-down altitude drops we were now a half mile from the rig, closing in at sixty knots two hundred feet above the water. The sky was black except for the blowing snow slamming against the window. "Half mile, two hundred feet," J.C. said as he made his final call looking into the radar. Now he was looking forward, with me, watching for the first signs of the rig.

Suddenly, the night turned from jet-black with blowing snow to extremely bright as the oil rig's massive 100-foot derrick, fully lit with hundreds of brilliant, beautiful lights welcomed us and signaled our safe arrival.

"Give me the gear," I said, completing our prelanding checklist as J.C. touched the lever and the landing gear extended. I brought the airspeed back, slowing our approach speed to fifty, forty, twenty, then ten knots, then slowly crossed the threshold of the rig, across the large rope net, and hovered twenty feet above the deck briefly and sat the aircraft onto the helideck firmly.

With the engine running, the aircraft safely on the deck, the passengers were escorted off the aircraft by the rig's helideck crew. J.C. and I watched from the cockpit while the passengers were led away, and the helideck crew refueled our helicopter. Someone handed us a cardboard box with two hot meals, to be eaten on the return flight.

When the aircraft was refueled, J.C. got out and checked to make sure the aircraft fuel cap and door was secured. Soon the outgoing passengers boarded, and we were ready to take off and fly back to St. John's.

Nighttime offshore landings are tense, but the takeoffs are far worse. I hovered over the helideck, and the incredibly bright, blinding light from the derrick lit up everything around it. J.C. called out our takeoff checklist, and I pulled the collective and pressed forward on the cyclic control steadily. Holding a fixed heading of 180 degrees, the aircraft slowly crossed the outer edge of the helideck, then over the water.

"Gear," I said. "Gear up," J.C. replied as he touched the lever, raising the landing gear.

"I'm on the gauges," J.C. said, as he watched the instrument panel carefully and called out our progress.

"I'm on the gauges now," I said, watching our takeoff and making sure I didn't let the bright light create a dangerous situation.

J.C. clearly stated each important step of our takeoff progress. "Heading one eight zero, twenty knots, thirty knots. Two hundred feet. Three hundred feet per minute, four hundred feet per minute."

And then, as dramatic as the blazing rig lights had been, we were instantly plunged into total, immense darkness, even more shocking to your sense of balance and orientation than the brilliant light. It is in this critical point of a night takeoff from an offshore platform that some pilots feel such an alarming change to their senses that they inadvertently turn back toward the rig, toward the comforting, alluring light source, and crash. For that reason, our crew call-out and response procedure was followed to the letter. One pilot controls the aircraft and the other pilot confirms the flight progress and major steps of the takeoff until the aircraft reaches the assigned altitude, heading, and airspeed.

Now with brilliant lights of the rig behind us, the horizon changed to the blackest of black and I felt the familiar incredible tension rise in me as I suffered a flashback from Vietnam.

Flying a Huey gunship over the jungle at night, the sky was a smoke-filled pale yellow as a mortar-launched flare illuminated my flight path. Enemy gunfire streaked across the night sky as tracers came dangerously close. Without warning, the pyrotechnic composition of the flare burned out, and in an instant the sky went pitch-black, except for the increased volume of orange AK-47 tracers now closer and seemingly larger. I held the controls tighter as sweat ran down my forearms onto my hands. Gunfire grew louder as I tried to keep the helicopter level in the blackest of black.

Louder now, J.C. called out, "Three hundred feet, sixty knots, heading one eight zero, now eighty knots,"

Deep in thought now, trying to forget Vietnam, I didn't respond. J.C., grew agitated, "Four hundred feet. Respond, Dave."

"Roger," I said. "Four hundred feet." I was back, and quickly put Vietnam out of my head. "I'm still on the gauges," I said. Because of the complete darkness and no horizon, I continued looking inside the aircraft at the instrument panel, 100% IFR.

J.C., glancing at me from time to time, continued his call-out, "Five hundred feet, six hundred feet, ninety knots, one thousand feet, level, level, one hundred and ten knots."

"I'm level at one thousand feet," I repeated, "and I'll switch to stabilization."

Our passengers, after spending two weeks offshore, were relaxing and would soon be sleeping in their comfortable high-back passenger seats. They were ready to go home to their families and were confident we could get them there safely.

J.C. made his radio call giving our time off the rig and our ETA to St. John's, as well as the other standard information. We were now flying into the wind toward St. John's, and it would be another two hours and twenty minutes before we made our IFR approach to the airport. Reaching across the cockpit, J.C. picked up the cardboard box with our meals inside. As he removed a large sandwich wrapped in aluminum foil, the amazing savory aroma of steak filled the cockpit.

With the torque and power at cruise settings, cockpit instruments and gauges steady, the aircraft flew quietly across the Atlantic toward the island of Newfoundland. We took turns eating our delicious sandwiches and watched carefully for any signs of changing weather or ice.

J.C. never asked why I was slow to answer as we came off the rig. Perhaps he knew. After all, he too was a Vietnam vet, and like me, suffered a few lingering reminders of the war.

Now the aircraft's radio was quiet, except for our fifteen-minute position checks, and the outside temperature held steady. On a nicer evening we would be able to see the water below us, but not tonight. Only snow.

After we ate, we would talk all the way to St. John's. Not because we wanted to, but to ensure neither of us went to sleep. Talk about our families, perhaps the aircraft, or even talk about Jim Johnson's dream of becoming a helicopter pilot.

That night we were to talk about many things as we flew westward searching for the distant, reassuring lights of St. John's. But, for some obscure, unspoken reason, we never spoke about blade icing, and we never mentioned Vietnam.

Chapter Thirty

In the crowded break room of a sheet metal shop in North Tulsa, Marve and one of his coworkers sat talking while they ate their brown-bag lunch. Pat had been one of the first people to welcome Marve to the company and stood by him while he learned the ropes. Short, but dignified in his well-worn, green cotton work slacks and matching long-sleeve shirt, Pat had a gentle tone and a way about him that invited respect.

The two, unlikely chums, had slowly formed a relationship as they swapped stories and quips about married life and an ungrateful boss. But lately they had begun to talk more openly about their lives, and Marve opened up about his past. Now for the second time Pat brought up the subject of his church and what an important role it played in his life. For once Marve listened.

At first, he had indulged Pat out of courtesy, not sure how to reply to some of the questions Pat asked him. A few times he wanted to change the subject, but began to be drawn in. Pat could see the gradual transition in Marve's eyes. He could tell the day he started listening out of interest. What he saw in this young man's face was hope.

As usual, Pat, always meticulous, laid out his lunch in a neat arrangement: sandwich cut in half, wrapped in wax paper on the right. Six neatly stacked Ritz crackers to the left of the sandwich. One winecrisp apple, which would soon be cut in six pieces, above the crackers. And finally, a light-green bottle of Coke, right in the middle. Glancing at his friend's lunch, arranged with the precision of a surgeon's operating instruments, Marve grinned. Pat lowered his voice and continued their conversation.

"Marve," he said. "your past is something you have to let God have. He died helping someone who had a life tougher than yours. Seems to me you're in a place in your life where you can truly let God help you."

"I know," Marve said. "I'm thinking about what you've told me. I appreciate it, really."

Again, Pat spoke quietly, but directly, now with more emotion than before. "I heard a man say something that you should know. It went something like this, 'The link between your soul and Christ isn't your goodness but your badness. It isn't your wealth but your need.' That man was talking to you, Marve." [4]

A moment passed while both men ate their homemade sandwiches and Marve considered Pat's words. Marve attended church services in several prisons and even got baptized in one of them, but still didn't feel he had lived his life in the right way to be a Christian. Without looking up, Marve whispered, "Tell me that last part again."

Pat took a sip of his Coke and gently placed the bottle on the wooden table. "A man once said, 'The link between your soul and Christ isn't your goodness but your badness. It isn't your wealth but your need.' That means God uses your down times and your regrets to build a link between Him and you. He uses your wounds and weakness."

"I like the sound of that, Pat," Marve said, cleaning up the scraps of paper and clutter on his table. Then standing to go, he said, "Let me think about it. I'll talk to Brenda and maybe I'll bring my family to visit your church one day soon."

Pat smiled and finished his last Ritz cracker. It was on his heart to help this young man, and he was going to keep at it. But for now, he knew he had said enough. Marve was coming around. It would take more time, but in his mind, he could see Marve and his family sitting in church in the not-too-distant future.

Pat glanced at the large clock on the break-room wall. Time to get back to work. He picked up the remnants of his lunch, tossed the trash in the wastebasket, then followed his tall friend out the door and into the shop. As they turned the corner, Marve glanced back at Pat for an instant, ready to say something, but before he spoke, he collided smack-dab into their boss. Brian, the loud, domineering manager fell backward onto the floor like a linebacker who got hit by surprise. Marve stifled a grin as he bent down to help the enraged supervisor. Brian waved him off, preferring to get up on his own, his face flushed with anger and obviously shaken by the spill.

"You could break a man's leg hurrying like that," Brian said, now furious. "If you stopped eating on time, you wouldn't have to run back to work." Marve, trying to think of the right thing to say, hesitated for a moment. Pat stepped forward and said, "Brian, it was my fault. I asked Marve a question and he turned to answer me. He left the lunchroom the same time that I did. We weren't late."

Brian bent over and brushed off his slacks. He looked at Pat, a scowl across his sullen face. "Get back to work, Pat. I'll let you know if I need your help." Brian leaned against the wall as Pat walked past him, leaving the two men alone. "Are you OK, sir," Marve said. Brian looked up at him with a coldhearted stare.

"I'm watching you," Brian said, waving his finger in Marve's face. "And I'm getting sick of your friend there taking up for you. I'm looking for a way to get rid of both of you, and don't worry, I'll find it. I'll give you plenty of rope, and I know you'll find a way to hang yourself and your asshole buddy over there."

Marve's right hand instinctively went forward to tear at this little weasel of a man. But he caught himself in time and pulled it back without touching Brian. But Brian saw it and smiled. Marve stood quietly as Brian walked away with a Napoleonic arrogance. Marve thought of how his friend Pat had stood up for him. Even if Marve lost his job, he couldn't let that happen to Pat.

As the noise of the machines grew louder and the continuous sounds of steel cutting steel echoed through the shop, Marve walked past his fellow workers toward his foot press. Across the room he watched as Pat worked on his massive Logan lathe. Marve was still upset with Brian, and he knew this would be one of the times in his life he was going to have to eat dirt to keep his job. He stood for a moment, and the noise from the room was somehow drowned out by his deep thoughts. He needed help to get through this. Not muscle; he had plenty of that. But another kind of help. What was it Pat had said? "Not my riches but my need." Right now, he thought, maybe God *is* the answer to my need.

Across the shop, Pat reached into a pile of long round pieces of steel and found one he liked. As he carefully placed it into the chuck, he turned toward Marve and gave a slight, innocent nod, as if to confirm Marve's wholesome thoughts.

For the rest of the afternoon, metal was cut, drilled, flattened, and shaped. Raw pieces were ground, bent, heat-treated and painted. And, like the transformation of metal going on all around him, the look and shape of Marve's brittle hope gradually changed as it was slowly processed, eventually turning something dubious into something meaningful.

***

Not long after I became a captain on the S-61, Mobil Oil moved their eastern drilling operations from St. John's to Halifax, Nova Scotia. The program became seasonal, which meant they drilled offshore part of the year near Nova Scotia and part of the year off the coast of Newfoundland.

Of course, this meant another move for my family, but I was careful not to tell Barbara until we were out for an evening with our friends Dave Whyte and his wife. At first Barbara hated the idea., but after I calmed her down and she agreed to spend a weekend in Halifax (just the two of us) enjoying a nice hotel and looking for a house, she changed her mind. After all the moves and difficult living conditions, she would now enjoy a home she could call her own. With Mobil's support, Okanagan graciously moved crews to Halifax and gave us a generous allowance for moving expenses.

This was the first time we were able to buy a home, and it wasn't as if we had accumulated a large amount of savings. In fact, like everyone else, we lived month to month and had no savings at all. But something unusual was going on in Nova Scotia, something called the "cooperative."

The Nova Scotia Housing Commission had a program which brought ownership of decent homes to low-income families. The program enabled first-time home buyers to build a home in stages, either contracting the work or doing the work themselves, thereby reducing the cost dramatically. We purchased a home that was built in the "co-op" section of Lower Sackville and wasn't quite finished. It needed to have the basement finished out, a yard and patio built behind the house, and a yard installed in the front. We were able to buy the home with an unheard-of 5% down payment, which was a little more than one thousand dollars. We had barely moved in when our third child, Kevin, was born.

Since our flights out of the Halifax Airport were well managed and crew changes were scheduled in advance, my flight schedule allowed me time to work on the house nearly every day. Each morning, weather permitting, we flew one or two flights, and then I drove home to work in the yard or basement.

The flights were shorter in distance and duration than the Newfoundland flights and there were fewer natural hazards to contend with. Our destination was an oil rig called the Sedco J, which was located near Sable Island. Often called the Graveyard of the Atlantic, Sable Island is 26 miles long and less than a mile wide at its widest point. It has a flat, sandy surface and got its nickname "graveyard" because of the three hundred ships which ran aground and wrecked there before the advent of radar. Sable Island is uninhabited except for a small herd of feral horses, whose ancestors, legend has it, survived a shipwreck several hundred years before. Living on their own, these hearty animals eat fescue, poe and marram grass, and have even been known to eat seaweed.

Our client, Mobil Oil, drilled several wells near Sable Island, a few of which were close enough that we often landed on the island, far from the horses while waiting for our next flight from the rig. And during those times when the rig was so near the island, there were rumors that some of the rig divers had swum underwater to a few of the shipwrecks to try and salvage gold from the sunken ships. I never found out if those rumors were true. But I doubt if it actually happened, because I never saw a rig diver who owned a Porsche or wore a Rolex watch.

Nova Scotia, Latin for New Scotland, has a rich history of Scottish settlers, Scottish festivals, and Gaelic music. In the 1970s Alasdair Gillies was a well-known Scottish performer in Eastern Canada, and I had the pleasure of appearing on his TV program weekly as part of a trio of backup singers. The show was called *Ceilidh*. Alasdair was an incredible Scottish entertainer, dazzling the audience with his beautiful voice and his unique ability to tell Scottish stories and tall tales.

One afternoon, after being chosen to be on the new TV show, I sat in the back yard having lunch with Barbara, discussing the show. We sat on our newly constructed patio with David Jr., who was old enough to tag along with me as I worked around the house. Barbara loved our house and, as usual, made new friends with our neighbors. Even though Leslie went to an elementary school less than a block from our house, and our youngest child, Kevin, was sleeping regularly, Barbara had few breaks from the rigors of raising three children.

It was my second week on the TV show, and Barbara finally arranged for one of our neighbors to watch the kids so she could come to the studio. I wouldn't be singing a solo, but Barbara was excited to see it all.

"So you're going to be at the studio around seven tonight?" I asked.

"Of course," Barbara said. "I wouldn't miss it."

"OK, we should be finished with the first rehearsal by seven, and when that happens, they bring in the audience and we videotape the show with the audience. They'll probably put you in the front row like they do all the pretty ladies."

"Sure," she said, unconvinced. "But I hope they don't. I'm there only to watch you. So no tricks. OK?"

Little David listened as he played nearby, "No tricks, Daddy," he said.

"OK," I agreed, smiling. "No tricks."

* * *

On a cold night in November, Marve drove along Harvard on his way home from work. As he passed Shorty's, one of his old hangouts during his single days, he noticed a familiar car parked in front. It was a two-door '55 Chevy Bel Air, gypsy red and white. No one in Tulsa drove a car like that except his old pal Charlie. He hadn't seen Charlie for more than three years, back around the time Marve got shot by a cop.

As he went past the bar, Marve turned in his seat to have another look, but kept driving south, knowing Brenda would have supper ready. She seemed to be easily agitated recently, ever since the day the doctor confirmed that she was pregnant. It was like being married to a different person.

Pat, his mentor at work, had smiled and congratulated Marve on his upcoming fatherhood. He made it sound like becoming a dad was the greatest thing in the world. But to Marve, it was more pressure at a time in his life when he could barely deal with the constant strain from keeping his wife happy or trying to hold down a job. Listening to a baby cry all night wasn't something he looked forward to.

Two blocks south of Shorty's, Marve made a quick decision. He did a blinding U-turn on Harvard, and in doing so, cut in front of four cars, annoying several drivers who honked loudly, and one who gave him the finger. He found a parking spot behind Shorty's, then walked into the dim, smoky bar. Even for a Friday afternoon, the place was busier than he expected. It took him a few minutes to adjust to the dark, crowded atmosphere. Several bikers wearing black vests and gang logos had pushed three tables together and were drinking pitchers of cheap beer. Two or three couples sat at the bar talking and listening to the jukebox. Like him, some of the men wore work clothes, having stopped in on their way home from work.

Marve walked past the long biker table, dodged an older man, bearded and staggering, then saw his friend sitting alone at a corner table. Charlie looked up as Marve approached, his smile wider than the whitewall tires on his Chevy. He had gained weight in the past three years and his hair was thinning, but he had the same broad, mischievous grin. A small collection of empty beer cans adorned his table, along with a pile of discarded peanut shells.

A young waitress walked by Charlie's table, long black hair, pretty face, holding three cans of beer. "Cindy," Charlie said, "bring a tall beer for my short friend, will ya."

"Sure, Charlie," she said, smiling at Marve. When she walked by, Marve caught her flirtatious glance and it felt good. "Sit down, sit down," Charlie said. "How the hell are you?"

"I'm doing all right," Marve said, glancing back at the waitress. "I saw your car parked outside and had to come in and see if you were still alive."

"It's been a long time, man. I heard you got married. Heard you're holding down a job and living the dream."

For the next few minutes Marve caught his friend up on his marriage, his job, his prick of a boss, and the news that he was about to be a father. The noise from the bar would have normally bothered Marve, but it had been so long since he was out on his own, it was invigorating. Before he knew it, he had consumed two large cans of beer. Then he remembered he needed to call Brenda.

"Back in a minute, Charlie," he said. "I've got to call my wife." As he stood up, Charlie smiled, "Oh hell, I wouldn't have you piss off the warden." Marve grinned, knowing Charlie was grinding him a little, but there was some truth to it. He didn't need his wife's permission to have a couple of beers with his old friend.

After he dialed the number, the phone barely rang once when Brenda answered. "Where are you," she said, more hateful than she had intended. Marve hesitated, then said, "I called to let you know I'm OK and I'm having a beer with an old buddy. But now I wish I hadn't called at all."

Brenda, worried and feeling nauseous after smelling food for the past hour, tried to hold back her anger, but couldn't. "I cooked a special supper tonight, and you promised Katy that after supper you were going to fix her bike. Oh, and another thing, did you remember to stop by the store and get those saltine crackers I like?" It was silent for a moment. "Well, did you?" she asked.

Marve took a deep breath and started to answer, but Brenda wasn't quite finished. "Today is payday, isn't it?

You better make sure you don't cash that check, do you hear me?" The minute she finished her sentence, she regretted speaking harshly to him.

Marve slammed down the receiver and cussed at the phone. He stood for a moment, then turned toward his friend. His face was beet red. He felt so pissed off he was ready to take on all the bikers if they said one word to him. When he sat down, Charlie looked at him carefully and summed up the situation. "Trouble in paradise?" he asked.

"Shut up, Charlie," Marve said, taking a long pull on his third beer. Charlie leaned in, and spoke more seriously, "I've got the cure for your problems, buddy. Let's have another drink, and I'll tell you all about it." As the cute waitress walked by, Charlie changed his order.

"Marve, how 'bout we switch it up and have a few shots of scotch?"

"Hell, yes," Marve said. "Bring it on."

Chapter Thirty-One

At 8:00 p.m., Marve's El Camino was parked in front of a stone-front, craftsman-style house. The headlights were off while Marve and Charlie talked quietly. The street was near Tulsa University, in a working-class neighborhood with large oak trees and well-kept yards. In the car, Charlie smoked nervously as he went over the details of a "collection" he needed help with. Marve looked in the rearview mirror to see if anyone was approaching them from behind. Charlie, coughing again, reassured him it would be easy.

"Like I said, Eagle, this guy is one of Bob Neilson's old buddies. He's a tweaker and he owes me some cash on another deal. Shit, he'll let us in, and I'll ask for my money, and if he won't pay, I'll demand some Flake. I know he's selling it. When we see where he keeps it, we'll strong-arm him. That's where you come in."

Marve rolled down his window to escape the noxious blue smoke and stared at a large, thick tree in the yard nearby. Lately he had enjoyed the mature trees around Brenda's house and found himself noticing the different types of trees around Tulsa. His mind wandered as Charlie continued to cough and ramble on. He wished now he hadn't switched to hard liquor. His mind wasn't clear, and he really wanted to get something to eat. He remembered that Brenda had fixed a special dinner. Even though they had quarreled, she would save him a big plate of food. She was nice like that.

"Are you ready, man," Charlie said, tossing his cigarette out the window. "Let's get this thing done."

Marve thought about backing out and started to say something, but Charlie was already out of the car. Reluctantly, Marve joined his nervous pal as they walked up the narrow sidewalk to the house. Charlie heavy-handedly knocked on the door, hard enough to make a person think it might be a cop. He grinned at Marve, and as the door opened resumed his brash, self-assured demeanor.

A few minutes later, Charlie and Marve stood in the living room talking to Charlie's low-end drug dealer. The man was dressed in brown pajamas and an old house coat, red with black stripes. His face was pale, sweat-soaked, and it appeared that he hadn't touched a razor or shaving cream since Easter. Bald except for the tuffs of unruly brown hair along the sides and back of his skull. He was friendly enough, but kept a close eye on Charlie's tall, brutal-looking friend. The guy had always despised tall men, and he found six-feet-four Marve even more disgusting since he had a full head of wavy black hair.

"Shit, Charlie," the dealer said, scratching his nose. "Like I told you, I got no cash right now, man. But come back on Sunday, I should be good." Marve walked closer to the sweaty stranger and the little man pulled back slightly, intimidated by Marve's sheer size. The dealer managed a slight grin and tried to make small talk, "You look familiar. What school did you go to? Rogers or Edison?" Marve leaned back, thoughtful for a moment, then answered colorlessly but truthfully, "Oklahoma State."

Surprise showed in the short man's sweaty face, "You went to OSU?"

"Hell, no. Not Oklahoma State University, Oklahoma State Penitentiary. And hey, let's cut the small talk, I got to get movin' here."

"OK, OK," he said, taking a step backward. "Charlie, how 'bout I give you something to get you by till Sunday? I got some good stuff."

Charlie, now standing in the hallway a few steps behind Marve, shook his head and took a deep breath, "Man, I don't know. I need the damn money, and it's already been a couple of weeks. And now you're about to get Marve pissed off. Buddy, you don't want to do that."

"That's right," Marve confirmed, his face dark, sinister.

"Wait, guys, wait," Gary said. "Stay right here, I'll be right back." Before Charlie could answer, the short drug dealer turned and walked through a swinging door into the kitchen. As he did, Charlie pulled a long knife out of his boot and handed it to Marve. Stunned by the size of the weapon, Marve stood for a moment and whispered, "What's this, man? We don't need this."

"Get in there, man," Charlie said. "Hurry."

In the kitchen, Gary stood in front of the stove with a metal lid in his left hand as he removed a small white bag from a heavy black skillet. The squeak of the kitchen door caused him to turn, and there stood Marve, knife in hand, a menacing stare on his rugged face.

Even more frightened now, he whined, "Here, take it all. Take it all. Just don't cut me." As he handed Marve several tiny white bags, a noise was heard from the front of the house. Two men walked into the house and, seeing Charlie, asked, "Who the hell are you?"

"Let's go, Marve," Charlie yelled. Marve hurried out of the kitchen, stuffing the plastic bags in his jean pockets. The two visitors stood still, surprised to see a huge man scurry out of the kitchen with a bowie knife in his hand. Marve ran past them and out the door with Charlie behind him.

Now in the yard, Marve ran ahead of Charlie and jumped into the El Camino. As he searched his jeans pockets for his keys, Charlie jumped into the passenger seat. Now there was a frantic commotion on the dealer's front porch. Marve found his keys and started the car. He glanced across the yard, and there with a rife in his hands, stood the dealer. At that moment, with a brilliant full moon lighting the yard in alluring golds and yellows, the man didn't appear short at all. He stood surprisingly tall, sculptured, and threatening.

***

Inside the CBC studio in Halifax, I took my place with the other two vocalists, one man and one pretty lady. We were the backup trio. The band warmed up their instruments, and the director called out over the loudspeaker while a couple of sound men checked the microphones.

The Scottish-themed program was called *Ceilidh*, pronounced kay-lee. The famous Alasdair Gillies hosted the show, dressed in a colorful knee-length kilt, pleated in the back, a symbol of traditional dress for men of the Scottish Highlands. Alasdair sang and spoke with a rich Scottish accent and kept the thirty-minute program moving with a boatload of good stories, traditional songs, and quick-time reels and jigs featuring the colorful tartan-clad Ceilidh dancers. Our job as the backup trio was to provide vocal harmony for Alasdair and do our own songs with the band when Alasdair and the dancers were busy performing one of their reels.

We rehearsed the music and audiotaped the songs without the studio audience present. When the director was satisfied the music was "in the can" or complete, the audience was invited in for the videotaping.

That evening the audiotaping went well, and it was a pleasant change from the stress of offshore flying and raising a young family. Silently, I thought it strange but fun to have an Oklahoma boy singing on a Scottish music program. Around seven, while I sat with the other two members of the trio, the director's voice came across the loudspeaker announcing he was good with the audiotapes and we were moving on.

Since we had a fifteen-minute break, I quickly stood and walked out of the brightly lit studio toward the lobby. I passed several members of the audience headed in the opposite direction to take their seats in the studio. They smiled and chatted, almost giddy as if entering another world. I guess I was a bit giddy, too, proud that Barbara would be there for the program.

I searched the lobby for my pretty wife, but failed to spot her. I looked back at the twenty or thirty strangers I had passed, but still, no Barbara. Glancing at my watch, I spun around and walked to the waiting area, empty except for the receptionist. I approached her counter.

"Ma'am," I said, "Have you seen a pretty young lady about 26 years old with blond hair and blue eyes? She's my wife, and she's supposed to be here tonight while we tape the show."

The receptionist casually glanced down at her notepad, then looked up at me with a serious expression. "Are you Dave Eagleston?" she asked.

"Yes, ma'am."

"Your wife called. You need to call her right away. It's important."

***

In the El Camino, Marve saw the determined look on the dealer's puffy face and quickly threw his truck into first gear. Charlie, closer to the shooter, was staring down the barrel of a rifle. He yelled at Marve, "Get the hell out of here."

Twenty feet away, the short man held his rifle to his shoulder, steadied it for a split second, and fired three shots.

As Marve pressed hard on the accelerator, the El Camino screeched onto the street, tires spinning as he sped away from the dealer's front yard. Front porch lights appeared in the peaceful neighborhood as the sound of gunfire and squealing tires alarmed the neighbors. The short, bald drug dealer along with his two visitors ran into the street and watched the El Camino as it turned left on 11th Street and drove out of sight.

Inside the car, Charlie, his head leaning back against the seat, grimaced in pain as he held his right shoulder. Blood oozed between his fingers and ran down his arm, dripping onto the clean black floor mats. "I'm screwed," Charlie said. "Asshole got me good."

"How could he miss?" Marve said weakly. "He was only ten feet away."

Charlie sat up, looked down at the broken glass on his lap, and brushed it off. "Damn, this hurts. I'll kill that son of a bitch."

He looked over at Marve. "You OK, Stud?" It was silent in the dark car for a moment as Charlie squinted, looking for blood or any signs of an injury on his friend. Marve coughed weakly, then wiped blood and broken glass off his face.

"Better get you to Hillcrest," Marve said.

"No, man," Charlie said. "I'll get this fixed. I know a guy. If we go to the hospital, the doctors will call the cops and we'll both get nabbed."

Marve cruised west on 11th, running stop signs and barely missing cars along the way. "Listen to me," he said. "We're headed to Hillcrest for you *and* for me. Your guy isn't going to fix this." He raised his right arm forward, painfully exposing a bloody hole in his brown leather jacket where the .30/30 round had struck him right below the shoulder. When the dealer fired three shots, the first round broke the passenger's window and hit Charlie on the edge of his right shoulder. The second round missed both Charlie and Marve, and shattered the driver's side window. The third round struck the dealer's main target.

The massive .30/30 cartridge, designed to bring down a deer or moose at distances up to two hundred yards, was incredibly destructive at such a short distance. With Marve's right arm forward gripping the steering wheel, the third round entered his right side, fracturing his sixth rib and penetrating his right lung. Marve was now bleeding internally, fighting desperately to stay alert as he turned left toward the hospital, then steered the mangled car under the portico in front of the emergency room.

**

Standing in the lobby of the CBC TV station, I dialed our phone number, feeling upset that Barbara wasn't there to watch the show. Most likely, the babysitter hadn't shown up or some other child-related crisis had taken place. I took a deep breath as the phone rang so I wouldn't come off too upset with my wife. I knew Barbara would try to sort things out at home, which was never easy with three children. But why tonight?

Finally, after five or six rings, Barbara answered.

"Hello," Barbara said, her voice quivering.

"Hi," I said, trying to choose my words carefully. "Did Leslie get hurt?"

"Dave," she said, now starting to cry. "Marve has been shot."

"What?" I asked. "What happened? Is he in the hospital?"

"No," she said through her tears. "He's ... he's dead."

The news hit me like a gunshot. I tried to say something, but couldn't speak. I guess I always knew down deep that my brother's life could end violently, but I was totally unprepared. I stood in the lobby with the phone in my hand and tears running down my face while Barbara, trying not to cry, explained what few details she knew.

After she told me everything, she promised to call and get an airline ticket so I could go to Tulsa the next day. I would be going alone because of the cost involved. When there was nothing else to say, I told her I would be home as soon as possible.

Walking down that hallway toward the studio was one of the hardest things I have ever done. I was in a daze, unsure of where I was or what I was supposed to do. The other two singers watched me as I walked in.

"What's wrong, Dave?" Bill asked.

"My brother," I said. "It's my brother."

Since we had already taped our vocals, I was able to finish the video session, simply mouthing the words. Surprisingly, the music provided a tranquil, soothing atmosphere, allowing me time to think and time to reflect before driving home. Reflect on a brother I loved deeply, but barely knew. A brother who would never know his own child and could only now forget his own childhood.

Music, melodic and spirited, spilled across the studio as the audience clapped their hands in rhythm and the band featured a bright fiddle solo. On both sides of me, my fellow singers smiled toward the camera, then glanced at me again as the camera focused on the silver-haired fiddler.

Being there was an escape from the reality I didn't want to face. I could sing without sounds and think without words. Two more songs, and then I would have to go home and face the truth. I wanted the music to last longer, but I knew it wouldn't. Two more songs. Just two more songs.

Chapter Thirty-Two

On the flight to Tulsa, I felt horribly alone and guilty. Even though I had called Marve several times during the past three years, I was never able to persuade him to come to Canada. He couldn't seem to escape the tether that tied him to a life of crime. Nothing I could say would ever convince him to leave his friends and the life he was so accustomed to. His friends . . . I had heard so much about his friends, and now I was about to meet some of them.

In Tulsa, during the next two days, I made the rounds attempting to learn as much as possible about the shooting. I visited the hospital to collect Marve's personal effects, then talked to the police. Of course, I spent time with my parents to try and ease their pain and to share any information that might help them. But mostly, I told them the basics and not the grim details.

The most interesting visits of all were with Marve's friends. Most of them were either on parole, wanted by the police, or addicted to some form of illicit drug. They all seemed eager to find out if I planned on tracking down his killer. After I assured them that I had no intentions of finding the shooter, they relaxed and spoke openly.

Marve's friends were mostly tough-looking men and women, hardened by years behind bars, and in some cases, years on the street. It wasn't surprising that he had friends who were ex-convicts, prostitutes, and drug dealers. But it was amazing that he had so many. I could tell they were uncomfortable chatting or drinking coffee with me, a clean-cut guy who they thought looked like a cop. But I worked at getting them to trust me. They were loyal, devoted, and saddened to have lost a friend. They seemed uncomfortable about attending his funeral service. I assured them they were welcome and mentioned there would be no police present. I let them know that they knew my brother better than I knew him and I would be disappointed if they didn't show up. Still, down deep I had my doubts.

Of all the visits that week, by far the most unusual and most helpful took place at the Hillcrest Medical Center. I went there to meet Charlie, who was with Marve the night of the shooting.

Dressed in a two-piece suit and wearing my hair short and neat, I walked down the hospital corridor displaying as much military decorum as I could muster. A bored police officer leaning back in his chair guarded Charlie's room.

"I'm here to interview your prisoner," I said. The sleepy cop, thinking I was a plainclothes officer, sat up straight and said, "Go on in, he's probably snoozing in there."

Inside the room there was a heavy, antiseptic smell, mixed with the faint, unpleasant scent of urine. Charlie was stretched out in the hospital bed reading a magazine. Tubes ran into him with various liquid dripping from them and a single handcuff connected his left arm to the bed. He looked at me suspiciously.

"My name is Dave, I'm Marve's brother."

"No shit," he said, now smiling. "You look like him, man. Hell, I thought you were a cop or something."

"No, I came by to find out how you're doing and try to understand what happened."

Charlie relaxed but kept his voice lower so that the cop in the hall wouldn't hear. He slowly explained his version of what had happened. Of course, he left out a few important details, like how he had talked Marve into the collection and why Marve had a bowie knife. And, his watered-down version featured Charlie as a hero since he was able to get Marve into the ER before he died.

I thanked him for his *honesty* and wished him well. At that point I didn't know all the details, but after talking with the police and Charlie and some of Marve's friends, I knew enough. Marve had stepped over the line once too often, and this time there was no going back.

Later that day I met with Marve's ex-wife, Brenda, who seemed more shocked than anyone. She was saddened by the violent death of the man she loved. I didn't know what to say to her, but even though she couldn't stand my father, I wanted her to continue to be part of the family and encouraged her to be at the funeral.

For the next day or so, I spent more time with my parents, my sister, and Marve's friends. In a short time, even though I didn't want to face it, it was time for his funeral.

Of course, like my brother's life, there was nothing normal about his funeral. My sister, Suzie, had made the arrangements for the service, and because of the respect for so many of Marve's friends, she had made sure we would have no police around. Of course, I knew it would be necessary to be around my parents that day, but I planned to avoid talking to my father.

As I turned off Admiral Place and drove through the gate of the funeral home, I was surprised at the group of strange-looking people standing next to their cars and motorcycles. There were bearded, brutish men, gloomy prostitutes, and older ex-cons, bloated and grizzled. A few young girls were delicately frail standing beside high-class hookers and worn-out pimps. Some were high on drugs and some drank beer openly.

They were a strange, disorganized group of weary people. But they had one thing in common; they had come to celebrate the life of my brother. Dressed in their own diverse, nonconforming styles, they stood in little groups. Men mostly wore blue jeans and muscle shirts, leather jackets, and black motorcycle boots. A few wore sports shirts, and more than a few sported colorful tattoos.

The ladies, however, outdid the men when it came to funeral fashion; several wore bell-bottom jeans with rainbow swirled blouses. A few sported sexy halter-neck tops, hot pants with matching headbands. There were sumptuous off-the-shoulder blouses revealing more cleavage than cotton material. Overgenerous tee shirts with no bras, short shorts with no shoes, and high heels with no limits. Long hair was worn in curls, straight, or frizzy. Most hair, long or short, was dyed, and only a few girls wore it natural.

This unusual group of friends and ex-cons ranged in age from late teens to mid-forties. Tough, streetwise, and nervous, they looked out of place in front of the splendid mausoleum, but they had all but abandoned their own comfort zones in order to be there. I was moved by their gesture of friendship.

These were Marve's people, fresh from his underground world, and they had collectively known him his entire adult life. I parked my car and looked closely at them and remembered some of the conversations over the past few days. I only knew the brother I had grown up with, but they knew the man he had become.

It was an unusual gathering; some, I'm sure, were wanted by the police or FBI, and judging by their body language and chatter, I suspected many of them had celebrated with booze or drugs before their arrival. Some sat in their cars, preferring to stay away from the crowd, but at least they showed up. They were at Marve's funeral, and they were paying tribute to him in their own way.

As I walked toward the unique little group of outsiders, I saw them through a different lens. Since I had met with most of them, it allowed me the luxury of seeing them from Marve's perspective instead of my own.

"You guys coming in?" I asked, shaking hands with a few of the rugged men. One man, a tall stocky guy, unshaven and shy, spoke to me. Under different circumstances, he could have easily been one of my Army buddies instead of an ex-con. He glanced at his friends, then back at me.

"We're cool right here," he said with no visible emotion.

"You're all welcome to come in," I offered.

"Thanks," he said, with a friendly tone.

"Well," I said, shaking his hand with a firm grip. "Thanks for being here; it really means so much that you came." I looked around at Marve's friends, as bizarre a group as I had ever seen, and I felt strangely comfortable in their presence. The group came closer, and a few men got out of their cars and joined the others. It was time for me to thank them.

"You all knew Marve better than I did," I said. "Marve and I weren't that close these last few years, and I'm sure you know that. Even though we were brothers, we seemed to have crawled out on separate branches of the family tree. Who knows why things work out the way they do. It could have been me spending time in prison instead of Marve. But, somehow I got some good breaks and he didn't. I don't know all the answers, I really don't."

It was quiet for moment. Nearby, someone on a Harley, arriving late, parked his noisy motorcycle and shut off the engine.

I grinned slightly, then continued. "I could tell you all some good stories about my big brother when we were kids. Sometimes he took up for me in neighborhood fights, and sometimes when we argued he would kick my ass."

One older man said, "And mine too." Several people grinned; a few laughed out loud. Then it was quiet again as the group listened attentively, thoughtfully, each I guess, reflecting on the man they knew. I looked down at the ground and thought for a moment. "I loved him very much," I said. "And I'll miss him forever. And I'll tell you something else. Though we lived our lives in different ways, I couldn't have loved him any more if he'd been a doctor or preacher or even an astronaut." I paused, and after a few seconds said, "Instead of an ornery ole bandit."

Several of the men chuckled, and some of the ladies had tears in their eyes. I looked over at the mausoleum and knew I needed to go inside to be with my parents and Marv's widow. When I looked back at the strange but affable group of Marve's people, I could hardly hold back my tears.

"Don't forget him," I said.

I walked into the chapel, and the service was about to begin. Inside, canned music played softly, and a shiny, pearl-gray casket held the remains of a life too short and too out of control to ever catch up with its full potential. It held what was left of a man after reality caught up with iniquity.

Later, after the service was finished and the family and friends had all gone home, I parked in the northeast section of the cemetery and walked across the grass toward Marve's grave. The sun slipped behind the trees on the western border of the cemetery and shade crept closer to the fresh pile of black soil marking the cemetery's newest resident. I stood alone, thinking of the finality of death, and recalled the words the preacher had read earlier:

"And all the rivers of all the years shall not carry away our remembrance of him." [5]

Tears fell onto my starched shirt as I took a closer look at the peaceful surroundings near Marve's section of the cemetery. For some strange reason, perhaps an oversight by the cemetery management, Marve was laid to rest in the part of the cemetery reserved for children.

The gravestones around him announced the short life span of the babies and toddlers who were now his neighbors. It was peaceful there. Looking around, I noticed something else—the nearby creek. I smiled as I realized that Marve's final resting place was in the section of the cemetery that he and I used to sneak into twenty years before. In those days this was an empty, unused area with no graves or markers of any kind.

I traveled along in my thoughts and recalled visiting Marve back in the Texarkana Prison. He had grinned and talked about the days when we came here to escape the constant uproar at home. It made him happy to recall coming out of the creek bed and into this peaceful section surrounded by tall cottonwood trees, fallen leaves, and green grass. A special place he called "a private heaven." Now, many years later, he'd finally made it back.

With sweet, but painful feelings, I looked down at the mound of fresh dirt above Marve's grave and the lovely flowers Mom and Suzie had placed there. Now my brother would never have to worry about parole or sentencing or holding down a job. He would never again be bothered by the police looking for him or concerned about our father not loving him. All of that was over now. He was near the creek he loved, surrounded by grass, trees, and little children. I smiled, thinking of the pleasant surprises life can bring us, even at a worrisome time like this.

In the distance a bird called out to one of its kind, and thick tree limbs creaked as they swayed in the evening breeze. From a neighborhood nearby came the faint sounds of children playing, reminding me of another time when Marve and I were young and innocent.

The wholesome smell of cold, loose dirt and fresh cut flowers hung in the air as leaves blew across the raised oblong shape in the earth. I turned and walked to my car, leaving him there. But he was not alone. No, not alone.

In death as in life, Marve will always be surrounded by interesting people.

***

One afternoon, several months after my brother's funeral, I worked in the backyard of our home in Nova Scotia. As usual, little David, our four-year-old son, worked with me in the backyard. A chubby-faced, blond-headed boy, David was as rough-and-tumble a little guy as you would ever meet. If he fell and cut his leg or hand on a rock or concrete like boys often do, he wouldn't cry or carry on. That was good, because it happened a lot. I enjoyed having him around as my helper, and I gave him a little children's wheelbarrow so he could pretend to move rocks or dirt.

That day we were working on a new fence in the backyard when little David saw a car pull into our driveway. He hurried to find out who was visiting us, then ran back to give me the news. "Man, Daddy," he said, pointing toward the driveway. "Man is here."

"That's good, son," I said. "Let's find out who it is."

In a moment, a man walked into the yard. He wore a brown leather jacket, and his hair was brown with a trace of gray, neatly cut. He stood beside the house for a long moment and scanned the backyard, taking it all in. "Jack Murphy!" I said. "You sure know how to surprise a guy."

"No more than you," he said, giggling. "Lord Jesus, is this the boy that was born in Gander?"

"Yes, sir," I said. "And I got another one in there with Barbara. She's gonna be happy to see you."

I took off my work gloves and shook hands with the man who had given me a chance to be a bush pilot four years ago. An opportunity to start a new life. That day he couldn't hide the fact that he was worried, and he may have spent a few sleepless nights concerned about his decision. But he gave me the chance that I begged him for.

Jack still had that strong, handsome grin and his endearing Newfoundland accent. I was thrilled to see him. "You haven't changed a bit, Jack."

Barbara must have heard us talking. She came out and gave Jack a hug, then made it clear he would be staying for dinner whether he had planned to or not. Immediately she went back in and started cooking. Little David loaded dirt in his wheelbarrow while Jack and I sat and talked about Jet Rangers, wildlife officers, and few people who had asked about me on the island. We had talked for over an hour when Barbara stuck her head out the back door to announce that supper was ready.

Walking toward the house, Jack said, "Saw you on that Scottish TV show the other night."

"Good," I said.

"What's the name of that show?"

"Don't ask me to pronounce it, Jack. I'm just a helicopter pilot." We both laughed, and I held the back door open as Jack stopped for a moment and turned toward me. He smiled and gave me a pat on the back.

"That you are, son, that you are."

The End

Author's Notes

People:

Jack Murphy: After retirement, the man who had been like a father to me continued to manage aviation operations and guide pilots, both young and old, through their stormy careers. Jack raised a wonderful family and continued to fly privately until his death in 2007. I still have the blue logbook Jack gave me in 1970. In it are records of aircraft, flight times, locations, and details of my years of flying. You will also find autographs of famous passengers, two of which were Pierre and Margaret Trudeau.

Paul Williams: My unsophisticated pal and Jet Ranger mechanic, Paul Williams, became president and co-owner of Universal Helicopters Newfoundland. Paul died of cancer when he was in his fifties. He was a father, successful businessman, and enthusiastic proponent of Newfoundland and Labrador culture.

Earl Pilgrim: The clever, dedicated wildlife officer continued his passionate fight for animal rights and became a well-known author and advocate for Newfoundland's precious environment. During his years as a Wildlife Enforcement Officer, Newfoundland won its frustrating and damaging battle with big game poachers. Today, Newfoundland has the highest ratio of moose per square mile of any place in the world.

J.C. Jones: J.C. was one of many capable pilots during the early offshore days in Newfoundland. As my friend, manager, and training captain, he was professional, patient, and talented. He used those and other skills outside the cockpit to move up through the ranks and become the president of Canadian Helicopters, one of the largest domestic and international helicopter companies in the world.

Dave Whyte: Even as a pilot, Dave's technical skills matched or exceeded that of a seasoned helicopter engineer. Dave assisted Okanagan during their expansion into international operations and eventually became chief pilot. Years later, Dave became part-owner of Alpine Helicopters Ltd in Kelowna, BC, Canada.

Jim Johnson: The spunky young mechanic who dreamed of becoming an S-61 pilot not only lived up to his ambitious prediction but went on to form a new company, **Cougar Helicopters.** Cougar is one of the most respected, innovative helicopter operators in the world. You may recall the beautiful overwater scene in the movie *Titanic*, where the elderly Rose arrived by helicopter at the explorer ship *Keldysh*. That shiny S-61 was one of Cougar's aircraft.

Pilots & Engineers: Those early years of offshore flying in Newfoundland and Nova Scotia were, in no uncertain terms, **Pioneering Years**. Today (2020) a student in middle school has more technical accuracy in their cell phone's GPS than we had 240 miles offshore in the Atlantic Ocean. Pilots were often faced with an ironic mixed bag of standards; on one hand, we used precise airline standards of IFR takeoff and landing procedures at the two international airports (St. John's and Halifax), and on the other hand, it was necessary to use seat-of-your-pants techniques when landing on an oil rig in thick fog or in a snowstorm at night. It took a unique breed of pilots to pull that off safely and professionally. Our confidence to fly in terrifying weather conditions came from the fact that we were supported by a wonderful team of hardworking, dedicated engineers.

In addition to those previously mentioned in this book or author's notes, some of the pilots and engineers I had the pleasure of working with in St. John's and Halifax are listed below,

PILOTS
Tony Adams
Rolf Ganong
Dan Hayes, dec.
Doug Hogan, dec.
Pierre Looten, dec.
Don MacKenzie, dec.
Mike McDonaugh, dec.
Didier Monier
Walter Ramsey
Jim Reid
Reg Rivard
Al Winter

ENGINEERS
Wally Boyle
Larry Gibbons
Phil McCully
Norm Noseworthy
Dave Palframan.
Rocky Pearson, dec.
Paul Stevens
Chuck Taylor, dec.

Marvin Eagleston (Marve): The dialogue and events in this book which pertain to my brother, Marvin Eagleston, are a mixture of truth and imagination. After years of research, interviews, letters, prison visits, vivid and often frightening memories, I attempted to re-create his heartbreaking life. By incorporating major facts and events from his troubled youth and prison life, I endeavored to walk in his shoes, if only for a short time. It is true, Marve was an inmate in the various jails and prisons depicted in this book as well as other jails and prisons not listed here. But the names, events, and details associated with my brother have been changed to protect the innocent and in no way attempt to blame anyone involved in his incarceration and/or death. Even though some of the dialogue was imagined, one fact is clear: Marve was a likable person with a magnetic personality, and he was blessed with a vast number of faithful, colorful friends. I would have to live another hundred years to accumulate half that many friends.

Barbara Eagleston: After twenty-two years of marriage, Barbara and I divorced. After reading this book, the reader can understand how difficult it must have been to be married to this author. Barbara re-married years later but passed away in 2018. She was a wonderful wife, mother, and grandmother.

Dave Eagleston: All the events depicted in this book that occurred in Newfoundland and Eastern Canada are true. And these were but some of those events. After Halifax, I entered the exciting field of international aviation as Okanagan expanded its offshore operations. Throughout my forty-six years of commercial aviation as a pilot, aviation advisor, buyer, seller, and broker of aircraft, I have had the pleasure of working in Thailand, the Philippines, Burma, Malta, Turkey, Egypt, Western Canada, Northwest Territories, Central America, South America, several US states, Africa, the Middle East, Kazakhstan, and Russia.

Sources

Page 111: Brown, Cassie, and Harold Horwood. *Death on The Ice: The Great Newfoundland Sealing Disaster of 1914*. Toronto, Ontario: Doubleday Canada, 1972.

Page 225: Gwyn, Richard J., Leanna Fong, Nathan Coschi. "Joey Smallwood," *The Canadian Encyclopedia*, last edited March 9, 2017. Retrieved from https://www.thecanadianencyclopedia.ca/en/article/joey-smallwood.

Page 258: Lotz, Jim. *Prime Ministers of Canada*. London, England: Bison Books, 1987.

Page 314: Graham, Billy. *Hope For Each Day: Words of Wisdom and Faith*. Nashville, Tennessee: J. Countryman, 2002. p. 301.
Page 336: Gibran, Kahlil. *Jesus, The Son of Man*. New York: Alfred A. Knopf, 1928. p. 67.

About Dave Eagleston

Dave Eagleston grew up in Tulsa, Oklahoma, and graduated from Will Rogers High School and Oklahoma State University. He worked for a few years as a cameraman and vocalist at KTUL-TV in Tulsa before joining the Army. After a tour as a combat helicopter pilot in Vietnam, Dave traveled the world as a commercial pilot and aviation advisor. He has had the privilege of living in such exciting locations as Burma, Russia, Kazakhstan, Thailand, the Philippines, Turkey, three provinces in Canada, as well as several beautiful cities in the United States. He has flown prime ministers, premiers, ambassadors, the US secretary of state, firefighters, roughnecks, game wardens, poachers, prisoners, movie stars, and a several thousand ordinary people. As a combat pilot, he was awarded two Purple Hearts, twenty-two Air Medals, and the Silver Star. As a commercial helicopter pilot, he received the Helicopter Association International (HAI) Safe Pilot Award. Dave lives in McKinney, Texas, with his wife Janie. Dave sings and plays the guitar professionally in the Dallas area and can be seen in plays and musicals as well as on television and the occasional low-budget short and feature films. You can watch his music videos on YouTube by simply searching for his name. Dave's first book, *West of Alva*, is available on Amazon.

For more about Dave, visit www.eagleston.com or email him at dave@eagleston.com, join him on Instagram at @daveeagleston follow him on Facebook: https://www.facebook.com/Dave-Eagleston-Author

Acknowledgements

Thanks to my beautiful wife, Janie, who gave me generous amounts of support, love, and encouragement while I struggled in my efforts to balance writing with family life.

And to my sister, Francis Sue Eagleston, who provided family stories that often included unpleasant, shameful details but added to this book's accuracy.

A special thanks to my good friend, Dave Whyte. For devoting your life to safety and professionalism in the commercial helicopter industry and supplying much-needed aviation oversight for this story.

Thanks to Warden Randy Workman and his assistant Terry Crenshaw at the Oklahoma State Penitentiary. They were kind enough to allow me full access to the giant McAllister, Oklahoma facility (Big Mac), and provided incredible insight into the life of inmates, rodeos, and correctional officers.

And finally, thanks to the courteous, gentle people of Newfoundland who opened their homes and hearts to a young man from Oklahoma. *May your boats be filled with cod, and your hearts be touched by God.*

Made in the USA
Middletown, DE
09 August 2021